END OF TEN

THE UNOFFICIAL AND UNAUTHORISED GUIDE TO *DOCTOR WHO* 2009

END OF TEN

THE UNOFFICIAL AND UNAUTHORISED GUIDE TO *DOCTOR WHO* 2009

STEPHEN JAMES WALKER

First published in England in 2010 by
Telos Publishing Ltd
139 Whitstable Road, Canterbury, Kent, CT2 8EQ

www.telos.co.uk

This edition 2021

Telos Publishing Ltd values feedback. Please e-mail us with any comments you may
have about this book to: feedback@telos.co.uk

ISBN: 978-1-84583-178-3

End of Ten: The Unofficial and Unauthorised Guide to Doctor Who *2009*
© 2010, 2021 Stephen James Walker

TABLE OF CONTENTS

INTRODUCTION

It was in a press release of 3 September 2007 that the BBC broke the news that there would be no full new series of *Doctor Who* in 2009 – the first time there had been such a hiatus since the show returned to TV in 2005. Instead, this 'gap year', as it quickly came to be known (and as it will be referred to in this book), would see the transmission of a succession of one-off, extended-length specials, initially envisaged as four in number (including the 2008 Christmas special) and eventually fixed as five. Furthermore, on 20 May 2008, it was announced that when the next series, Series Five, did finally reach the screen in spring 2010, the show would have a new production team at the helm, with Steven Moffat taking over from Russell T Davies as showrunner and Piers Wenger succeeding Julie Gardner as his fellow executive producer. [1] Phil Collinson, the producer for most of Series One to Four, had already left to take up a new BBC post elsewhere, and would have to be replaced. The closing months of 2008 then brought the revelation that the show's hugely popular star, David Tennant, would also be leaving, handing over the reins to a new Doctor at the end of the last of the five specials. Clearly, then, these specials would mark the end of an era for *Doctor Who* in more ways than one, and represent an important landmark in the show's long history.

End of Ten, the latest in Telos Publishing's series of comprehensive annual guides to *Doctor Who*, gives a full overview of this extraordinary 18 month period. The first section of the book notes all the main events, news stories, promotional activities and so forth that occurred in the *Doctor Who* world between the end of Series Four and the close of the tenth Doctor's era in 'The End of Time', in what is designed to serve as a useful record of this time from the 'outside looking in' perspective of the viewing public. Following this, there are capsule biographies of all the main cast and production team members who worked on the gap year specials. Then comes the most substantial section of the book, which consists of a detailed guide to and analysis of all five specials. Lastly there are seven appendices, covering: the animated adventure 'Dreamland'; the *Doctor Who at the Proms* event; Series Five of *Doctor Who Confidential*; the specials' ratings and fan rankings; the final entries in BBC Books' original tenth Doctor novels range; the last of the original tenth Doctor comic strip stories; and other officially-sanctioned original *Doctor Who* fiction published during this period.

If you are reading this book, the chances are that you are already an avid follower of the good Doctor's adventures, but I hope that in the following pages you will find much to interest, inform and enlighten you, and ultimately to enhance your appreciation and enjoyment of the latest run of episodes in what is undoubtedly my favourite TV series of all time!

Stephen James Walker
10 June 2010

---

[1] For full details of these announcements, see *Monsters Within: The Unofficial and Unauthorised Guide to Doctor Who 2008* (Telos Publishing, 2008).

PART ONE
THE GAP YEAR AS IT HAPPENED

CHAPTER ONE
THE NEXT DOCTOR ...?

For *Doctor Who* fans, the period between the transmission of the Series Four finale 'Journey's End' on 5 July 2008 and that of the Christmas Special 'The Next Doctor' on 25 December 2008 was filled with much speculation – and some anxiety – about the show's future.

The 'fake regeneration' cliff-hanger ending to 'The Stolen Earth', the episode prior to 'Journey's End', had already got people talking about the possibility of a change of leading man in the offing. While many hoped that the gap year would be just a temporary hiccup in a long ongoing run for the tenth Doctor – needed simply because David Tennant had agreed to star in a new Royal Shakespeare Company production of *Hamlet* being previewed from 24 July at the Courtyard Theatre in Stratford-upon-Avon – others feared that it would mark the end of his era. The *Sun* newspaper added fuel to the fire of debate on 18 July when, in a story curiously headed 'Tennant is Dr Glue', it reported, 'Beeb bosses are more hopeful than ever that David Tennant *will* stay on as Doctor Who – after wooing him with a £1.5 million deal. They had feared the Scot, 37, was sure to quit after filming four more specials of the BBC One sci-fi hit.[2] But last night a source said he could stay as the Time Lord for the fifth series to be screened in 2010.' With hindsight, however, the veracity of this story seems doubtful, given that it ended by asserting, erroneously, 'David's real-life love Georgia Moffett, 23, returns as his daughter Jenny for one of the *Who* specials.'

On 19 July, the *Daily Mail* claimed that Steven Moffat had 'turned down a £500,000 movie deal with Steven Spielberg' so that he could become *Doctor Who*'s new showrunner. This related to the fact that Moffat had written the first script for a planned series of Spielberg-produced moves about the famous Belgian detective character Tintin but had to pull out of further work on the project in order to take on the *Doctor Who* post. Moffat was quoted as saying: 'I was under contract to do the first two of the three Tintin films. I completed the first one and then the Hollywood writers' strike happened and I couldn't work. I was offered the *Doctor Who* job and accepted immediately. I hope you won't make what happened sound too dramatic. I talked to Steven and he understood completely. I could not work on the second Tintin film and work on *Doctor Who*. So I chose *Doctor Who*. Steven is a fan and he understood my passion for the series completely.' Two days later, however, Moffat told the BBC News website that the *Daily Mail*'s report had been 'a bit misleading'; the suggested £500,000 figure was 'entirely speculative and wildly inaccurate' and Spielberg was not really a fan of *Doctor Who*, although he 'knew and admired' the show.

---

[2] Press reports and the like frequently make reference to *Doctor Who* being 'filmed'. This is incorrect, as the show is actually video-recorded on tape. However, references to 'filming' have been retained in this book where directly quoted from other sources.

At the end of July, Issue 398 of *Doctor Who Magazine* confirmed that David Morrissey, Dervla Kirwan and Velile Tshabalala would be the guest stars in the forthcoming Christmas special – the title of which had still to be revealed at that stage – and that it would be produced by Susie Liggat and directed by Andy Goddard. It was also announced that Russell T Davies would be writing the four subsequent specials, although two of them would be co-written by Gareth Roberts and Phil Ford respectively.

A sold-out concert showcasing a selection of Murray Gold's incidental music from *Doctor Who* received a rapturous response from the audience when staged on Sunday 27 July at the Royal Albert Hall in London as part of the BBC's annual Proms series. It was also broadcast live on BBC Radio 3 and recorded for future TV screening and DVD release.[3]

The official opening of the RSC's *Hamlet* on 5 August brought much press coverage and many positive reviews, both for Tennant's performance in the title role and for the production as a whole. *The Times*'s Benedict Nightingale commented, 'Gregory Doran's fluent, pacey, modern-dress revival of *Hamlet* gives Tennant the chance to show the world that he has the range to tackle the most demanding classical role of all – and, praise be, he seizes it. I've seen bolder Hamlets and more moving Hamlets, but few who kept me so riveted throughout.'

Award nominations and successes continued to roll in for *Doctor Who* throughout this period. On 9 August, the website for the prestigious US-based Hugo Awards for science fiction revealed that Steven Moffat had won the Best Dramatic Presentation, Short Form category for the third year in succession. This was for his script for the Series Three episode 'Blink' (2007) (his previous Hugos having come for 'The Empty Child'/'The Doctor Dances' (2005) and 'The Girl in the Fireplace' (2006)). Then, on 23 August, *Doctor Who* was announced as having won the award for the best programme of 2008, as judged by a panel of industry executives and journalists, at the Edinburgh International Television Festival. Interviewed at the Festival by BBC News, Moffat responded to questions about the possibility of a *Doctor Who* movie by saying he would not be opposed to the idea, provided it did not get in the way of making the series itself. The BBC News report continued:

> Moffat went on to rule out introducing an older Doctor Who, if and when David Tennant leaves the show. 'It's a practical issue. This is a show that's hard for even the young, super-fit David Tennant to keep up with. It might kill someone over 60,' he said. 'If the Doctor turned into an old man you would be a bit pissed off … I think he'll always probably tend to be around 40.'

Further talk about the possibility of a movie version was prompted two days later, when it was revealed that *Doctor Who* had topped a *Radio Times* online poll, conducted over the previous two months, of TV shows that readers would most like to see adapted for the cinema.

The accolades kept on coming on 8 September when the ceremony for the reader-voted annual TV Quick/TV Choice awards took place at London's Dorchester Hotel and saw David Tennant being named as Best Actor for the second time, Catherine

---

[3] See Appendix B for further details.

Tate as Best Actress, and *Doctor Who* itself as Best-Loved Drama for the third year running.

On the same day, the *Sun* boasted another *Doctor Who* scoop when it broke the news that Catherine Tate, John Simm and Bernard Cribbins would all be appearing in one of the forthcoming specials.

Meanwhile, rumours about a possible *Doctor Who* movie continued to abound. Various newspapers carried stories about this on 10 September, all apparently based on a piece in the *Sun*'s TV Biz column, which stated:

> *Doctor Who* heartthrob David Tennant is negotiating to play the role in a movie version as part of his big comeback deal … We can now reveal that the star has agreed to make a full fifth series in 2010 if the big screen role can be tagged on to the deal. Beeb chiefs are in talks about funding for a movie. At the moment Tennant is only signed up to star in four specials next year, as well as a Christmas episode. Last night, a show source said: 'It looks like the film is going to happen in the next few years. For ages, BBC Worldwide held the rights and were planning to make a movie, but it got held up and former BBC One boss Lorraine Heggessey decided to bring back the TV series in 2005. But everyone is keen now and the fans are clamouring. Part of David's conundrum is that he wants to do films, so this looks like it would solve both issues.'

The *Sun* carried yet another *Doctor Who* story on 11 September, claiming that one of the forthcoming specials would see Paul McGann reprise his role as the eighth Doctor in an extended flashback to the events of the Time War. This report was quickly denied by the BBC.

Further speculation about the identity of Tennant's eventual successor was prompted by the 16 September publication in *The Times* of some serialised extracts from the forthcoming book *The Writer's Tale* by Russell T Davies and *Doctor Who Magazine* scribe Benjamin Cook, detailing a lengthy exchange of e-mails between the two about the making of Davies's *Doctor Who*. The source of the speculation was a comment made by Davies in one of his e-mails to Cook to the effect that actor Russell Tovey – who had appeared as Midshipman Frame in 'The Voyage of the Damned' (2007) – would make a good candidate for the role of the eleventh Doctor. This was deemed sufficiently newsworthy to form the basis of stories by numerous online and print journalists, including in the *Guardian* and the *Daily Mirror*.

On 23 September, the BBC Press Office announced that the 2008 Christmas special would be called 'The Next Doctor' – a title that immediately prompted a fresh wave of speculation as to whether or not David Tennant would soon be leaving the show. Although it had already been made clear prior to this that Tennant would be starring in all of the gap year specials, many fans began to wonder if 'The Next Doctor' would afford an early glimpse of his eventual successor, perhaps through some twisting of the laws of time, as in other multi-Doctor stories such as 'The Five Doctors' (1983) and, more recently, 'Time Crash' (2007).

A brief respite from all the conjecture came on 29 September, when the Periodical Publishers' Association announced that the *Radio Times* cover for the week of 30 April 2005, showing a Dalek outside the Houses of Parliament, had come top in an online poll to decide Britain's greatest magazine cover ever. This striking image, headlined 'Vote Dalek!', which had cleverly promoted both the transmission of the episode 'Dalek' and the BBC's coverage of the 2005 General Election, reportedly received more than a quarter of the 10,000 votes cast in the poll.

Sunday 12 October saw the *News of the World* making its own contribution to the speculation surrounding David Tennant's future commitment to *Doctor Who* with the following story:

> David Tennant is in talks to stay on as Doctor Who until 2011 ... The negotiations mark a stunning U-turn for the 37-year-old actor who had planned to walk away from the BBC role after filming four specials next year. But, following pleas from BBC chiefs and fans, Tennant is now considering continuing as the telly Time Lord. Insiders say TV bosses are prepared to offer him a big increase on his current £1 million deal. So far Tennant ... has stopped short of signing because of a potential Hollywood film deal and offers from rival TV channels. But an insider said: 'The BBC is determined to make sure David doesn't go without a fight. He is an integral part of the series.'

Several other newspapers meanwhile chose the same date to report a rumour about a special *Doctor Who* scene supposedly being recorded for the BBC's 2008 *Children in Need* telethon. The story on the *Daily Mirror*'s website, headed 'All Surviving Doctor Who Actors to Appear in One-Off TV Special', read:

> The seven surviving Doctor Whos are to appear together in a one-off TV special. Ten actors have played the Time Lord since the BBC sci-fi series began in 1963. The surviving Doctors – including current one David Tennant – are getting together for the first time for *Children in Need* on 14 November. A BBC source revealed: 'It's a pretty ambitious idea and it's still being finalised. Everything is being kept under wraps but *Doctor Who* fans are in for a big treat.'

Russell T Davies provoked a brief flurry of controversy when, during a 12 October guest appearance at the annual Cheltenham Literary Festival, he jokingly commented that Prince Charles was a 'swine' for having declined an invitation to make a cameo appearance in *Doctor Who*. This was picked up by a number of the national newspapers, and a report on the BBC News website noted that the invitation had actually been turned down not by Prince Charles himself but by a member of his staff acting on his behalf and without his awareness. A spokesperson was quoted as saying, 'We receive a great many requests and it's impossible to accept them all.'

Issue 401 of *Doctor Who Magazine*, which went on sale in the week beginning 13 October, saw the first significant snippets of news released about the second gap year special, due to be transmitted at Easter 2009. Davies's co-writer was confirmed as Gareth Roberts, and the director was announced as James Strong, who had been responsible for a number of well-received episodes previously.

17 October saw the BBC Press Office issue information regarding the *Children in Need* event on 14 November. This confirmed that there would indeed be a *Doctor Who*

scene featured. However, no comment was made about the rumoured 'seven Doctors' team-up and, as a number of the actors concerned denied in interviews that they had been contacted about any such project, realisation began to dawn amongst fans that those rumours were actually baseless. A week later, on 24 October, the BBC revealed that *Doctor Who*'s contribution to the telethon would actually consist of a preview of the first couple of minutes of 'The Next Doctor' rather than any specially-shot material. The preview would be introduced by Captain Jack actor John Barrowman, who would also be singing as part of the evening's entertainment.

There were more awards for *Doctor Who* on 29 October, at the National Television Awards ceremony. The show was named Most Popular Drama, while David Tennant received the Outstanding Performance gong. Of far greater significance, however, was the fact that Tennant used the opportunity of his acceptance speech, carefully timed to be beamed live from Stratford-upon-Avon during an interval in that evening's performance of *Hamlet*, to end all the speculation by announcing that the forthcoming specials would indeed mark the end of his time in *Doctor Who*. This news had actually been leaked a little earlier in the day on the website of the *Guardian* newspaper, apparently on the basis of a press release that the BBC Press Office had prepared as a contingency measure in case something went wrong with the live link-up to Tennant or he did not actually win the award. That press notice should not have been issued, however, and the *Guardian*'s story was taken down shortly after it appeared, leaving the way clear for Tennant to drop the bombshell himself.

The BBC's official *Doctor Who* website subsequently reported Tennant's decision as follows:

> 'I've had the most brilliant, bewildering and life changing time working on *Doctor Who*. I have loved every day of it,' the actor says. 'It would be very easy to cling on to the TARDIS console forever and I fear that if I don't take a deep breath and make the decision to move on now, then I simply never will ... I'm still the Doctor all next year but when the time finally comes I'll be honoured to hand on the best job in the world to the next lucky git – whoever that may be.' Tennant added that he 'always thought the time to leave would be in conjunction with Russell T Davies and Julie Gardner who have been such a huge part of it all for me. Steven Moffat is the most brilliant and exciting writer, the only possible successor to Russell, and it was sorely tempting to be part of his amazing new plans for the show. I will be there, glued to my TV when his stories begin in 2010.' He furthermore says that he feels 'very privileged to have been part of this incredible phenomenon, and whilst I'm looking forward to new challenges I know I'll always be very proud to be the tenth Doctor.'

As fans were still trying to take in this momentous news, the media went into overdrive, losing no time in bandying about the names of potential successors, while the bookmakers started offering odds on those considered to be the leading contenders. The favourite was David Morrissey, already announced as playing the titular character of 'The Next Doctor', while others at relatively short odds included Paterson Joseph, James McAvoy, James Nesbitt and Robert Carlyle.

An interview by Tennant on the BBC's *Breakfast* programme on Monday 3 November only heightened the astonishing media frenzy when the actor responded to a question about a possible female Doctor by jokingly suggested that his former co-star Billie Piper might make a good candidate. A number of journalists apparently took him more seriously than he'd intended, judging by the reports that followed, such as the *Daily Mail*'s 4 November piece headed 'Billie Piper Leads the Space Race to Become the New Doctor Who', while at the bookmakers, the odds on a female Doctor fell from 20/1 to 12/1.

14 November saw the promised preview clip of 'The Next Doctor' being transmitted on *Children in Need*, and also placed on the BBC's official *Doctor Who* website. David Morrissey was still the bookies' favourite to take over from David Tennant the following year, but in a 20 November interview on the BBC News website, one of the other leading contenders, Paterson Joseph, made it clear that he would certainly be interested in the role, commenting, 'Any actor would love the challenge'. He refused to be drawn on his chances, however, saying, 'I'm afraid I can't make any comment on it. I'm not a gambler. And I don't approve of gambling unless it's for the Grand National.' Over the following week, the odds on Joseph taking the role fell dramatically, and a number of media websites suggested that he would indeed be announced as the next Doctor quite soon. Other names being bandied about in the press – which continued to devote a huge amount of coverage to the issue – included Colin Salmon, Rhys Ifans, Chiwetel Ejiofor and Benedict Cumberbatch. Two actors who appeared to rule themselves out of the running when questioned by journalists were John Simm and *Spooks'* Rupert Penry-Jones, the latter of whom was quoted by the 24 November *Daily Mirror* as saying, 'I haven't been asked to take over in *Doctor Who*. I took over from someone in *Spooks*, and I was never quite comfortable with that … so I wouldn't like to take over something else. I'd like to stick with original things.'

On 28 November, Russell T Davies visited Buckingham Palace to be presented by Prince Charles with an OBE for his services to drama. 'Writers are the lifeblood of a lot of stuff that gets made,' he was quoted as saying on the BBC News website. 'So I was really honoured to accept [the OBE] on behalf of everyone slaving away at keyboards.'

The following day, the issue of *Radio Times* for the week beginning 6 December went on sale in Britain's newsagents, and featured a photograph of Davids Tennant and Morrissey from 'The Next Doctor' on the front cover, with an extensive preview article about the special inside, including dramatic pictures of the Cybermen.

From the beginning of December, the BBC's promotional effort for 'The Next Doctor' stepped up a gear. The official website launched its annual 'advent calendar' feature, many of the daily items in which related in some way to the forthcoming special, and also presented a video Christmas message from David Tennant. Meanwhile a number of previously-unseen clips from 'The Next Doctor' were included in an new trailer covering all of the BBC's major festive drama offerings, which was placed online and began to be shown in selected programme breaks on BBC One. On 5 December, the BBC Press Office confirmed that the special would be shown at 6.00 pm on Christmas Day in an hour-long slot. Also revealed was the scheduling of the *Doctor Who at the Proms* programme, which would go out at 1.50 pm on New Year's Day, likewise on BBC One. The Christmas double issue of *Radio Times*, which hit the shops the following week, contained another preview of 'The

Next Doctor', this time in the form of an piece by Russell T Davies.

A worrying news story broke on 9 December, when it emerged that David Tennant had been unable to take part in the previous evening's performance of the RSC's *Hamlet*, which had now transferred to the Novello Theatre in London, due to what was described as a flare-up of a 'long-standing back injury'. As further details emerged, it seemed that Tennant would have to undergo surgery on his back on 11 December, and would then be out of action until at least Christmas while he recuperated. Given that recording on the next *Doctor Who* special was due to begin in January, this raised concerns amongst fans that his participation in that might also be affected.

Issue 403 of *Doctor Who Magazine*, which went on sale on 11 December, carried amongst other things an interview with David Morrissey, in which he expressed surprise at the level of interest his casting in 'The Next Doctor' had sparked, and at the number of texts and e-mails he had received from people quizzing him on whether or not he would indeed be succeeding Tennant as the show's leading man.

18 December saw the BBC holding a press launch for 'The Next Doctor', at which an invitation-only audience of journalists was treated to a preview screening of the special. Instant reactions soon began to appear on a number of media websites – although, to their credit, they all abided by the request made at the screening by Jane Tranter, BBC Controller of Fiction, not to spoil the twist of the identity of David Morrissey's character. The *SFX* magazine website commented:

> Andy Goddard directs with a lot of style, atmosphere and an eye for striking imagery, though he does seem out of his depth in a couple of the action scenes, which lack a certain oomph. However, a set-piece scene in the graveyard is shot very effectively and the opening encounter with a Cybershade is hilarious. The production design is stunningly good, really bringing to life a snowy Victorian London and providing some wonderful cyberpunk additions. So, yeah, there's a lot of lightweight fluff here, and one very cheesy moment, but the Next Doctor mystery provides the emotional core of the episode. Other than that I'm saying no more, as any discussion of it will give away too many clues.

Neither Morrissey nor Tennant was present at the screening (unsurprisingly in the latter case, in view of his recent surgery), but Russell T Davies was on hand to answer questions. As reported in a piece headed 'Tennant Expected Fit for New *Who*' on the BBC News website, he quelled fears over the impact of Tennant's operation on the next special by saying he was 'hopeful' the actor would be ready to start recording on 19 January, adding, 'We'll have to be very careful. I don't think we'll be swinging him on a wire on his first day back.' Davies went on from the screening to guest on the Victoria Derbyshire show on BBC Radio 5 Live, again fielding questions about 'The Next Doctor'.

On 19 December, BBC One's early evening magazine programme *The One Show* featured a behind-the-scenes look at 'The Next Doctor', presented by impressionist John Culshaw and including on-set interviews with Tennant and Morrissey.

22 December saw the RSC issue a press notice, stating that Tennant was recovering well from his operation but that it was too soon to say when he might be

able to return to the lead role in *Hamlet*, which in the interim was being played by his understudy Edward Bennett. Tennant was quoted as saying: 'I am so grateful for all the terrific medical attention I have received and although it is frustrating to have to take it easy whilst all my friends and colleagues continue at the Novello Theatre every night, I am aware that I must listen to the experts and take my time. I am impatient to be back at work and sincerely hope to make it back some time before the end of the run.'

The week leading up to transmission of 'The Next Doctor' as part of the BBC's prestigious Christmas Night schedule saw the publicity blitz continuing, with many of the national newspapers and online media outlets running previews and other items about the special, and continuing their speculation about the identity of Tennant's successor. In a 22 December interview in the *Metro* free newspaper, Davies refused to be drawn on the subject of the next Doctor, commenting: 'I'm not naming any names – if I do, there'll be a van-load of journalists turning up at some actor's house asking him if he's doing the show. A separate team is casting the next Doctor and I honestly don't know who they are auditioning … When we brought *Doctor Who* back, the role was considered such a joke that names such as Paul Daniels were mentioned. Now it's serious actors. That shows how much the perception of the show has changed.' On the subject of Tennant's eventual departure, he noted: 'Well, something dreadful has to happen to make David Tennant change into the next Doctor, so there's some joy in heading towards that. At the same time it's quite sad as I know it will traumatise some children. If you're six it's a huge event. I really hope we'll write something those six-year-olds will remember in 50 years' time.'

The transmission of 'The Next Doctor' brought with it the revelation of the title of the next special: 'Planet of the Dead'. Overnight ratings figures that became available the next day indicated that 'The Next Doctor' itself had been viewed by at least 11.7 million people – a phenomenal 50.5 percent of the total TV audience at that time. Overall, Christmas Day had been a triumph for BBC One, with it taking the top seven places in the ratings chart. *Doctor Who* came in at number two, behind the animated comedy *Wallace and Gromit: A Matter of Loaf and Death*. The best ITV had been able to manage was 7.4 million viewers for *Coronation Street*. The national newspapers all reported on the BBC's ratings domination, the *Sun* stating:

> The BBC triumphed with its Christmas Day offerings – pulling in nearly 16m viewers with a new episode of *Wallace and Gromit*. Nick Park's *A Matter Of Loaf and Death* was the most-watched Christmas TV show yesterday, peaking with an audience of 15.8m and averaging 14.3m. The rating was the highest of the year – even beating the *X Factor* final, which saw a peak of 14.6m viewers tune in to see Alexandra Burke win the series. Viewing figures show BBC One had nine of the 10 most-watched programmes on Christmas Day. The second most popular was the *Doctor Who* Christmas special, 'The Next Doctor', which averaged at 11.7m and featured Dervla Kirwan and David Morrissey as another Doctor.

With Morrissey's character now revealed to be school teacher Jackson Lake rather than a future incarnation of the Doctor, fans and media alike continued to speculate about the true identity of Tennant's successor – and they didn't have long to wait to find out. The BBC News website announced on 2 January 2009 that the name of the eleventh Doctor would be finally revealed the next day, in a special *Doctor Who Confidential* programme being broadcast at 5.35 pm on BBC One and also shown on big public-area screens in a number of cities around Britain. Fans had suspected for some days that there might be some exceptional significance to this programme, as *Doctor Who Confidential*, usually a BBC Three show, had never before been accorded such a prominent slot; and now they had definite confirmation. The BBC News report noted:

> The casting decision has been a priority for the show's new creative team, led by executive producers Steven Moffat and Piers Wenger. The BBC said that in Saturday's *Doctor Who* special 'the actor playing the new Doctor will be giving his or her initial reaction' to becoming TV's most famous time traveller. Wenger, head of drama at BBC Wales, said: 'We believe the actor is going to bring something very special to the role and will make it absolutely their own. I just can't wait to tell everyone who it is – it has been a nail-biting Christmas trying to keep this under wraps!'

Remarkably, the secret had indeed been kept, with no hint of the chosen actor's identity having leaked out – although at the bookmakers, Paterson Joseph remained the strong favourite. The press continued to have a field day, with the possibility of a female Doctor remaining a popular topic. The *Guardian* on 3 January commented: 'It is understood that those hoping for the first female doctor will be disappointed. *Doctor Who*'s new executive producers, *Coupling* creator Steven Moffat and BBC Wales head of drama Piers Wenger, are said to have stuck with tradition and cast a man in the role. However, Moffat and Wenger are thought to have steered away from the more obvious names that have been linked to the role.'

The BBC's *Breakfast* programme had entertainment correspondent Lizo Mzimba and *Doctor Who Adventures* editor Moray Laing as studio guests to discuss the forthcoming announcement, and although both effectively refused to speculate about the identity of the next Doctor, a pre-recorded report by Mzimba ran through some of the oft-mentioned names such as Chiwetel Ejiofor, Paterson Joseph and Russell Tovey, and also one previously undiscussed one, Matt Smith.

Completely overshadowing the welcome news of David Tennant's return to the stage in *Hamlet*, his back surgery having now had sufficient time to heal, the transmission of the *Doctor Who Confidential* special on the evening of 3 January finally ended the weeks of conjecture by revealing the eleventh Doctor to be the man first brought into the spotlight by Mzimba's report that morning: Matt Smith.

The BBC Press Office issued a full press release to accompany the announcement. This gave biographical details for Smith and included quotes from the actor and BBC executives, including the following from Steven Moffat: 'The Doctor is a very special part, and it takes a very special actor to play him. You need to be old and young at the same time, a boffin and an action hero, a cheeky schoolboy and the wise old man of the universe. As soon as Matt walked through the door, and blew us away with a bold and brand new take on the Time Lord, we knew we had our man.'

This press release quickly became the basis for numerous newspaper and online articles over the next couple of days – some of them even in other countries, including the USA and Australia. In its piece, under the heading 'New Doctor Actor is Youngest Ever', the BBC News website reported:

> At 26, Smith is three years younger than Peter Davison when he signed up to play the fifth Doctor in 1981. Smith will first appear on TV screens as the eleventh Doctor in 2010. He was cast over Christmas and will begin filming for the fifth series of *Doctor Who* in the summer. Tennant is filming four specials in 2009. Smith was named as Tennant's replacement in Saturday's edition of *Doctor Who Confidential* on BBC One. The programme was watched by an audience of 6.9 million people at its peak, according to official overnight figures. The actor said: 'I feel proud and honoured to have been given this opportunity to join a team of people that has worked so tirelessly to make the show so thrilling. David Tennant has made the role his own, brilliantly, with grace, talent and persistent dedication. I hope to learn from the standards set by him. The challenge for me is to do justice to the show's illustrious past, my predecessors, and most importantly, to those who watch it. I really cannot wait.' Piers Wenger, Head of Drama at BBC Wales, said that as soon as he had seen Smith's audition he 'knew he was the one. It was abundantly clear that he had that "Doctor-ness" about him ... You are either the Doctor or you are not. It's just the beginning of the journey for Matt.'

Most of the articles that appeared at this time commented on the issue of Smith's age. Many observers found it surprising that someone so young had been cast in the role, and even some fans questioned whether or not an actor still in his mid-twenties would be able successfully to portray a character hundreds of years old. Nevertheless, the general mood was one of cautious optimism, and it seemed that an exciting new era of *Doctor Who* was just around the corner.

Before that, though, there were four more David Tennant-starring specials still to be made and transmitted.

CHAPTER TWO
INTO THE GAP YEAR PROPER

There had been nothing unusual about the six-month break in transmission of *Doctor Who* between 'Journey's End' and 'The Next Doctor'; each year since the show had returned to TV in 2005, there had been an equivalent break between the end of that year's series and the Christmas special. It was only at the start of 2009 that the gap year proper began, and it really hit home to fans that they would have to wait a further 15 months or so until the next full new series of the Time Lord's adventures hit the screen. In the meantime, there would be just four more specials to come, seeing out the end of the tenth Doctor's era.

At the beginning of January 2009, media interest was actually still focused more on the arrival of Matt Smith's Doctor than on the departure of David Tennant's. In amongst the many comment pieces on Smith's accession to the role, the *Daily Telegraph*, in its 5 January edition, turned its attention to the subject of his future co-star. In a piece headed 'Search for New Doctor Who's Partner Begins', it said:

> The singer Lily Allen is an early favourite; while sources say *Strictly Come Dancing* stars Rachel Stevens and Kelly Brook are high on the BBC's wish-list. Producers are looking for someone who is famous outside the world of acting – replicating the success of former Doctor's assistant Billie Piper, who was better known as a teenage pop star and the wife of DJ Chris Evans when she landed the role but proved a hit with viewers. Auditions will take place over the coming months and filming begins in the summer. Piers Wenger, executive producer of the BBC One show, said: 'Having got the casting of the Doctor out of the way, the companion role is where we will be looking next. Someone terribly exciting like Billie Piper, who was at the beginning of her acting career but who had a profile for other reasons, would be great. We are looking for someone whose light can burn brightly.'

The following day, the BBC's in-house staff magazine *Ariel* carried an article describing the enormous lengths that had been gone to in order to maintain the secrecy over the announcement of Matt Smith's casting. Apparently the arrangements regarding the special *Doctor Who Confidential* programme had all been made verbally, with no written communications exchanged, and Smith's on-camera interview had been conducted in secret by a two-man crew on the very day that he signed his *Doctor Who* contract. He had then on Christmas Eve attended a photo shoot in the basement of the BBC's Television Centre, with none of those involved being made aware of what it was for; the pictures taken of Smith were later digitally combined with shots of the TARDIS in an alleyway to create some promotional images.

Also at this time, the BBC started looking for a new permanent producer for the 2010 series, issuing a detailed job description for the post.

On 16 January, a blog by journalist Gareth McLean on the guardian.co.uk website effectively confirmed rumours that had been circulating amongst fans for some time that 'Planet of the Dead' would feature some recording carried out in the unusually far-flung location of Dubai. McLean was far from positive about this move, however, delivering a lengthy diatribe prefaced by the following:

> Picture the scene: the TARDIS materialises in a windswept desert under a blistering sun and the Doctor steps out on to an undulating dune. Beyond the sands, there is a glittering capital full of futuristic skyscrapers, extravagant edifices and peoples from all over the planet in pursuit of pleasure in the metropolis's plentiful fun palaces. But there is a sinister side to this sparkling city. It is built on slave labour, at an enormous ecological cost, and some of its population is criminalised just for being who they are. Moreover, it is ruled by a rich-as-Croesus dynasty unwilling to give its people that most basic of rights – the vote – while its police and judiciary are no strangers to excessive force and Kafka-esque machinations. In short, it's just the sort of place that the Doctor … would find cause to fight for right and justice. Right? Wrong. For this is not the plot of an episode of *Doctor Who* … Rather it is the story of an episode of *Doctor Who* – one of the upcoming specials … For the BBC, in its infinite wisdom, has decided to film some of said special in Dubai. That's the Dubai that isn't a democracy. Dubai with its dubious human rights record, appalling treatment of migrant workers and flagrant disregard for the environment. Dubai, where you can be arrested for being gay and jailed for up to 10 years.

On a lighter note, 18 January saw Catherine Tate spoofing *Doctor Who* in some sketches performed while appearing as a guest host on Channel 4's irreverent comedy show *The Sunday Night Project*, at one point even dressing up as the tenth Doctor, complete with wig and fake sideburns.

Recording on 'Planet of the Dead' got under way on schedule on 19 April, not in Dubai initially but in the more familiar setting of Cardiff. The National Museum of Wales was the venue for the first scenes to be taped, featuring Michelle Ryan as Lady Christina de Souza. A number of newspapers, including the *Daily Mirror* in its 18 January edition, had got the wrong end of the stick about this, suggesting that Ryan was under consideration for the role of the eleventh Doctor's companion, but fans who visited the Cardiff location quickly realised the truth of the matter.

Further 'Planet of the Dead' casting news came on 23 January when the BBC officially confirmed Ryan's involvement and announced that comedian Lee Evans would also be appearing, as would Noma Dumezweni, reprising her role from 'Turn Left' (2008) as UNIT's Captain Erisa Magambo. Evans had meanwhile verified his participation in person in an interview recorded a couple of days earlier for the 23 January edition of *Friday Night With Jonathan Ross*.

On 27 January, the *Sun*'s TV Biz column had some news on one of the later specials, in a piece headed 'Look Who's Back Again':

Doctor Who will be reunited with ex-sidekick Martha Jones yet again, TV Biz can reveal. Bosses are lining up Freema Agyeman to make a surprise return in one of this year's four specials marking David Tennant's last hurrah as the Time Lord. The move has surprised fans as Freema, 29, reportedly annoyed *Who* chiefs after she signed up for ITV1's *Law and Order: London*.[4] Show creator Russell T Davies was then forced to tear up scripts for *Who* spin-off *Torchwood*, in which she'd been given a starring role. But sources confirmed the Londoner will reprise Martha for the BBC One hit later this year. An insider said: 'Freema's on board. It's early days so it's unclear what exactly Martha will be up to in the new show. Whatever happens, it's good news for Freema and shows that whatever friction there was between her and *Who* bosses has gone.'

On 28 January, news broke that one of two double-decker buses acquired by the *Doctor Who* team to be used during recording of 'Planet of the Dead' had been seriously damaged in transit to Dubai. The BBC News website reported:

Doctor Who writers were forced to change the script for the show's Easter special after a double-decker bus was damaged ahead of filming in Dubai. 'Planet of the Dead's plot sends David Tennant's Doctor and guest star Michelle Ryan on a dangerous bus trip. One bus is being used for filming scenes in Cardiff, but the top deck of the second vehicle was damaged as it arrived in Dubai. A spokeswoman said that shooting was 'continuing as normal'.

Two days later, it was reported on the Newsarama media website that the director of the final two tenth Doctor specials would be Euros Lyn, who had also recently been responsible for the *Torchwood* mini-series 'Children of Earth', for which promotional activities were now starting to be undertaken prior to its planned summer transmission – one example being that a minute-long trailer would be shown on 5 January at the New York Comic Con, which Lyn was attending, and also placed on the official *Torchwood* website.

On 2 February, the official *Doctor Who* website uploaded a short video diary made by David Tennant marking his return to recording on the show, the worst effects of his back surgery the previous month having now passed. Also on this date, reports surfaced that the BBC had acquired a third double-decker bus for use in recording of 'Planet of the Dead'. This was to accommodate some shots rescheduled in light of the damage to the bus in Dubai.

Issue 405 of *Doctor Who Magazine*, which went on sale on 5 February, contained some more snippets of news about the forthcoming specials, perhaps the most significant of which was that they would see *Doctor Who* being recorded and transmitted for the first time in high definition – a move previously resisted by the production team on the grounds that it would increase costs, including on effects work. This meant amongst other things that the specials would be shown on the BBC

---

[4] *Law and Order: London* was the working title for the ITV1 show eventually transmitted as *Law and Order: UK*.

HD channel as well as on BBC One.

A BBC press release of 13 February announced that the Dubai location recording for 'Planet of the Dead' had got under way. Producer Tracie Simpson was quoted as saying: 'We rarely take *Doctor Who* abroad although we did visit Rome for Series Four's "The Fires Of Pompeii" [2007], which gave us some spectacular footage. The locations in Dubai are a perfect match for writer Russell T Davies's vision of the episode and we expect to film some incredible scenes while we are here.'

The 16 February edition of the *Sun* had an intriguing story about a *Doctor Who* stage show apparently being planned for later in the year, enthusing:

> The TARDIS could soon be landing in your home town – after *Doctor Who* bosses decided to launch a megabucks *stage* version of the TV hit. The multi-media extravaganza will feature a state-of-the-art light and sound show including many of the cult hit's best-loved characters. The Doctor will take on flying *Daleks*, croaky *Cybermen* and stocky *Sontarans* in the family event.

This story was subsequently picked up by a number of other media outlets.[5]

On 18 February, by which point recording on 'Planet of the Dead' was reaching its conclusion, some important casting news broke about the following special, the Scottish *Daily Record* newspaper reporting that distinguished actress Lindsay Duncan was to take on the guest star role of Adelaide. 'Lindsay is an incredibly talented actress and I've been an admirer of her work for some time,' Russell T Davies was quoted as saying. 'We are delighted to announce that she will be joining the team and playing the Doctor's most strong-minded companion yet.' The BBC officially confirmed this report the following day.

By late February, recording for that next special – tentatively scheduled for a November transmission – had got under way. A 2 March story in Cardiff's local newspaper, the *Western Mail*, described the scene at one location:

> Fans of *Doctor Who* were treated to a glimpse of the Time Lord's new assistant as filming for a new special episode got under way in Wales. Around 60 diehard fans of the hit BBC One Wales show queued overnight to see Lindsay Duncan's performance as the Doctor's assistant … Shooting took place in Newport in the early hours of Saturday morning, with Victoria Place closed off to accommodate the filming. One onlooker said: 'They closed the streets off and brought in a huge snow machine to cover the road with snow … David Tennant was looking very cold as they waited around and was drinking plenty of tea to keep himself warm. Lindsay Duncan had a big, thick coat on, because it was freezing.'

The *Daily Mirror* meanwhile reported on the same date that a new TARDIS interior was to be designed for Matt Smith's first season, and the police box exterior given a make-over too. This story was reiterated by a number of other newspapers.

---

[5] As things transpired, it would not be until the autumn of 2010 that the stage show would finally come to fruition, as *Doctor Who Live*.

CHAPTER TWO: INTO THE GAP YEAR PROPER

In an interview published on 6 March on the wired.com website, director Euros Lyn spoke about the *Torchwood* mini-series 'Children of Earth' and also whetted readers appetites for the last two tenth Doctor specials, noting: 'I've seen the scripts, and they're amazing. I'm being very careful not to give anything away, but I think fans will be thrilled with David's farewell and how we set up the eleventh Doctor. I have to approach the project as I would any other. From the script's perspective, the past or the significance of the episode isn't relevant. You have to start with the script from day one … We're in post-production on *Torchwood* now, and I'm already into prep for *Doctor Who*.'

On 17 March, the *Daily Mirror* carried a brief story about the special currently in production:

> David Tennant will have to fight creatures from Mars in his last days as Doctor Who. Among those he takes on will be ex-soap actor Peter O'Brien, who played Shane Ramsay in *Neighbours*. He told reporters in Sydney he will appear as a villain in the story. Glamorous actress Gemma Chan has also been lined up as a baddie.

Two days later, the official *Doctor Who* website announced that BBC One's forthcoming John Barrowman-presented Saturday evening family entertainment show *Tonight's the Night* was launching an exciting competition:

> If you know of any mature aliens with an original name, home planet and background story who can design their very own home made alien outfit, why not get them to enter this exciting Alien Talent Search. They could be the lucky winner, and if so, experience a chance of a lifetime to work with an award winning BBC team spending several hours on set filming their very own special scene. This will appear on *Tonight's the Night* [on] BBC One in April/May 2009 (subject to scheduling) … The first phase is to get your mature alien to enter the 'Online Selection' stage, this is where the fun begins and they get the chance to show how creative they are by making an original alien outfit … Once all the entries have been received, they will be judged by a team of BBC programme-makers with up to 50 of the most outstanding applicants being invited to Phase Two of the competition, which will take place in London. This will be the 'Alien Activity Day' where the lucky few will get a chance to impress the Doctor's assistants in his search for a new alien race! … The final ten aliens will be required to face the expert panel individually and may be assessed on vocal, movement and scene stealing abilities. Three finalists will then face a final series of alien orientated challenges, but only one will win this once in a lifetime experience.

22 March saw a trailer for 'Planet of the Dead' being shown on large screens around the Millennium Stadium in Cardiff during the half time interval in an international rugby match between Wales and Ireland. The trailer consisted of numerous previously-unseen clips from the forthcoming special.

On 26 March, the BBC Press Office confirmed that 'Planet of the Dead' would air in the week beginning 11 April. Initially it was noted as being scheduled for the Saturday evening, but this was quickly changed to describe it as 'unplaced'. The following brief details were given:

> When a London bus takes a detour to an alien world, the Doctor must join forces with the extraordinary Lady Christina, in this one-off seasonal special. But the mysterious planet holds terrifying secrets, hidden in the sand. And time is running out, as the deadly Swarm gets closer.

On this day, the Press Office finally confirmed that 'Planet of Dead' would be broadcast at 6.45 pm on Easter Saturday. The first TV trailer for the special, featuring different clips from the Millennium Stadium one, went out on the evening of 1 April, during a programme break on BBC One. It would be aired on numerous further occasions over the days that followed, and was also placed online on the official website.

In addition, 1 April saw the *Sun* printing (without credit) a photo previously posted online by a fan, showing David Tennant performing a scene with Bernard Cribbins outside Tredegar House in Newport. This was from the location recording now getting under way for the final two tenth Doctor specials.

The following day's *Sun* had an interview with Paul McGann, the eighth Doctor, in which he made some tongue-in-cheek comments on the casting of the eleventh:

> Ex-Doctor Who Paul McGann claims Matt Smith got the Time Lord gig because of his crazy hair. McGann says his own locks landed him the role in 1996. And the eighth Doctor Who insists big hair is top of the Beeb's checklist when recruiting. McGann, 49, revealed: 'Matt said that in the auditions they could not stop talking about his hair. They were telling him his hair was wonderful – that's exactly what happened to me when I got the part ... Basically, if you've got long or big hair, you've got the job.' Paul added: '[Matt] is an absolute knockout choice – a fabulous actor with a very odd quality about him, which you need as the character.'

2 April saw the publication of an interview with Russell T Davies on the website of the London listings magazine *Time Out*; this also appeared subsequently in the print edition of the magazine. Asked if he would reveal how Tennant's Doctor would be written out, he joked: 'Ha ha! Yeah – an elephant falls on his head. Death by circus.' More seriously, he added: 'I've known exactly how he would die for a couple of years, just as I did with Chris Eccleston. The detail has changed, but I always have an end point in mind. The journey has changed – some characters and so on – but I knew the why, the how and what the reaction would be. Ha ha! Like it's real!' On the subject of the accidental damage to the bus in Dubai prior to recording of 'Planet of the Dead', he recalled: 'I actually laughed and laughed. There was frantic work for a lot of people, but I thought of the solution in about a minute flat: that's just what happens when a bus goes through a wormhole, it looks a bit worse for wear. You won't even notice the rewrite. The most important thing was that no-one was hurt. A

damaged double-decker looks beautiful in a way. There were other options, but they would have twisted the plot so badly that it would have broken in half.'

The *Sun* had yet more to say about *Doctor Who* on 3 April, reporting a comment from Michelle Ryan about her involvement in 'Planet of the Dead': 'I see Christina as someone who is around for this one-time adventure. Please don't put your bets on me being the next assistant. You would be wasting your time. *Doctor Who* is amazing but I think people presume, "Why wouldn't I want to do it as a regular thing?" I'm a commitment-phobe.'

Also on 3 February, the gay-interest magazine *Pink Paper* carried an interview with Davies's 'Planet of the Dead' co-writer, Gareth Roberts, in which he talked about working both on *Doctor Who* and *The Sarah Jane Adventures*.

As the flurry of pre-transmission press interest in 'Planet of the Dead' continued, *The Times* of 5 April printed an in-depth interview with Davies and Tennant. On the subject of 'Planet of the Dead', Davies noted: 'People are going to be *Doctor Who*-deprived this year, so it's got everything in it: CGI monsters, prosthetic monsters, army, police, an alien planet ... It's our last chance to have a bit of a laugh. Now the Doctor's facing the end of his life, it's going to get dark.' Asked if they had made a pact to leave the show at the same time, Tennant responded: 'We talked about it. It wasn't a pact ... I'd sort of decided. But then I nearly changed my mind again ... I kept my options open as long as I could!' Tennant also said that he cried when he read the script for his final episode.

Another interview with Davies appeared on the same day in the *Scotland on Sunday* newspaper, talking in depth about his writing.

Guesting on the sofa on the BBC's *Breakfast* programme on 7 April, Davies again promoted 'Planet of the Dead', production on which he said had been finally completed the previous evening. He also confirmed Bernard Cribbins' involvement in the last two Tennant-era specials.

8 April saw Tennant doing the rounds of a number of radio shows to give further publicity to 'Planet of the Dead'. First he guested on Christian O'Connell's breakfast show on Absolute Radio, where he said that not only Bernard Cribbins but also Catherine Tate would be appearing in his last two specials; then he moved on to the Jo Whiley show on BBC Radio 1; and lastly he spoke to Colin Murray, standing in for Simon Mayo on BBC Radio 5 Live's afternoon show. Michelle Ryan meanwhile did her bit to promote 'Planet of the Dead', appearing both on the CBBC children's magazine show *Blue Peter* and on Channel 4's *The Paul O'Grady Show*.

The morning of 11 April saw Tennant back on the radio, this time alongside Catherine Tate, when they were joint guest hosts of the Jonathan Ross show on BBC Radio 2. John Barrowman also popped in for a chat, and there was live music from one of Tennant's favourite groups, the Proclaimers.

The same day's edition of the *Daily Telegraph* carried another interview with Davies, an extended version of which was published on the newspaper's website. In this, Davies described 'Planet of the Dead' as 'a great big spectacular ... a little bit *Indiana Jones*, a little bit *Flight of the Phoenix*.'

The main event on 11 April, though, was of course the transmission of 'Planet of the Dead' itself that evening, simultaneously on BBC One and BBC HD, at the end of which the title for the next special was finally announced: 'The Waters of Mars'.

CHAPTER THREE
ON COURSE FOR MARS

Once 'Planet of the Dead' had been transmitted, fans had about seven months to wait until the next new *Doctor Who* reached the screen in the form of 'The Waters of Mars'. However, there was still plenty going on in the meantime to maintain their interest.

Location recording was continuing on David Tennant's final two specials, spawning occasional reports from local and national press – not to mention, as usual, from fans who attended the locations to observe what was going on, some of whom posted accounts on online forums such as Gallifrey Base (at www.gallifreybase.com).

On 15 April, the BBC announced the identities of the two new permanent producers who would work under executive producers Steven Moffat, Piers Wenger and Beth Willis on Series Five: Tracie Simpson and Peter Bennett, both of whom already had long behind-the-scenes associations with the show. Bennett had also recently produced the *Torchwood* mini-series 'Children of Earth', promotion of which continued apace, including with a preview screening of the first episode at the BFI South Bank in London on 12 June, with stars John Barrowman and Eve Myles and director Euros Lyn in attendance to answer audience questions afterwards.

The *Sun*'s 15 May edition meanwhile had a piece of casting news for the final Tennant-era specials, under the headline 'Licensed to Exterminate':

> Former James Bond Timothy Dalton is to play a baddie in one of David Tennant's final episodes of *Doctor Who*. Details are being kept under wraps but Dalton has already flown in from his home in Los Angeles for filming. An insider said: 'Timothy Dalton is a big coup for *Doctor Who* because he's pretty iconic. He's in the UK right now and is shooting scenes over the next few weeks. It's a good gig for him as it will be one of the most memorable episodes yet.' … The final episode will feature *all* the Doctor's sidekicks – Billie Piper, Freema Agyeman and Catherine Tate. John Simm will also feature as the Doctor's arch enemy the Master.

On 18 May, *Doctor Who* was again showered with awards, this time winning two BAFTA Craft Awards – for visual effects (the Mill) on 'The Fires of Pompeii' (2008) and editing (Philip Kloss) on Series Four overall – and four main BAFTA Cymru Awards – for sound (sound team), editing (Philip Kloss) and writing (Russell T Davies) on 'Midnight' (2008) and direction (Euros Lyn) on 'Silence in the Library' (2008).

21 May brought an interview with Russell T Davies on BBC Wales's *Wales Today* programme. Speaking from the TARDIS set, Davies reflected on his time as *Doctor Who* showrunner, which was shortly to come to an end – recording on the last of the specials was due to be concluded the following day. Asked if he had any favourite memories, he said that he had particularly enjoyed working with some wonderful

actors, including the Doctors and their companions. Invited to give a 'farewell message' to any cast and crew who were watching, he said, 'It's just been a joy to do this in Wales, and to [have] Welsh crews and so many Welsh actors, and the staff in the office are Welsh, and it's just been a joy, I think; and to have been welcomed into Cardiff in the way we have been. I'd like to say thank you. It's just been brilliant.'

The winning entrant in the *Tonight's the Night* Alien Talent Search competition, launched on 19 March, was finally announced on the 23 May edition of the programme: it was fan Tim Ingham, whose creation was the blue-skinned alien Sao Til from the planet Aminopius. The special scene made as the prize was shown during the programme, and lasted approximately three minutes. Written by Russell T Davies, it started with John Barrowman, in his Captain Jack Harkness guise, encountering Ingham, as Sao Til, on the TARDIS set. Sao Til initially tries to pass himself off as a new incarnation of the Doctor, but Captain Jack quickly sees through this when the alien brandishes a weapon attached to his right arm. As the confrontation reaches its climax, David Tennant enters the TARDIS, wearing everyday clothes, and it becomes apparent that what the viewer has been witnessing is not a piece of drama but simply Barrowman and Ingham playing around on the set. As Tennant leaves, warning them that he will be keeping his eyes on them, they resume their antics.

The producers of *Tonight's the Night* had originally wanted Davies to write a *bona fide Doctor Who* scene for them involving Sao Til, but he had been unwilling to do this, partly because it would have been the very last scene he ever wrote for the tenth Doctor, and he did not think that would be fitting. Consequently the scene ended up being more in the form of a comedy sketch in which, by the end, the actors were clearly appearing as themselves rather than genuinely in character.

The end of May brought a flurry of significant announcements. On 26 May, news broke of two more performances that David Tennant would be giving as the tenth Doctor outside of the gap year specials themselves. First, he would be guest-starring in a two-part story in the forthcoming new series of CBBC's *The Sarah Jane Adventures*. Secondly, he would be voicing the Doctor for a new animated *Doctor Who* serial, 'Dreamland', to be transmitted later in the year, initially on the BBC's Red Button interactive service.[6] The BBC Press Office issued a press release about the appearance in *The Sarah Jane Adventures*, quoting Sarah Jane actress Elisabeth Sladen as saying: 'When I heard the news that David was going to be joining us I was absolutely over the moon. Not only has it made my day but it will also make the viewers' day. It's fantastic news that Sarah Jane is going to spend some time working with the Doctor again and is testament to just how successful this CBBC series is.' Russell T Davies added, with a touch of hyperbole: 'Viewers thought they may have to wait until November for the next full episode of *Doctor Who*, but this is an extra special treat. And it's not just a cameo from David – this is a full-on appearance for the Doctor, as he and Sarah Jane face their biggest threat ever.'

Davies had previously promised fans that Tennant would be involved with three 'special projects' before bowing out as the Doctor: his performances in *The Sarah Jane Adventures* and the 'Dreamland' animation were the first two of these, but the third still remained under wraps for the time being.

On 27 May, the website of the American entertainment industry magazine *Variety*

---

[6] See Appendix A for full details of 'Dreamland'.

reported that BBC America would be giving the debut Stateside transmissions to the five gap year specials, starting with 'The Next Doctor' on 27 June. Previously, all new-era *Doctor Who* episodes had debuted on the Sci-Fi Channel in the States, so this marked a significant change. *Variety* noted:

> BBC America doesn't have a traditional upfront – the net acquires comparatively short seasons of Brit programmes and airs them year-round, sometimes combining them to make a US-length season. Because of the way BBC Worldwide is funded, BBC America has to outbid any interested Stateside nets, even for programming that appears on its sister network in the UK. The unique structure has occasionally resulted in a success story for BBC America that has turned into a success story for another net when the time came to renew the show. For *Doctor Who*, the reverse would appear to be true. The net has back a quintessentially British show that BBC Worldwide America [President] Garth Ancier wishes had always been on BBC America (he came onboard after the deal was made). 'If I'd been here,' Ancier said, 'we wouldn't have sold it, to be quite honest.'

The last of the month's big announcements came on 29 May, when BBC Press Office put out another press release, revealing the identity of the actress who would play the eleventh Doctor's first companion. It was Scottish born Karen Gillan, who had previously appeared in the minor role of a soothsayer in the Series Four episode 'The Fires of Pompeii':

> With filming due to begin this summer, Gillan beat off dozens of hopefuls to land one of television's most coveted roles. Gillan said: 'I am absolutely over the moon at being chosen to play the Doctor's new companion. The show is such a massive phenomenon that I can't quite believe I am going to be a part of it. Matt Smith is an incredible actor and it is going to be so much fun to act alongside him – I just can't wait to get started!' Lead writer and executive producer, Steven Moffat, added: 'We saw some amazing actresses for this part, but when Karen came through the door the game was up. Funny, and clever, and gorgeous, and sexy. Or Scottish, which is the quick way of saying it. A generation of little girls will want to be her. And a generation of little boys will want them to be her too.' Executive producer and Head of Drama BBC Wales, Piers Wenger, said: 'We knew Karen was perfect for the role the moment we saw her. She brought an energy and excitement to the part that was just fantastic. And when she auditioned alongside Matt we knew we had something special. It is a partnership that is ready to take on the universe!'

Also issued were some promotional images of Gillan standing on a flat rooftop beside the familiar shape of the TARDIS police box.

In Australia, 31 May saw 'Planet of the Dead' being transmitted for the first time on ABC1, *Doctor Who*'s traditional channel down under. Like most recent episodes of the show, it gained excellent ratings – over a million viewers in the five major capital cities combined – and garnered some very positive press coverage and reviews.

More news about the show's transmission overseas came on 1 June, when BBC America announced that *Torchwood*: 'Children of Earth' and 'Planet of the Dead' would together launch their new BBC America HD channel, the former screening over five nights from 20 July and the latter on 26 July in what the network was promoting as 'a special sci-fi week'. These transmissions would be simultaneous with those on the standard BBC America channel. This announcement was also notable for the fact that it actually preceded confirmation of the scheduling of 'Children of Earth' in the UK.

In Canada, meanwhile, the Doctor Who Blog website was reporting that it was not just in the US that *Doctor Who* would have a new home channel: in future, viewers in that country would be able to see the show on the Space Channel rather than the Canadian Broadcasting Corporation (which back in 2005 had even been credited as a co-production partner on the episodes). The Space Channel would also be broadcasting 'Children of Earth' over the same week as BBC America.

June was actually a relatively quiet time in the *Doctor Who* world. There was however a flurry of publicity for 'Children of Earth' toward the end of the month. On 18 June, it was revealed that the BBC One debut transmission of the mini-series would take place over five consecutive weekday evenings from 4 July. The week beginning 29 June then saw three new *Torchwood* audio plays being broadcast on BBC Radio 4. The issue of *Radio Times* that went on sale on 30 June, covering the following week's programmes, had a *Torchwood* fold-out cover featuring John Barrowman as Captain Jack Harkness. Lastly, Russell T Davies was interviewed on the 30 June edition of BBC Radio 4's *Front Row* programme, talking briefly about *Doctor Who* and *The Sarah Jane Adventures* as well as about *Torchwood*.

Torchwood also dominated the *Doctor Who* landscape in the early part of July, as 'Children of Earth' finally reached the screen, to exceptionally good viewing figures and great critical acclaim. 9 July did however bring one piece of news about *Doctor Who* itself, when the BBC Press Office put out a 'drama showreel', comprising a compilation of clips from all of the BBC's major autumn drama offerings, including 'The Waters of Mars'. The same date saw further promotional material for that forthcoming special being added to the official *Doctor Who* website, including a minute-long clip from one scene.

On the morning of 20 July, BBC News's entertainment correspondent Lizo Mzimba was back on the couch of the *Breakfast* programme to talk about *Doctor Who*, this time alongside *Doctor Who Magazine* reporter and *The Writer's Tale* co-author Benjamin Cook. The specific subject under discussion on this occasion was the eleventh Doctor's costume, the first photograph of which had just been released. The photograph showed Matt Smith sitting alongside co-star Karen Gillan on the steps of a location trailer, just prior to the start of their first day's recording on Series Five. The accompanying press release from the BBC Press Office quoted Steven Moffat as saying: 'And here it is, the big moment – the new Doctor, and his new best friend. And here's me, with the job I wanted since I was seven. 40 years to here! If I could go back in time and tell that little boy that one day all this would happen, he'd scream, call for his mum, and I'd be talking to you now from a prison cell in 1969. So probably best not then. Matt and Karen are going to be incredible, and *Doctor Who* is going to come alive on Saturday nights in a whole new way – and best of all, somewhere out there, a seven-year-old is going to see them, fall in love, and start making a 40-year plan ...' The full name of Gillan's character was also revealed for the first time in this press release as Amy Pond.

The photo of Smith and Gillan in costume generated a huge amount of media interest, and spawned many news and comment stories over the next couple of days, including from style magazines such as *Esquire* and *GQ*, which were generally complimentary about the Doctor's new look, and even the Chairman of the Harris Tweed Authority, who enthusiastically anticipated that the choice of a tweed jacket would be emulated by lots of youngsters. Reaction in the national press was more lukewarm. The *Guardian*'s Hadley Freeman wrote in the paper's 22 July edition:

> Hey, check out the new Burberry model, hanging out in the VIP section of Glastonbury, en route to meet Emma Watson and Pixie Geldof. Oh no, wait a fashion moment minute – it's Matt Smith, the all-new Doctor Who, on set in Cardiff. I'm going to be honest here: I hate this look. Hate it ... Because it commits the ultimate fashion crime: it is trying too hard. It is a patchwork of '*Grazia* told me this is very fashionable right now' looks, and that is just wrong. A Time Lord should not read *Grazia*. DM boots and all their lookalike cousins have, incredibly, been having what magazines insist on calling a 'comeback' for some time, mainly on the basis that Agyness Deyn likes them. The shortened trousers are the signature style of the perennially trendy menswear designer, Thom Browne. Thanks to the joyless likes of Pharrell Williams, bow ties are very in now but, like, ironically (that sound you hear is the sound of style dying), and, yes, you can buy them at American Apparel.

The *Sun*'s Sara Nathan was equally, though less eloquently, sceptical, writing on 21 July:

> New Time Lord Matt Smith films his first *Doctor Who* episodes – dressed like a geography teacher. It looked like the latest Doc had travelled back in time to the place fashion forgot. He donned a tweed jacket with elbow patches, braces and a bow tie for the latest series, which is set to feature the Time Lord's *wife* – played by Alex Kingston. Matt, 26, also wore black boots and rolled-up trousers. The preppy, old-fashioned look recalled bow-tie wearing Patrick Troughton, who played the second Doctor in the 1960s. It's a far cry from the current Doctor, David Tennant, who described his sharp suited and baseball boot look on the BBC One sci-fi hit as 'geek chic'.

This report in the *Sun* was accompanied by a number of paparazzi photographs taken during the previous day's location shoot on Southerndown Beach in Ogmore Vale, Bridgend (previously featured as Bad Wolf Bay in 'Doomsday' (2006) and 'Journey's End' (2008)). The photographs showed Smith and Gillan performing scenes alongside Alex Kingston as River Song, the enigmatic archaeologist character who had been introduced in 'Silence in the Library'/'Forest of the Dead' (2008) and whom many fans did indeed believe to be the Doctor's future wife. This first day's recording on Series Five, which had been attended by showrunner Steven Moffat and unveiled a new TARDIS police box in a slightly different shade of blue to the previous one, itself became the subject of much media discussion, including a short video report by Lizo Mzimba viewable on the BBC News website.

On 26 July, Russell T Davies, Julie Gardner, David Tennant and Euros Lyn answered questions on stage at the huge Comic-Con event in San Diego, California. They received a rapturous reception from the assembled throng, who were also treated to trailers for 'Planet of the Dead', 'The Waters of Mars' and – in a notable first – Tennant's last two specials, ending with the caption: 'The End of Time. Christmas 2009'.

In the UK, meanwhile, the trailer for 'The Waters of Mars', consisting of a 74-second montage of clips, was placed on the official *Doctor Who* website, which also confirmed that John Simm would be reprising his role as the Master in Tennant's swansong – as attendees of the San Diego event had already seen in some of the clips included in the trailer for that.

The San Diego event was also notable for the fact that it saw Russell T Davies being presented with a plaque commemorating *Doctor Who* receiving its second Guinness World Record – this one for being the most successful science fiction series ever. (The first one had been for being the longest-running science fiction series on TV.)

Issue 412 of *Doctor Who Magazine*, which went on sale on 20 August, confirmed that Tennant's last specials as the Doctor would be presented as a two-part story, the latter part of which would be entitled 'The End of Time', and that the guest stars would include Timothy Dalton, Bernard Cribbins, Catherine Tate, John Simm and comedy legend June Whitfield. It also indicated that the final part would be around 75 minutes long, as opposed to the usual 60 minute length of the specials.

Also on 20 August, fans who wanted to learn more about the 'Dreamland' animation, due to debut toward the end of the year, were given an opportunity to do so when the official *Doctor Who* website launched a blog on the making of the story, with a video introduction by Russell T Davies. Over the weeks that followed, this blog would include content such as interviews, artwork and clips of the finished production.

On 24 August, the US-based Airlock Alpha website (recently renamed from SyFy Portal) reported that Catherine Tate had won its annual Portal Award for best actress for her role as Donna Noble, as voted for by thousands of the website's readers'.

Meanwhile, recording of Series Five was continuing in Cardiff, with a green-painted Dalek and actor Bill Patterson being spotted on 27 August on the rooftop of Cardiff University's Glamorgan Building. There was more Series Five news on 8 September, too, when distinguished screenwriter Richard Curtis told the *Sun* that he would be writing an episode for Matt Smith's Doctor:

> Dad of three Richard confessed that he signed up for *Doctor Who* in a bid to impress his kids who are massive fans of the Time Lord. He said: 'It's tremendously good fun and a treat for my children. These days the things you can watch together as a family are much fewer so when you get something like *Doctor Who* or *The X Factor* it is such

a pleasure to sit down as a family.' It is also a chance for Richard to indulge his fascination with time travel – something that cropped up in *Blackadder*. He added: 'I am very interested in time travel for some reason or other. I am writing a film about it but on a low budget with no spectacular special effects. Maybe it's a desire to get out of being old. Sometimes you do just love the idea that you could go back in time and change things.'

Curtis confirmed his involvement in a video interview with Lizo Mzimba placed on the BBC News website on 15 September.

19 September saw *Doctor Who* winning the inaugural British Fantasy Award for Television at the annual FantasyCon event in Nottingham. The award was collected on Russell T Davies's behalf by Rob Shearman, the writer of 'Dalek' (2005).

Another piece of Series Five news hit the media on 5 October when the new *Doctor Who* logo and insignia – the latter consisting of a graphic made up of the letters 'DW' in a police box shape – were unveiled in a BBC press release. Steven Moffat was quoted as saying: 'A new logo. The eleventh logo for the eleventh Doctor – those grand old words, Doctor Who, suddenly looking newer than ever. And, look at that, something really new – an insignia! DW in TARDIS form! Simple and beautiful, and most important of all, a completely irresistible doodle. I apologise to school notebooks everywhere, because in 2010 that's what they're going to be wearing.' The logo and insignia were further shown off in an animated teaser trailer placed on the official *Doctor Who* website, which ended with the simple caption, '2010'.

On 6 October, CBBC's *Blue Peter* launched a competition in which young viewers were invited to submit designs for a new TARDIS control console, with the promise that the winner's entry would be used in a future episode of *Doctor Who* itself.

9 October brought the sad news that former *Doctor Who* producer Barry Letts had died at the age of 84. Letts had been in charge of the show throughout virtually all of the third Doctor's era, had been responsible for casting Tom Baker as the fourth Doctor and had made numerous other contributions to the show and its tie-ins in other media.

A happier development came on 15 October when the third series of the highly successful spin-off *The Sarah Jane Adventures* began its on-air run on BBC One/CBBC with the opening episode of 'Prisoner of the Judoon', the first of six two-part stories. Three weeks later, on 29 October, viewers saw the first part of the story featuring David Tennant's Doctor, *The Wedding of Sarah Jane Smith*. The second part was transmitted the following day. No doubt due to Tennant's presence, these episodes drew about double the number of viewers that *The Sarah Jane Adventures* usually got – 1.6 million and 1.5 million respectively – and exceptionally good Appreciation Index figures – 87 and 89 respectively.

On 4 November, the BBC Press Office announced the scheduling of the animated adventure 'Dreamland':

Described as '*Doctor Who* meets a '50s monster B-movie', 'Dreamland', a new six-part animated adventure, premières daily on BBC Red Button and the *Doctor Who* website (bbc.co.uk/doctorwho) from Saturday 21 November. Written by Phil Ford (*Doctor Who*, *Torchwood*, *The Sarah Jane Adventures*),

'Dreamland' sees the iconic TARDIS touch down in the desert in the USA. Stumbling across a mysterious alien artefact in a local diner, the Doctor is led to Area 51, also known as Dreamland, the US's most secret base. He then finds himself on a momentous mission to rescue Rivesh Mantilax from the threat of the ruthless Viperox and the clutches of the American military. Created in eye-catching high-definition 3D animation, the series sees the Doctor, played by David Tennant, hook up with two new companions – Cassie (Georgia Moffett) and Jimmy (Tim Howar) – and pits him against a new alien race, the monstrous Viperox, led by Lord Azlok (David Warner). The multiplatform offering will be enhanced by a brand-new mobile comic reader application.

For five days from 9 November, David Tennant joined disc jockey Christian O'Connell each morning to co-present his breakfast show on Absolute Radio. During the first show, Tennant announced that he would be auctioning off his own bed for charity, donating the proceeds to the BBC's *Children in Need* appeal. (In the event, this auction did not take place as the bed was damaged beyond repair while being stored at the Absolute Radio studios; a donation was made to the charity instead.)

The edition of *Radio Times* that went on sale on 10 November once again had a *Doctor Who* cover, this time depicting David Tennant's Doctor in the spacesuit he would be seen wearing in 'The Waters of Mars', which would receive its debut transmission the following Sunday, 15 November. By this point, it had also been confirmed that the special would air in New Zealand on 29 November, in Australia on 6 December and in the USA and Canada on 19 December, meaning that viewers in all of these major markets would have got to see it within little more than a month of their UK counterparts.

In Issue 415 of *Doctor Who Magazine*, which went on sale on 12 November, Russell T Davies confirmed that this year's *Children in Need* telethon, to be transmitted on 20 November, would again feature a *Doctor Who* item. Like the previous year's, this would take the form of a preview clip from the forthcoming Christmas special – the title of which had still to be revealed at this point, although Davies said that it would be six words long.[7]

15 November then brought the much-anticipated transmission of 'The Waters of Mars'. There was perhaps rather less advance publicity this time around than there had been for either 'The Next Doctor' or 'Planet of the Dead', despite most of the national newspapers as usual running preview pieces in their weekend editions, but this certainly didn't seem to have any adverse impact on the ratings: the final figures, released just over a week later, showed that the special had been seen by some 9.94 million viewers on BBC One and an additional 0.38 million on BBC HD; excellent numbers by any standards.

Now, though, aside from the 'Dreamland' animation, there were only two more specials remaining before fans would have to bid farewell to the tenth Doctor.

---

[7] At this point, the intention was that the Christmas special would be entitled 'The Last Days of Planet Earth'. Only later was it decided to give David Tennant's last two specials the overall title 'The End of Time'.

CHAPTER FOUR
THE END IS NIGH

Christmas is traditionally a time of happiness and celebration, but for *Doctor Who* fans, the 2009/2010 festive season would be tinged with sadness, as they witnessed David Tennant's departure from the show.

Following transmission of 'The Waters of Mars', there was little over a month to wait before the next special went out on Christmas Day 2009. On 19 November, the official *Doctor Who* website revealed that the title of that special would be 'The End of Time' Part One, making this the first time since the show returned to TV in 2005 that the episodes of a multi-part story had not had different individual titles. The following day, the promised clip from the special was aired during the *Children in Need* programme. This was of almost three-and-a-half minutes' duration, and showed the Doctor arriving on the Ood-Sphere, from just after the opening titles. The 15-minute segment of *Children in Need* including this clip was reported the following day to have been watched by 11.9 million BBC One viewers, the highest rating on any channel that day, equating to a remarkable 49.5% audience share.

Over the six days from 21 November, the six-part 'Dreamland' animation was broadcast as planned on the BBC's Red Button service, where – according to figures released by the BBC some weeks later – it was seen by almost one million viewers. The complete story was then screened in omnibus form on BBC Two at 10.00 am on 5 December.

On 23 November – the forty-sixth anniversary of the day *Doctor Who* began – the BBC Press Office released advance information about Christmas programming on all of the BBC's channels, along with a 10-minute trailer of clips, including for both parts of 'The End of Time'.

The new edition of *Radio Times* that went on sale on 28 November again saw *Doctor Who* grace the front cover, with an image of a grim-faced tenth Doctor outside the TARDIS on a snowy landscape and the headline 'Death of a Doctor'. Inside the magazine was a three-page preview of 'The End of Time', featuring interviews with Russell T Davies and Bernard Cribbins.

29 November saw the British Academy Children's Awards being presented at the Hilton Hotel, London. Cribbins was the recipient of this year's Special Award for his many contributions to children's programming over the decades. In the days leading up to this, he gave a number of interviews, including one on the BBC's *Breakfast* show, reminiscing about his career and commenting on his *Doctor Who* roles.

Hopeful news for *Torchwood* fans came on 30 November when, interviewed on the *Steve Wright in the Afternoon* show on BBC Radio 2, John Barrowman stated that he had signed up for a fourth series, currently expected to be a full 13-episode run, although it was unknown exactly when this would go into production.

The start of December as usual brought an upswing in publicity for the forthcoming Christmas special. On 1 December, the official *Doctor Who* website launched its annual 'advent calendar' feature, which would see new items unveiled on a daily basis, many of them relating to 'The End of Time'. The following day, the BBC Press Office revealed scheduling information for the major Christmas programmes, indicating that Part One of 'The End of Time' would go out at 6.00 pm on Christmas Day and Part Two at 6.40 pm on New Year's Day.

David Tennant gave a flurry of interviews over the course of December, including in that month's issue of *Readers' Digest*, and made numerous TV and radio guest appearances, including on *Blue Peter* (BBC One/CBBC), *Never Mind the Buzzcocks* (BBC Two), *QI* (BBC One), *Breakfast* (BBC One) and *Desert Island Discs* (BBC Radio 4). He would also be seen on BBC Two on Boxing Day playing the lead role in *Hamlet*, a TV version of the RSC's acclaimed production of a year earlier. Many of his co-stars in 'The End of Time' also made promotional appearances this month, on a wide variety of TV and radio chat shows, news programmes and entertainment round-ups.

By the beginning of December, fans had also gleaned the nature of the third 'special project' that Russell T Davies had promised involving the tenth Doctor: a set of four special Christmas idents for BBC One. The main one, lasting 30 seconds, involved the Doctor hooking up a team of six reindeer to a snowbound TARDIS and flying it through the air, looping the loop around a BBC One logo, in the style of Father Christmas on his sleigh. The others, lasting five seconds each, consisted of, respectively, the Doctor starting to dig the TARDIS out of the snow with a shovel; a reindeer beside the TARDIS; and a reindeer snorting at the camera.

On 4 December, the MediaGuardian website was the first to reveal the cover of this year's Christmas edition of *Radio Times*. This came in two variants: the first depicted Father Christmas winding up a pair of toy ballroom dancers – alluding to the popular BBC One show *Strictly Come Dancing* – while the second showed him winding up a clockwork Dalek – making this yet another *Doctor Who*-related cover. The issue went on sale a few days later, and included a lot of *Doctor Who* content, including an interview with David Tennant. The festive editions of the UK's other TV listings magazines, all published around this time, also carried preview pieces on 'The End of Time', and in some cases their own interviews with Tennant.

4 December also saw the BBC debuting on its YouTube channel a new trailer covering both 'The End of Time' Part One and an unrelated programme, the animated children's drama *The Gruffalo*, which would be transmitted just before it on Christmas Day. This trailer would later receive numerous airings between programme breaks on the main BBC channels.

5 December brought an opportunity to see a number of previously-unpublished publicity images from 'The End of Time', presented in a gallery on the official CBBC website.

The edition of the weekly London listings magazine *Time Out* that went on sale on 8 December was notable for featuring ten different *Doctor Who* covers – one for each Doctor to date. However, while the full set was available to buy online, only the David Tennant one could be found in shops.

A flurry of press reports was sparked on 10 December when the familiar police box shape of the TARDIS was spotted atop the inner east gatehouse tower of Caerphilly Castle in Wales. Some fans initially assumed that this was part of a location shoot for a Series Five story, but it turned out that it was actually a promotional stunt for the Castle's Christmas fair that weekend.

On 11 December, the BBC placed two Christmas video messages from David Tennant, in character as the tenth Doctor, on its YouTube channel. These had been recorded during the same session and on the same set as the BBC One Christmas idents. In the first, the Doctor said: 'Christmas presents. I love opening Christmas presents. Although, I'm always slightly disappointed when they're not bigger on the inside. Have a very merry Christmas with BBC One.' In the second, he said: 'Christmas! Brilliant! I love Christmas. In fact, when it's over, I'm going to pop back and do it all over again. Have a very merry Christmas with BBC One.'

Russell T Davies remained busy on the promotional trail. In a *Western Mail* interview published on the Wales Online website on 15 December, he commented: 'David deserves this, and the programme deserves this – it deserves to go out on a high. The audience deserve it too, they've been so faithful to us and loyal and devoted. I don't mean just the fans, I mean the kids, and the parents who sit with the kids. It's Christmas and New Year, so you want people to be happy, to sit down and enjoy something together, to laugh, to be sad. It's all there in these final two episodes. It's like all your Christmas presents rolled into one, right from your big present to the tiniest thing at the bottom of the stocking.'

New showrunner Steven Moffat was meanwhile interviewed by broadcaster and *Doctor Who* fan Matthew Sweet on BBC Radio 3's *Night Waves* programme between 9.15 and 10.00 pm on 15 December, talking about his plans for the show and revealing for the first time that the Weeping Angels from 'Blink' would be making a return appearance.

On 17 December, a short interview with David Tennant, conducted by Lizo Mzimba, was placed on the BBC News website. Recorded earlier in the year, when 'The End of Time' was still in production, it saw Tennant reflecting on his time as the Doctor and his imminent departure from the show, and speaking enthusiastically about his swansong story, a number of clips from which were shown by way of illustration.

Also on 17 December, 'The End of Time' Part One received a press screening at the BBC's Television Centre. The very end of the episode, featuring the reveal of Timothy Dalton's character, was removed from this in order to preserve the surprise of the cliff-hanger. Tennant was not present at the screening, but it was attended by other members of the cast, including John Simm, Catherine Tate, Bernard Cribbins, Claire Bloom, David Harewood and Alexandra Moen, as well as outgoing and incoming showrunners Russell T Davies and Steven Moffat. Initial media reaction to the special came in a number of reports over the next few days, and was largely positive. Paul Collins of the Total Sci-Fi Online website marked it 9/10, and commented:

> With the return of Wilf and the Master – not to mention Ood Sigma, and Donna and her Mum – this episode could easily have become bogged down in continuity, and off-putting for a Christmas Day audience, but once again Russell T Davies has pulled off the trick of pleasing long-term fans within the confines of an easy-to-understand, rollicking fantasy adventure. The perfect example of this is the resurrection of the Master, which manages to be both a brief and functional device to get the story moving, yet also pivotal to the development of the character. True,

the story relies on a few flashbacks and some linking narration to fill in gaps that might have been more artfully explained, but Davies has never been one to miss an opportunity, and there's a definite sense that 'The Narrator' will turn out to be much more than just a narrator … So whether fan or gran, viewers should find this the perfect Christmas present when they settle down after the biggest dinner of the year, and one entirely deserving of the fanfare BBC One has afforded it.

Excitement about the forthcoming two-parter was not confined to the UK. Media items about the show were also appearing in other countries, perhaps most notably the USA, where a number of newspapers and websites presented interviews with David Tennant, currently living in Los Angeles while playing the leading role in a pilot being made for a possible new NBC comedy-drama series entitled *Rex is Not Your Lawyer*. BBC America meanwhile continued to enjoy considerable success with *Doctor Who*. Its transmission of 'The Waters of Mars' on 18 December won the channel its highest ever primetime ratings, as 1.1 million viewers tuned in.

On 23 December, the *Daily Mirror* had an interview with Russell T Davies, the main focus of which was his fears for the BBC's future if the Conservative Party were to win the next General Election. Headed 'Tories Will Exterminate BBC If They Get Elected', it did however contain some brief comments about 'The End of Time'. 'From New Year's Day I should feel happy, but could feel terrible,' said Davies. 'I shed a tear when I finished writing it – it is emotional. Saying goodbye, for me and David, has been a long process. If it had happened overnight I'd [be] bereft and grieving, but we've had a long time to get used to the idea.'

The following day, another interview with Davies appeared in print, this time in the *Guardian*, revealing a perhaps surprising inspiration behind his approach to *Doctor Who*:

They have both revived Saturday night television, but on the face of it, *Pop Idol* and *Doctor Who* would appear to have little in common. But as fans of the sci-fi drama prepare to witness the death of David Tennant's Doctor this Christmas, it has emerged that the talent show forerunner of *The X Factor* was a key inspiration for the Time Lord's creative rebirth. 'It was the biggest Saturday night show then,' said *Doctor Who*'s executive producer, Russell T Davies. 'We used to gather around at a friend's house to watch the final and vote, and I wanted to do that with drama. If we could have the voice at the beginning of *The X Factor* introducing each episode I would do it.'

Christmas Day saw 'The End of Time' Part One being transmitted as scheduled, concluding with the shocking revelation of the Time Lords' return.

On 26 December, David Tennant and Catherine Tate fulfilled what was becoming something of a regular engagement for them, standing in for Jonathan Ross on his BBC Radio 2 show. Their guests included Bernard Cribbins and fifth Doctor actor Peter Davison. Then, at 8.00 pm that evening, BBC Radio 4 broadcast an hour-long programme about the 108 episodes of 1960s *Doctor Who* currently missing from the BBC's archives. This was produced by Shaun Ley, who had also been responsible for a 12 December documentary on the same channel entitled *Shelved*, looking at a number of abandoned and unbroadcast BBC productions from the 1970s, including the *Doctor Who* story 'Shada'.

The 27 December editions of all the national newspapers reported on the initial ratings figures for Christmas Day's programmes, which had again seen the BBC securing a dominant position. The *Daily Star* noted:

> Huge audiences for *The Royle Family, Doctor Who* and *Gavin & Stacey* made the BBC the clear winner in this year's ratings battle, where they landed nine of the top ten shows on Christmas Day for the second year running. *The Royle Family* had an average of 10.2 million viewers and was the second most watched show after *EastEnders* – followed by *Doctor Who*, seen by 10 million. The only ITV programme to make the Top 10 was [*Coronation Street*], the sixth most popular show. BBC One Controller Jay Hunt said yesterday: 'I am thrilled.'

The Times' arts editor Peter Brooks was alone in putting a negative slant on things, in a piece headed 'Doctor Who Fails to Top Christmas TV Ratings':

> The great Christmas slump in front of the television screen may have had its day. This year's most hyped programme for 25 December, David Tennant's penultimate appearance as Doctor Who, managed to attract just 10m viewers, 1.4m fewer than last Christmas's *Doctor Who* instalment. Even the most-watched programme, *EastEnders*, won only 10.9m viewers. On 25 December 2008, by contrast, *A Matter of Loaf and Death*, the *Wallace and Gromit* Christmas special on BBC One, drew an audience of 14m. The increasing time that Britons spend in front of computer screens – whether playing games, surfing the internet or shopping online – appears to be cutting into television viewing.

Of 'The End of Time' Part One itself, the *Daily Mirror* commented approvingly:

> Part One of Tennant's farewell to *Doctor Who* – 'The End of Time' – was terrific. An amazing supporting cast included David Harewood, Claire Bloom, Timothy Dalton, June Whitfield and the inestimable Bernard Cribbins. The storyline consisted of a classic duel between the Doctor and the Master. John Simm revelled in the Master's madness, shooting lightning bolts from his fingers, devouring chickens whole and doing a good impression of Keith from the Prodigy. 'Breaking news!' he cackled as he escaped his Hannibal Lecter chains. 'I'm everyone. And everyone in the world is me.' Russell T Davies's trump card has always been the scale of his ambition. Let's hope he goes out in style on New Year's Day.

CHAPTER FOUR: THE END IS NIGH

29 December saw BBC Radio 2 broadcasting an hour-long programme entitled *Who on Who?*, in which David Tennant interviewed Russell T Davies (and, at times, vice versa) about his work on *Doctor Who*. A previously-unheard audio clip from 'The End of Time' Part Two was played. This same clip was then used with picture as well as sound, on that evening's edition of Channel 4's *Alan Carr: Chatty Man*, accompanying an interview with Tennant and Catherine Tate.

Ever keen to stir up controversy, the *Daily Mail* printed on 30 December a story headed 'How Doctor Who (With a Little Help from Hamlet) Took Over the BBC':

> He is about to make his final bow after nearly five years as one of the most popular incarnations of Doctor Who. But it seems the BBC are squeezing as much as they can out of the success of David Tennant. By the end of the Christmas period, the actor will have made 75 appearances in three weeks on the Corporation's TV channels and radio stations. As well as his two-part farewell as the time-traveller in *Doctor Who*: 'The End of Time', the 38-year-old has starred in a production of *Hamlet*, been a presenter and panellist on celebrity quiz shows and read stories for a children's programme. He has also been featured as a guest on *Desert Island Discs* and even popped up on a programme about the *Open University* – all between 14 December and 3 January. Just 28 of his appearances come in new programmes, while 47 are repeats. Tennant has also appeared regularly in BBC One's promotional 'idents' in between shows.

This story was subsequently picked up in a number of other media reports.

31 December saw Tennant giving some parting reflections on his time in *Doctor Who* in an interview on the BBC's *Breakfast* programme and in a BBC Radio 5 Live phone-in. Then, the following evening, the moment that all of the tenth Doctor's fans had been dreading finally arrived, as his era came to an emotional close at the climax of 'The End of Time' Part Two.

With Tennant's departure came also that of Russell T Davies and his fellow executive producer Julie Gardner. This meant that all of the major players responsible for the hugely successful 2005 revival of *Doctor Who* had now gone; it was the end of an era in more ways than one. However, proof that the show would go on came a little later on the evening of 1 January 2010, when viewers of BBC One were treated to a minute-long trailer of clips from Series Five, incorporating captions reading: 'Coming Spring 2010. The End is Just the Beginning'.

The dawn had broken on a new era of *Doctor Who*.

PART TWO
BIO-DATA

CHAPTER FIVE
MAIN CAST

DAVID TENNANT (THE DOCTOR)

David Tennant was born David John McDonald in Bathgate, West Lothian, on 18 April 1971 and grew up in Ralston, Renfrewshire, where his father was a Church of Scotland minister. His later stage name, adopted in order to avoid confusion with another actor called David McDonald, was taken from that of pop star Neil Tennant of the Pet Shop Boys. He became a fan of *Doctor Who* at a young age and, partly inspired by that, made it his ambition to become an actor. He joined a Saturday youth theatre while still attending Paisley Grammar School and went on to train at the Royal Scottish Academy of Music and Drama, to which the youth theatre was affiliated. In his twenties he joined a radical Scottish theatre company called 7:84, making his professional debut in their production of *The Resistible Rise of Arturo Ui*. He broke into TV with small parts in *Strathblair* (BBC One, 1992) and a 1993 episode of *Rab C Nesbitt* (BBC Two, 1988-1999) and then won his first lead role, as a manic-depressive, in a drama called *Takin' Over The Asylum* (BBC Two, 1994). After moving from Scotland to London, where he rented rooms from actress Arabella Weir of *The Fast Show* (BBC, 1994-2000), he gained more theatre work, including in numerous Royal Shakespeare Company productions. He also made his feature film debut in *Jude* (Universal Pictures/PolyGram Filmed Entertainment, 1996), in which he shared a scene with its star Christopher Eccleston, later to play the ninth Doctor. Further film roles followed, including in Stephen Fry's *Bright Young Things* (Film Four, 2003) and *Harry Potter and the Goblet of Fire* (Warner Brothers, 2005). It was for his TV work that he became best known, however, taking parts of increasing prominence in programmes such as: *The Mrs Bradley Mysteries* (BBC One, 1999), in which he appeared opposite fifth Doctor actor Peter Davison; *Randall and Hopkirk (Deceased)* (BBC One, 2000-2001); a first season episode of *Foyle's War* (ITV, 2002-); and *He Knew He Was Right* (BBC One, 2004). His rise to star status came with major roles in two acclaimed series in quick succession: as DI Carlyle in *Blackpool* (BBC One, 2004) and, even more memorably, as the title character in Russell T Davies's *Casanova* (BBC Three, 2005), which gained him his first front cover picture on *Radio Times*. *Casanova* effectively served as Tennant's 'audition' for the part of the tenth Doctor, for which he was the only actor seriously considered when Eccleston departed. He accepted the role after a brief hesitation, and quickly became a household name following his full debut in 'The Christmas Invasion' on Christmas Day 2005. This was not in fact his first connection with *Doctor Who*: he had previously played voice parts in a number of Big Finish's audio CD dramas – 'Colditz' (2001); 'Sympathy for the Devil' (2003); 'Exile' (2003) (one of the *Doctor Who Unbound* range); the spin-off series *Dalek Empire III* (2004); 'Medicinal Purposes' (2004); and 'The Wasting' (2005), an episode of the *UNIT* spin-off – and also in an episode of the webcast story 'Scream of the Shalka' (2003). His portrayal of the tenth Doctor was, however, the first time he had been associated with the series in the general public's eyes, and it saw him becoming Britain's most popular TV actor, winning numerous awards and other accolades. He still found time to take on a number of other roles during breaks in production on *Doctor Who*, including in the TV plays *Recovery* (BBC One, 2007) and *Learners* (BBC One, 2007), and has made numerous guest appearances on talk shows and the like. Following completion of work on the 2008 *Doctor Who* Christmas special, he joined the Royal Shakespeare Company to appear in new productions of *Hamlet* – as Hamlet – and *Love's Labour's Lost* – as Berowne. After leaving *Doctor Who*, he lived in Los Angeles for a time, and starred in an unaired pilot for a new US show entitled *Rex is Not Your Lawyer*.

DAVID MORRISSEY (JACKSON LAKE)

David Morrissey was born on 21 June 1964 in Everton, Liverpool. Having trained at Liverpool's Everyman Theatre and at RADA, he made his on-screen debut in Willy Russell's *One Summer* (Channel 4, 1983). He then worked mainly in the theatre for a time, including for two years in the Royal Shakespeare Company. Other early TV credits included *Cause Célèbre* (ITV, 1987), *The Storyteller* (ITV, 1990), *Between the Lines* (BBC One, 1993), *The Knock* (ITV, 1994) and *Out of the Blue* (BBC One, 1995). He also made a number of appearance in movies, including *Drowning by Numbers* (1988), *Robin Hood* (1991), *Waterland* (1992) and *Being Human* (1993). He came to greater prominence after taking on the role of the main protagonist in *Holding On* (BBC One, 1997), which won him the Royal Television Society's Best Actor award. Also well received was his portrayal of Bradley Headstone in an adaptation of Dickens' *Our Mutual Friend* (BBC One, 1998). Further film roles followed, including in *Hilary and Jackie* (1998), *Fanny and Elvis* (1999), *Some Voices* (2000) and *Captain Corelli's Mandolin* (2001). He also turned his hand to directing, initially on *Sweet Revenge* (BBC One, 2001). Two of his most prominent roles to date came in Paul Abbot's six-part drama *State of Play* (BBC One, 2003) and Stephen Frears' TV movie *The Deal* (Channel 4, 2003), in the latter of which he portrayed future Prime Minister Gordon Brown. Next he co-starred with David Tennant in the musical drama serial *Blackpool* (BBC One, 2004). A period of work in Hollywood followed, as the male lead opposite Sharon Stone in *Basic Instinct 2* (2006) and in *The Reaping* (2007). Further notable TV work came next, in the serials *Cape Wrath* (Channel 4, 2007) and *Sense and Sensibility* (BBC One, 2008). He then won another movie role in *The Other Boleyn Girl* (2008). A spell in the theatre followed, in *In a Dark Dark House* at the Almeida Theatre in London. Following his appearance as Jackson Lake in 'The Next Doctor', Morrissey continued to take on a variety of high-profile film and TV roles, and also continued to work as a director, including on his first feature-length project, *Don't Worry About Me* (BBC Two, 2010).

MICHELLE RYAN (CHRISTINA DE SOUZA)

Michelle Claire Ryan was born on 22 April 1984 in Enfield, Middlesex. As a child she joined a local theatre group, and at the age of 15 she won a coveted part as Zoe Slater in the hugely successful BBC One soap opera *EastEnders*. This was a role she was to play for some five years, from 2000 to 2005. Following that, she took a wide variety of TV roles, including one in Steven Moffat's *Jekyll* (BBC One, 2007). Shortly after this, she starred in the short-lived US revival of a 1970s cult classic, *Bionic Woman* (NBC, 2007). When that was cancelled – its chances of success having been damaged by the US writers' strike at that time – she resumed her career as a TV actress in the UK, the role of Lady Christina in 'Planet of the Dead' being just one of many in which she could be seen at the end of the 2000s.

LINDSAY DUNCAN (ADELAIDE BROOKE)

Lindsay Vere Duncan was born on 7 November 1950 in Edinburgh, Scotland. She studied acting at the Central School of Speech and Drama in London, then worked extensively in the theatre for a number of years, mainly in supporting parts. From the 1980s, she turned her attention more to TV, taking increasingly prominent roles. She appeared in, amongst others, *Reilly, Ace of Spies* (ITV, 1983), *Dead Head* (BBC Two, 1986), *Kit Curran* (ITV, 1986), *Traffik* (Channel 4, 1989), *G.B.H.* (Channel 4, 1991), *A Year in Provence* (BBC One, 1993), *Jake's Progress* (Channel 4, 1995), *Get Real* (ITV, 1998) and *Oliver Twist* (ITV, 1999). She never abandoned the theatre, however, and from 1985 to 1987 performed to great acclaim as La Marquise de Merteuil in the Royal Shakespeare Company's production of *Les Liaisons Dangereuses*, in Stratford-upon-Avon, London and New York. This won her the Laurence Olivier Award for Best Actress in 1986. Amongst her most notable roles subsequently were that of Servilia in the series *Rome* (BBC/HBO/RAI. 2005-2007) and that of Lord Longford's wife Elizabeth in *Longford* (Channel 4, 2006). In 2008, she appeared in the play *That Face* at the Duke of York's Theatre in London's West End, opposite future eleventh Doctor Matt Smith. Following her role as Adelaide Brook in 'The Waters of Mars', she played Alice's mother in Tim Burton's movie *Alice in Wonderland* (2010). She was awarded a CBE in the 2009 Queen's Birthday Honours list.

JOHN SIMM (THE MASTER)

John Ronald Simm was born on 10 July 1970 in Leeds, West Yorkshire, and raised in the small town of Nelson in Lancashire. He initially followed in the footsteps of his musician father Ronald, learning to play the guitar and accompanying him on stage for performances at working men's clubs and the like under the name Us2. This led on to him becoming the guitarist in the band Magic Alex during the 1990s and singing backing vocals on an album by Ian McCulloch, former leader of Echo and the Bunnymen, with whom Magic Alex had toured as a support act. In the meantime, he had been studying acting, first at Blackpool Drama College for three years from the age of 16, and then at the Drama Centre in London. While still performing as a musician, he started to take acting jobs as well, winning his first TV role in a 1992 episode of *Rumpole of the Bailey* (ITV, 1975-1992). Further notable TV parts came in a 1995 episode of *Cracker* (ITV, 1993-1996, 2006), in two series of *The Lakes* (BBC One, 1997-1999) and in a 2000 episode of *Clocking Off* (BBC One, 2000-2003). He also found work in feature films, with roles in *Boston Kickout* (CNC, 1995), *Diana & Me* (BVI/Village Roadshow Pictures, 1999), *Understanding Jane* (Scala Productions, 1998), *Human Traffic* (Metrodome/Miramax, 1999), *Wonderland* (Universal Pictures, 1999), *Miranda* (First Look/ Pathé/Film Four, 2002) and *24 Hour Party People* (United Artists, 2002), the latter of which saw him playing Bernard Sumner of the group New Order and led on to him performing a song live on stage with them at a concert in Finsbury

Park, London, the same year – by which point he had otherwise effectively given up working as a musician to concentrate fully on acting. With his reputation steadily growing, he returned to TV with parts in productions including *Crime and Punishment* (BBC Two, 2002), *State of Play* (BBC One, 2003), *The Canterbury Tales* (BBC One, 2004) and *Sex Traffic* (Channel 4, 2004), before taking on the starring role for which he is now best known, as policeman DI Sam Tyler in *Life on Mars* (BBC One, 2006-2007). After completing work on the second season of *Life on Mars* and portraying artist Vincent Van Gogh in the biographical drama *The Yellow House* (Channel 4, 2007), Simm took up temporary residence in Cardiff to play the Master in 'Utopia'/'The Sound of Drums'/'Last of the Time Lords' (2007). Subsequent credits included prominent parts in *The Devil's Whore* (Channel 4, 2008) and the TV movie *Skellig* (Sky1, 2009). Following his return to the role of the Master in 'The End of Time', he appeared in the play *Speaking in Tongues* (2009) at London's Duke of York theatre.

BERNARD CRIBBINS (WILFRED MOTT)

Bernard Cribbins was born Bernard McDermott on 29 December 1928 in Oldham, Lancashire. He joined the Oldham Repertory Theatre at the age of 14 and served an eight year apprenticeship, with a break for National Service in the Parachute Regiment in his late teens. His early work was in the theatre, and he made his West End debut in 1956 at the Arts Theatre playing the two Dromios in Shakespeare's *A Comedy of Errors*. He went on to co-star in the first West End productions of the farces *Not Now Darling*, *There Goes the Bride* and *Run For Your Wife*. From the late 1950s he started appearing in TV shows and films, in increasingly prominent roles. He also developed a talent for musical comedy, and in 1962 recorded the two hit novelty records 'Right Said Fred' and 'Hole in the Ground'. Some of his most well-remembered film roles came over the next decade, including in the comedies *Carry On Jack* (1963) and *Carry On Spying* (1964), as hapless policeman Tom Campbell alongside Peter Cushing's Dr Who in *Daleks' Invasion Earth 2150 AD* (1966) and as station porter Perks in *The Railway Children* (1970). By the end of the 1960s, he had become one of Britain's best-loved character actors, specialising in comedy roles, and was even given his own series, *Cribbins* (BBC One, 1969). In the 1970s he remained a familiar face in a wide variety of TV shows. He also narrated the animated children's TV series *The Wombles* (BBC One) and a celebrated BBC radio adaptation of *The Wind in the Willows* and provided voices for the Tufty character in the Green Cross Code road safety films and for Buzby, a talking cartoon bird that served as the mascot for the then GPO, which later became BT. He holds the record as the most prolific contributor to the BBC's children's story reading programme *Jackanory*, with over a hundred appearances stretching from the 1960s to the 1990s. His other notable TV credits include a 1975 episode of *Fawlty Towers* and a 2003 stint as the regular character Wally Bannister in *Coronation Street* (ITV1). His role in the 2007 *Doctor Who* Christmas special 'Voyage of the Damned' was originally intended to be a one-off, with his character named Stan, but at producer Phil Collinson's suggestion he was brought back to play Donna Noble's grandfather, named Wilfred Mott by Russell T Davies, after Howard Attfield, who had been intended to reprise his role as her father Geoff, died shortly after recording began. The closing credits of 'Voyage of the Damned' were amended before transmission to reflect the change of the character's name.

CHAPTER SIX
PRINCIPAL CREATIVE TEAM

RUSSELL T DAVIES OBE (SHOWRUNNER, EXECUTIVE PRODUCER, LEAD WRITER)

Russell T Davies was born in Swansea, South Wales, in 1963. (The 'T' does not stand for anything: he was born Stephen Russell Davies, decided to use the name Russell Davies for professional purposes and started using 'T' as an initial in the 1980s in order to distinguish himself from an actor, journalist and broadcaster also called Russell Davies.) He was educated at Olchfa School, a huge comprehensive, and had an early involvement with the West Glamorgan Youth Theatre in Swansea. He then studied English Literature at Worcester College, Oxford University, graduating in 1984. His TV career began with posts as a floor manager and production assistant at the BBC, where in the late 1980s he also trained as a director and gained a presenting credit on *Play School* (1987). He produced the children's series *Why Don't You ...?* for BBC Manchester from 1988 to 1992, during which time he also started to work as a writer, gaining credits on *The Flashing Blade* (1989), *Breakfast Serials* (1990) and *Chucklevision* (1991). His writing career moved up a gear when he was responsible for the acclaimed BBC children's serials *Dark Season* (1991) – which he also novelised for BBC Books – and *Century Falls* (1993). In 1992, he moved from the BBC to Granada, where he produced and wrote for the popular children's drama *Children's Ward* (1992-1996). He also started to gain writing credits for family and adult programmes, including *Cluedo* (1993), *Families* (1993), *The House of Windsor* (1994) and *Revelations* (1994). He worked briefly as a storyliner and writer on *Coronation Street* (1996) and contributed to Channel 4's *Springhill* (1996). It was at this time that he had his first professional association with *Doctor Who* – having been a long-time fan of the series – when he wrote the New Adventures novel *Damaged Goods* (1996) for Virgin Publishing. The following year, he was commissioned to contribute to the ITV period drama *The Grand* (1997), and ended up scripting the whole series after a number of other writers dropped out. He subsequently left Granada and joined a company called Red Productions, where he had a major success as creator, writer and producer of *Queer as Folk* (1999-2000), a groundbreaking two-season drama series for Channel 4 about a group of gay men in Manchester, which also spawned a US remake. Since then, his career has gone from strength to strength, with writer and executive producer credits on *Bob and Rose* (2001) and *Mine All Mine* (2004) for ITV and *The Second Coming* (2003), *Casanova* (2005) and of course *Doctor Who* (2005-2009), *Torchwood* (2006-) and *The Sarah Jane Adventures* (2007-) for the BBC. On 20 May 2008, it was announced that he would be relinquishing his showrunner responsibilities on *Doctor Who* the following year, leaving him free to pursue new projects. He has since moved to Los Angeles to develop scripts for BBC Worldwide America. He is frequently cited as one of the most influential and powerful people in the British TV industry, and was awarded an OBE for services to drama in the Queen's 2008 birthday honours.

JULIE GARDNER (EXECUTIVE PRODUCER)

Julie Gardner was born in South Wales, near Neath, in 1969. Having gained a degree in English at London University, she began her working life as a teacher of English to secondary school pupils in Wales. In her mid-twenties, however, she decided that this was not the career for her, and she successfully applied for a job at the BBC, as the producer's secretary on the series *Our Friends in the North* (1996). She quickly ascended the ladder of promotion to script reader in the Serial Drama Department, then to script editor and then to producer, working on shows including *Silent Witness* (1996), *Sunburn* (1999) and *The Mrs Bradley Mysteries* (2000). In 2000, she left the BBC and took up a post as development producer at London Weekend Television. There she was responsible for dramas including a controversial modern-day retelling of Shakespeare's *Othello* (2001) and *Me and Mrs Jones* (2002). She was working on further ideas at LWT when, in 2003, she was head-hunted to become Head of Drama at BBC Wales. The new *Doctor Who* series gave her one of her first executive producer credits, and she went on to fulfil a similar role on *Torchwood* and *The Sarah Jane Adventures*. Other projects she oversaw at BBC Wales included *Casanova* (2005), *Girl in the Café* (2005) and *Life on Mars* (2006-2007). On 21 September 2006 it was announced that she had been promoted to the post of the BBC's Head of Drama Commissioning, and would have special responsibility for implementing a cohesive independent drama strategy across the UK. She would however remain as Head of Drama, BBC Wales, for the time being, and would continue as executive producer of *Doctor Who*, *Torchwood* and *The Sarah Jane Adventures*. Her role on those shows ended in 2009, when she handed over responsibility to Piers Wenger. She has since moved to Los Angeles to work as executive producer of scripted projects for BBC Worldwide America.

SUSIE LIGGAT (PRODUCER)

Susie Liggat's TV credits have come mainly as a first assistant director, including on series such as *Teachers* (Channel 4, 2001-2004) and *Casanova* (BBC Three, 2005). In 2006 she produced both *The Sarah Jane Adventures*: 'Invasion of the Bane' and, standing in for Phil Collinson, one recording block of Series Three of *Doctor Who*, comprising the story 'Human Nature'/'The Family of Blood' (2007). She then served as producer on five episodes of Series Four and the Christmas special 'The Next Doctor'. After leaving *Doctor Who*, she produced *Blood and Oil*, a two-part drama for BBC Two, transmitted early in 2010.

TRACIE SIMPSON (PRODUCER)

Tracie Simpson started her TV career as a production co-ordinator on BBC Wales shows including *Tiger Bay* (1997), *Jack of Hearts* (1999) and *Care* (2000). She was associate producer on another BBC Wales show, *The Bench* (2001), before becoming production manager on *Doctor Who* from the start of Series One until mid-way through Series Four. She returned to the show to produce 'Planet of the Dead' and 'The End of Time' and was then appointed as one of the two permanent producers for Series Five.

CHAPTER FIVE: MAIN CAST

NIKKI WILSON (PRODUCER)

Nikki Wilson, *née* Smith, started out as an actress. She then turned her hand to script editing, initially on the first five series of the police procedural drama *Trial and Retribution* (ITV1, 1997-), the latter of which also saw her serving as head of development and taking a small role as a showgirl. Other script editor credits came on Lynda La Plante's *Mind Games* (ITV1, 2001), *The Bill* (ITV1, 2003) and the *Doctor Who* story 'The Sontaran Stratagem'/'The Poison Sky' (2007). She then took over from Matthew Bouch as producer of *The Sarah Jane Adventures* for its second and third series. 'The Waters of Mars' was her first *Doctor Who* producer credit.

LINDSEY ALFORD (SCRIPT EDITOR)

Lindsey Alford studied Psychology and Zoology and joined the BBC's Natural History Unit as a researcher on wildlife programming. She then transferred to BBC One's *Casualty*, progressing from researcher to storyliner to script editor over a period of several years. Moving to BBC Wales in 2006, she gained further script editor credits on *Doctor Who* ('Daleks in Manhattan'/'Evolution of the Daleks' (2007) and 'Human Nature'/'The Family of Blood' (2007)), the whole of the first series of *The Sarah Jane Adventures*, and the *Torchwood* episode 'Adrift' (2008). She then became the principal script editor on Series Four of *Doctor Who*, and continued in this role for the first two gap year specials.

GARY RUSSELL (SCRIPT EDITOR)

Gary Russell was born in Maidenhead, Berkshire on 18 September 1963. He began his working life as a child actor, winning notable TV roles in *The Phoenix and the Carpet* (BBC One, 1976), *The Famous Five* (ITV, 1978), *Dark Towers* (BBC One, 1981) and *Schoolgirl Chums* (BBC One, 1982). A lifelong *Doctor Who* fan, he edited his own fanzine, *Shada*, in the 1980s, and contributed to a number of others. This led to a new career as a freelance writer and editor. He contributed to the official *Doctor Who Magazine* and was its editor between 1992 and 1995; wrote a number of *Doctor Who* novels between 1994 and 2005; co-wrote with Philip David Segal the non-fiction book *Regenerations* (HarperCollins, 2001) about the 1996 TV movie; and was producer and occasional director of the Big Finish *Doctor Who* audio CD dramas between 1998 and 2006. He then joined BBC Wales, initially to administer product licensing for *Doctor Who, The Sarah Jane Adventures* and *Torchwood*. He served as director for the animated *Doctor Who* series 'The Infinite Quest' (2007) before starting work as a script editor on episodes of Series Two of *Torchwood*. His first *Doctor Who* script editor credits came on 'The Waters of Mars' and 'The End of Time'. He has also written *Doctor Who – The Inside Story* (BBC Books, 2006), *Doctor Who – The Encyclopedia* (BBC Books, 2007), *The Sarah Jane Adventures: Warriors of Kudlak* (BBC Books, 2007), *Torchwood: The Twilight Streets* (BBC Books, 2008), *The Torchwood Archives* (BBC Books, 2008), *The Sarah Jane Adventures: The Lost Boy* (BBC Books, 2008) and stories for IDW Publishing's *Doctor Who* comic book series, which launched in 2008. Outside of the *Doctor Who* world, his most notable work as an author has been on a number of non-fiction titles related to the movies based on Tolkien's *The Lord of the Rings*. These include: *The Lord of the Rings: Gollum: How We*

Made Movie Magic (Houghton Mifflin, 2003), co-written with Andy Sirkis; a range of books about the movies' art and design work, culminating in the best-of collection *The Art of The Lord of the Rings* (Houghton Mifflin, 2004); and *The Lord of the Rings: The Official Stage Companion: Staging the Greatest Show on Middle Earth* (HarperCollins, 2007).

GARETH ROBERTS (WRITER)

Gareth Roberts was born in 1968. He studied drama at college and worked as a clerk at the Court of Appeal while also pursuing an interest in writing. In the 1990s he authored seven acclaimed *Doctor Who* novels, plus novelisations of two episodes of *Cracker* (ITV, 1993-1996), for Virgin Publishing. He also wrote for *Doctor Who Magazine* and for Big Finish's tie-in audio CD drama range before coming to work on the TV series via the digital mini-adventure 'Attack of the Graske' (2005) and the 'Tardisode' teasers for Series Two. He has written the new series novels *Only Human* (BBC Books, 2005) and *I Am A Dalek* (BBC Books, 2006) and several *Doctor Who* short stories. He has also written numerous episodes of *The Sarah Jane Adventures*. His other TV credits include: storylines for *Springhill* (Sky One, 1996-1997); episodes of *Emmerdale* (ITV1, 1972-) in 1998; episodes of *Brookside* (Channel 4, 1982-2003) over a four year period from 1999; and co-written episodes of *Randall and Hopkirk (Deceased)* (BBC One, 2000-2001) and *Swiss Toni* (BBC Three, 2004-2004).

PHIL FORD (WRITER)

Phil Ford gained his first TV writing credits in 1998 on episodes of ITV1's *Taggart*, *Coronation Street* and *Heartbeat*. He went on to contribute scripts to a number of other ITV1 series, including *The Bill* (2001), *Footballers' Wives* (2002), *Bad Girls* (2005-2006) and *Bombshell* (2006). It was, however, his work on *Gerry Anderson's New Captain Scarlet* (ITV1, 2005), for which he wrote the majority of the episodes, that caught the attention of Russell T Davies and his team. He was commissioned to provide the stories 'Eye of the Gorgon' and 'The Lost Boy' for Series One of *The Sarah Jane Adventures* and was then elevated to head writer on Series Two and Three. For *Torchwood*, he wrote 'Something Borrowed' (2008); the 'alternate reality' online game presented on the official website; and the novel *Skypoint* (BBC Books, 2008). 'The Waters of Mars' gave him his first *Doctor Who* credit, quickly followed by the animated story 'Dreamland'. His other recent TV commissions include two episodes of the BBC One series *Waterloo Road* (2007).

ANDY GODDARD (DIRECTOR)

Andy Goddard began his career as a writer and director on the award-winning short film *Little Sisters* (1997), *Yabba Yabba Ding Ding* (Film Four 1999), *Kings of the Wild Frontier: 'New Found Lands'* (STV, 2000) (co-written with Ian Rankin) and *Rice Paper Stars* (BBC Scotland, 2000). He then focused increasingly on directing rather than writing, and was responsible for episodes of *G4CE* (CBBC, 2001), *Stacey Stone* (CBBC, 2001), *Taggart* (ITV1, 2003), *Casualty* (BBC One, 2003), *The Bill* (ITV1, 2003-2004), *Twisted Tales* (BBC Three, 2004), *Murphy's Law* (BBC One 2004-2005), *Hex* (Sky One) and *Wire in the Blood* (ITV1 2005-2006). His first contact with the *Doctor*

Who world came when he directed six episodes across Series One and Two of *Torchwood*. This led on to his assignment on 'The Next Doctor'. He has since directed several episodes of *Law & Order: UK* (ITV1, 2009-2010).

JAMES STRONG (DIRECTOR)

James Strong's first TV credits were as a documentary maker, on *Critical Mass* (Carlton, 1998), *World in Action* (ITV, 1998/99), *My FC* (Channel 5, 2000) and *Crimewatch UK* (BBC1, 2000). He then moved into directing comedy and drama programmes, including *Otis Lee Crenshaw* (Channel 4, 2000), *Jack Dee's Happy Hour* (BBC One, 2001), *Doctors* (BBC One, 2000-2001), *Nothing but the Truth* (ITV1, 2001), *Blood on her Hands* (ITV1, 2002), *Mile High* (Sky One, 2002), *Holby City* (BBC One, 2002-2004), *Casualty* (BBC One, 2004), *The Good Citizen* (BBC One, 2004) and *Rocket Man* (BBC One, 2005) He both wrote and directed the comedy short film *Sold* (2002) and the TV dramas *Lady Jane* (ITV1, 2003) and *Billie Jo* (ITV1, 2004). For the new-era *Doctor Who* he directed 'The Impossible Planet'/'The Satan Pit' (2006), 'Daleks in Manhattan'/'Evolution of the Daleks' (2007), 'Voyage of the Damned' (2007), 'Partners in Crime' (2008) and 'Planet of the Dead'. He also directed 'Cyberwoman' (2006) and 'They Keep Killing Suzie' (2006) for the first series of *Torchwood*.

GRAEME HARPER (DIRECTOR)

Graeme Harper was born on 11 March 1945. He started his working life as a child actor, appearing in TV adaptations of *The Pickwick Papers* (Associated Redifussion, 1956) and *The Silver Sword* (BBC, 1957), amongst other productions, before becoming a floor assistant at the BBC in 1965. It was in the latter capacity that he first worked on *Doctor Who*, on stories including 'The Power of the Daleks' (1966). He was promoted to assistant floor manager in 1969, being assigned to *Doctor Who* again on 'Colony in Space' (1971), 'Planet of the Daleks' (1973) and 'Planet of the Spiders' (1974). His next promotion, in 1975, was to production assistant, in which capacity he worked on 'The Seeds of Doom' (1976) and 'Warriors' Gate' (1981). He then successfully completed the BBC's directors' course. The fifth Doctor's swansong 'The Caves of Androzani' (1984) was the first job he got as a freelance director, after handling some of the final episodes of the hospital drama *Angels* (BBC One, 1975-1983) in-house at the BBC. He went on to direct one further classic series story, 'Revelation of the Daleks' (1984), and would also have handled the third story of Season 23 had the series not then been put on temporary hiatus by Michael Grade, Controller of BBC One at that time. He subsequently became one of Britain's most sought-after TV directors, building up an impressive list of credits on shows such as: *The District Nurse* (BBC One, 1984-1987); *Star Cops* (BBC Two, 1987); *Boon* (ITV, 1986-1992); *The House of Elliot* (BBC One, 1991-1994); numerous episodes of *Casualty* (BBC One, 1986-); *The Royal* (ITV, 2003-); some 2003 and 2005 episodes of *Byker Grove* (BBC One, 1989-2006); and three episodes of *Robin Hood* (BBC One, 2006-). He came close to working on *Doctor Who* again both in 1989, when he was approached to direct 'Battlefield' (an assignment he was prevented from taking on as he was already committed to *Boon*), and in 1993, when he was scheduled to helm the planned, but ultimately unmade, thirtieth anniversary story 'The Dark Dimension'. He finally returned to direct numerous new-era *Doctor Who* episodes, including the special 'The Waters of Mars'. In addition, he has directed several episodes of *The Sarah Jane Adventures*.

EUROS LYN (DIRECTOR)

Euros Lyn was born in Wales in 1971 and educated at Ysgol Gyfun Ystalyfera and the University of Manchester. He began his career as a TV director in 1997, and gained some of his earliest credits on several episodes of the BBC Wales drama *Belonging* in 2000. Aside from the numerous episodes he has directed for *Doctor Who*, from 'The End of the World' in 2005 to 'The End of Time' in 2009/10, he has also worked on, amongst others, *All About George* (ITV1, 2005), *Jane Hall* (ITV1, 2006) and *George Gently* (BBC One, 2007). In addition, he directed all five episodes of *Torchwood*: 'Children of Earth' (BBC One, 2009).

EDWARD THOMAS (PRODUCTION DESIGNER)

Edward Thomas took a foundation course in art and design after leaving school, and then studied at the Wimbledon School of Art, from which he graduated with a BA (Hons) degree in 3-D Design, specialising in theatre. He began his career as a designer on a wide variety of commercials and a number of theatrical productions, including *Turandot* for the Royal Opera Company at Wembley Arena, *Under Milk Wood* for the Dylan Thomas Theatre Company and Shakespeare's *Twelfth Night* and *Cymbeline* for the Ludlow Festival. This was followed by work on numerous feature films, including over a dozen South African productions in the early 1990s and *The Mystery of Edwin Drood* (1993), *Resurrection Man* (1998), *Darkness Falls* (1999) and *The Meeksville Ghost* (2001). He also gained credits on a wide range of TV shows including, for BBC Wales, *Jones, The Coal Project* and, of course, *Doctor Who* (2005-), *Torchwood* (2006-) and *The Sarah Jane Adventures* (2007-). He has sometimes been credited as Edward Alan Thomas or simply as Ed Thomas, and is represented by the Creative Media Management agency.

PART THREE
PRODUCTION CREDITS

DOCTOR WHO
THE NEXT DOCTOR (4.14)
PLANET OF THE DEAD (4.15)
THE WATERS OF MARS (4.16)
THE END OF TIME – PART ONE (4.17)
THE END OF TIME – PART TWO (4.18)

PRODUCTION CREDITS[8]

Producer: Susie Liggat (4.14), Tracie Simpson (4.15, 4.17, 4.18), Nikki Wilson (4.16)

1st Assistant Director: Richard Harris (4.14), John Bennett (4.15), William Hartley (4.16), Peter Bennett (4.17, 4.18)
2nd Assistant Director: Jennie Fava (4.14), James Dehaviland (4.15, 4.16, 4.17, 4.18)
3rd Assistant Director: Heddi Joy Taylor (4.14, 4.17, 4.18*), Sarah Davies (4.15, 4.16)
Location Manager: Gareth Skelding
Unit Manager: Beccy Jones (4.14), Geraint Williams (4.15, 4.16), Rhys Griffiths (4.17, 4.18*)
Production Co-ordinator: Jess Van Niekerk
Production Secretary: Claire Thomas (4.14), Kevin Myers (4.15, 4.16, 4.17, 4.18*)
Production Runner: Sian Warrilow (4.14, 4.16, 4.17*, 4.18*)
Driver: Wayne Humphreys (4.14, 4.16*, 4.17*, 4.18*), Kevin Kearns (4.06, 4.14), Malcolm Kearney (4.16*, 4.17*, 4.18*)
Floor Runner: Nicola Brown (4.14, 4.15, 4.16*, 4.17*), Tom Evans (4.14, 4.16*, 4.17, 4.18*), Bobby Williams (4.14), Alison Jones (4.16, 4.18*), Chris Goding (4.18)
Assistant Production Accountant: Carole Wakefield (4.16*, 4.17, 4.18)
Contracts Assistants: Kath Blackman (4.14*, 4.16*, 4.17*, 4.18*), Lisa Hayward (4.14*, 4.16*, 4.17*, 4.18*)
Continuity: Non Eleri Hughes (4.14, 4.17, 4.18), Llinos Wyn Jones (4.15, 4.16)

---

[8] Where an episode number (or more than one) appears in brackets after a person's name in the listing, this means that they were credited only on the episode (or episodes) indicated. Otherwise, the person concerned was credited on all episodes. The numbering follows the convention used by the show's production team, who effectively treated these five specials as a continuation of Series Four, even though they were made months apart. Some production roles were credited only on certain episodes. Where an asterisk appears beside an episode number, this means that the person concerned was credited only on the DVD and Blu-Ray versions of the episode, not on the transmitted version.

Script Editor: Lindsey Alford (4.14, 4.15), Gary Russell (4.16, 4.17, 4.18)

Camera Operator: Roger Pearce (4.14, 4.16), Joe Russell (4.14, 4.15, 4.17, 4.18), James Leigh (4.15), Rory Taylor (4.16), Alwyn Hughes (4.17, 4.18)

Focus Puller: Jamie Southcott, Duncan Fowlie (4.14), Steve Rees (4.15, 4.16, 4.17, 4.18)

Grip: John Robinson (4.14, 4.15, 4.16), Clive Baldwin (4.17, 4.18)

Camera Assistant: Jon Vidgen (4.16, 4.17*, 4.18), Tom Hartley (4.16, 4.17*, 4.18)

Boom Operator: Glen Jenkins (4.14), Patrick O'Boyle (4.14), Jeff Welch (4.14*, 4.15, 4.16, 4.17*, 4.18), Bryn Thomas (4.14*, 4.15, 4.16, 4.17*, 4.18)

Gaffer: Mark Hutchings

Best Boy: Peter Chester

Electrician: Alan Tippetts (4.14), Steve Guy (4.14), Clive Johnson (4.14), Gavin Riley (4.14), Steve Slocombe (4.15, 4.16*, 4.17, 4.18*), Clive Johnson (4.15, 4.16*, 4.17, 4.18*), Ben Griffiths (4.16, 4.17*, 4.18*), Jonathan Cox (4.16, 4.17*, 4.18*)

Stunt Co-ordinator: Tom Lucy (4.14), Lee Sheward (4.15, 4.17, 4.18), Abbi Collins (4.16)

Stunt Performer: Gordon Seed (4.14*, 4.16*, 4.17*, 4.18*), Dean Foster (4.14*), Jason Hunjan (4.14*), Maurice Lee (4.14*), Nick Wilkinson (4.14*), Sarah Franzl (4.17*, 4.18*), Paul Herbert (4.17*, 4.18*), Marlow Warrington Mottei (4.17, 4.18*), Tony Lucken (4.18*)

Choreographer: Ailsa Berk

Chief Supervising Art Director: Stephen Nicholas[9]

Associate Designer: Julian Luxton (4.14), James North (4.15, 4.16, 4.17, 4.18)

Art Department Co-ordinator: Amy Pope (4.15, 4.16, 4.17, 4.18)

Standby Art Director: Ciaran Thompson (4.14, 4.16), Nick Murray (4.15), Keith Dunne (4.17, 4.18*)

Art Department Production Manager: Jonathan Marquand Allison (4.14*, 4.18*)

Graphic Designer: Christina Tom (4.14*, 4.16*, 4.17*, 4.18*)

Model Maker: Al Roberts (4.14*)

Concept Artist: Peter McKinstry (4.14*), Sarah Payne (4.14*)

Storyboard Artist: Shaun Williams (4.14*, 4.16*, 4.17*, 4.18)[10]

Design Assistant: Al Roberts (4.16*, 4.18)

Concept Artist Trainee: Lee Bryan (4.16*, 4.17*, 4.18*)

Standby Props: Phill Shellard (4.14, 4.15, 4.16, 4.17, 4.18*), Jackson Pope (4.14, 4.15, 4.16, 4.17, 4.18*)

Set Decorator: Keith Dunne (4.14), Julian Luxton (4.15, 4.17, 4.18), Joelle Rumbelow (4.16)

Props Buyer: Ben Morris (4.14*), Catherine Samuel (4.16*), Adrian Anscombe (4.17*, 4.18)

Production Buyer: Ben Morris (4.16*, 4.17*, 4.18)

Props Master: Paul Aitkin (4.14, 4.15, 4.16, 4.17, 4.18*)

Props Chargehand: Phil Lyons (4.14*)

Design Chargehand: Matt Wild (4.16*, 4.17*, 4.18*)[11]

---

[9] Credited as 'Supervising Art Director' on 4.16 and 4.18.

[10] Credited on 4.16*, 4.17* and 4.18* as 'Storyboard and Concept Artist', and on 4.16*, 4.17* and 4.18 under the name 'Richard Shaun Williams'.

[11] Credited on 4.17* as 'Dressing Chargehand'.

Forward Dresser: Matt Wild (4.14*)

Props Dresser: Pat Deacy (4.14*)

Dressing Props: Stuart Wooddisse (4.16*), Rhys Jones (4.16*, 4.17*, 4.18*), Phil Lyons (4.17*, 4.18*)

Props Driver: Tom Belton (4.16*, 4.17*, 4.18*)

Props Dailies: Austin Curtis (4.16*, 4.17*, 4.18*), Ian Davies (4.16*, 4.17*, 4.18*), Jayne Davies (4.16*, 4.17*, 4.18*), Matt Watts (4.16*, 4.17*)

Practical Electrician: Albert James (4.14*, 4.16*, 4.17*, 4.18*)

Props Fabrication Manager: Penny Howarth (4.14*, 4.16*, 4.17*, 4.18*)

Props Makers: Nicholas Robatto (4.14*, 4.16*, 4.17*, 4.18*), Jon Grundon (4.14*, 4.16*, 4.17*, 4.18*)

Construction Manager: Matthew Hywel-Davies

Construction Chargehand: Scott Fisher (4.14*, 4.16*, 4.17*, 4.18*)

Workshop Manager: Mark Hill (4.14*, 4.16*, 4.17*, 4.18*)[12]

Scenic Artist: John Pinkerton (4.16*, 4.17*, 4.18*), John Whalley (4.16*, 4.17*, 4.18*), Lou Bohling (4.16*, 4.17*, 4.18*), Steve Fudge (4.16*, 4.17*, 4.18*), Janine Little (4.16*, 4.17*, 4.18*)

Carpenter: Chris Daniels (4.16*, 4.17*, 4.18*), Brian Jones (4.16*, 4.17*, 4.18*), Joe Painter (4.16*, 4.17*, 4.18*), Mark Painter (4.16*, 4.17*, 4.18*), Chris Selley (4.16*, 4.17*, 4.18*), Chris Stephens (4.16*, 4.17*, 4.18*), Nick Stephenson (4.16*, 4.17*, 4.18*), Justin Williams (4.16*, 4.17*, 4.18*)

Standby Painter: Julia Challis (4.14*)

Standby Carpenter: Will Pope (4.14*, 4.16*, 4.17*, 4.18*)

Standby Rigger: Keith Freeman (4.14*, 4.16*, 4.17*, 4.18*)

Graphics: BBC Wales Graphics

Assistant Costume Designer: Rose Goodhart

Costume Supervisor: Lindsay Bonaccorsi

Costume Assistant: Barbara Harrington, Louise Martin

Make-Up Artist: Pam Mullins, Steve Smith (4.14, 4.15, 4.16), Morag Smith, Cathy Davies (4.17, 4.18)

Casting Associate: Andy Brierley

Casting Assistant: Alice Purser (4.16, 4.17, 4.18*)

Post Production Supervisor: Samantha Hall, Chris Blatchford

Post Production Co-ordinator: Marie Brown

SFX Co-ordinator: Ben Ashmore (4.14*), Paul Kelly (4.16*, 4.17*, 4.18*)

SFX Supervisor: Danny Hargreaves (4.14*, 4.16*, 4.17*, 4.18*)

SFX Technician: Dan Bentley (4.14*, 4.16*, 4.17*, 4.18*), Henry Brook (4.14*, 4.16*, 4.17*, 4.18*), Gareth Jolly (4.14*, 4.16*, 4.17*, 4.18*)

SFX Trainee: Felix Rowberry (4.16*, 4.17*, 4.18*)

Prosthetics Designer: Neill Gorton (4.14*, 4.16*, 4.17*, 4.18*), Rob Mayor (4.14*)

Prosthetics Studio Manager: Rob Mayor (4.16*, 4.17*, 4.18*)

Prosthetics Administration Manager: Martina Hawkins (4.16*, 4.17*, 4.18*)

Prosthetics Studio Co-ordinator: Kate Walshe (4.16*, 4.17*, 4.18*)

Prosthetics Crew[13]: Pete Hawkins (4.14*), Jon Moore (4.14*), Sarah Lockwood (4.14*, 4.16*, 4.17*, 4.18*), Lauren Wellman (4.14*), Alex Wathey (4.14*, 4.16*, 4.17*, 4.18*),

---

[12] Credited on 4.16*, 4.17* and 4.18* as 'Construction Workshop Manager'.

[13] Credited on 4.16*, 4.17* and 4.18* as 'Prosthetics Technicians'.

Lenny Sant (4.14*), Jill Reeves (4.14*), Karen Spencer (4.14*, 4.16*, 4.17*, 4.18*), Darren Nevin (4.14*, 4.16*, 4.17*, 4.18*), Martina Hawkins (4.14*), Kate Walshe (4.14*), Lisa Crawley (4.14*), Pete Tindall (4.16*, 4.17*, 4.18*), Valentina Visintin (4.16*, 4.17*, 4.18*), Valter Cosotto (4.16*, 4.17*, 4.18*), Gilles Paillet (4.16*, 4.17*, 4.18*), Lauren Wellman (4.16*, 4.17*, 4.18*), Fiona Walsh (4.16*, 4.17*, 4.18*), Vikki Muse (4.16*, 4.17*, 4.18*)

On Line Editor: Mark Bright (4.14*), Matthew Clarke (4.14*)

VFX Editor: Ceres Doyle (4.14, 4.16), Matt Mullins (4.17), Joel Skinner (4.18)

Colourist: Mick Vincent

Online conform: Mark Bright (4.16*, 4.17*, 4.18*), Matthew Clarke (4.16*, 4.17*, 4.18*)

Assistant Editor: Carmen Roberts (4.14, 4.16*, 4.17*, 4.18), Lee Bhogal (4.15, 4.16*, 4.17*)

3D Supervisor: Jean Claude-Deguara (4.14*, 4.16*, 4.17*, 4.18*), Nicholas Hernandez (4.16*, 4.17*, 4.18*)

3D Artist: Nicholas Hernandes (4.14*), Matthew McKinney (4.14*, 4.18*), Jean-Yves Audouard (4.14*, 4.17*, 4.18*), Nick Webber (4.14*, 4.16*, 4.17*), Neil Roche (4.14*, 4.17*, 4.18*), Serena Cacciato (4.14*, 4.17*), Adam Burnett (4.14*), Jeff North (4.14*, 4.17*, 4.18*), Edmund Kolloen (4.14*, 4.16*, 4.17*, 4.18*), Will Pryor (4.14*, 4.16*, 4.17*, 4.18*), Andy Guest (4.14*, 4.16*, 4.17*), Wayde Duncan-Smith (4.14*, 4.17*, 4.18*), Sam Lucas (4.14*, 4.17*, 4.18*), Bruce Magroune (4.14*, 4.16*, 4.18*), Ruth Bailey (4.14*, 4.17*, 4.18*), Grant Bonser (4.14*, 4.16*, 4.17*, 4.18*), David Jones (4.14*, 4.16*, 4.17*, 4.18*), Emily Pearce (4.14*), Virgil Manning (4.14*), David Bennett (4.14*, 4.18*), Ross Stansfield (4.18*), Nick Bell (4.18*), Zahra Al Naib (4.18*)

2D Supervisor: Peter Barber (4.14*), Sara Bennett (4.16*, 4.17*), Murray Barber (4.18*)

2D Artist: Sara Bennett (4.14*, 4.18*), Michael Harrison (4.14*, 4.17*, 4.18*), Tim Barter (4.14*), Russell Horth (4.14*), Arianna Lago (4.14*, 4.16*, 4.17*, 4.18*), James Etherington (4.14*), Adriano Cirulli (4.14*, 4.16*, 4.17*, 4.18*), Simon C Holden (4.14*), Joe Courtis[14] (4.14*, 4.16*, 4.17*, 4.18*), Loraine Cooper (4.14*), Lyndall Spagnoletti (4.14*, 4.16*, 4.17*, 4.18*), James Moxon (4.14*, 4.16*, 4.17*, 4.18*), Julie Nixon (4.14*, 4.16*, 4.17*, 4.18*), Murray Barber (4.16*, 4.17*), Greg Spencer (4.16*, 4.17*, 4.18*), Bryan Bartlett (4.17*, 4.18*), David Bowman (4.17*, 4.18*), Rosemary Chester (4.17*, 4.18*), Martin Davison (4.18*), Frank Hanna (4.18*)

Senior Digital Matte Painter: Simon Wicker (4.16*)

Digital Matte Painter: Simon Wicker (4.14*, 4.17*, 4.18*), David Early (4.14*, 4.16*, 4.17*, 4.18*), Charlie Bennett (4.14*, 4.16*, 4.17*, 4.18*), Alex Fort (4.16*, 4.17*)

VFX Co-ordinator: Jenna Powell (4.14*), Rebecca Johnson (4.14*), Kamila Ostra (4.14*, 4.16*, 4.17*, 4.18*), Marianne Paton (4.16*), Alex Fitzgerald (4.17*, 4.18*)

VFX Production Assistant: Marianne Paton (4.14*), Alexander Fitzgerald[15] (4.14*, 4.16*)

VFX Supervisor: Tim Barter (4.14*, 4.17*, 4.18*)[16]

Dubbing Mixer: Tim Ricketts

Supervising Sound Editor: Paul McFadden

---

[14] Credited on 4.16*, 4.17* and 4.18* as 'Joseph Courtis'.

[15] Credited on 4.16* as 'VFX Assistant' under the name 'Alex Fitzgerald'.

[16] Credited on 4.17* and 4.18* as 'On Set VFX Supervisor'.

CREDITS

Sound FX Editor: Paul Jefferies
Dialogue Editor: Matthew Cox (4.15), Douglas Sinclair (4.16)
Foley Editor: Kelly-Marie Angell (4.14*), Will Everett (4.16*, 4.17, 4.18*)
Finance Manager: Chris Rogers (4.14*)

With thanks to the BBC National Orchestra of Wales
Conducted and Orchestrated by: Ben Foster (4.17, 4.18)
Mixed by: Jake Jackson (4.17, 4.18)
Recorded by: Gerry O'Riordan (4.17, 4.18)

Crouch End Festival Chorus (4.17, 4.18)
Conducted by: David Temple (4.17, 4.18)
Counter Tenor: Mark Chambers (4.18)

Original Theme Music: Ron Grainer
Casting Director: Andy Pryor CDG
Production Executive: Julie Scott
Production Accountant: Oliver Ager (4.14), Adam Olley (4.15), Dyfed Thomas (4.16), Ceri Tothill (4.17, 4.18)
Sound Recordist: Julian Howarth
Costume Designer: Louise Page
Make-Up Designer: Barbara Southcott
Music: Murray Gold
Visual Effects: The Mill
Executive Visual FX Producer: Will Cohen (4.16*, 4.17*, 4.18*)
Visual FX Producer: Will Cohen (4.14*), Marie Jones (4.14*, 4.16*, 4.17*, 4.18*)
Visual FX Supervisor: Dave Houghton (4.14*, 4.16*, 4.17*, 4.18*)
Special Effects: Any Effects
Prosthetics: Millennium FX
Editor: Richard Cox (4.14), Mike Jones (4.15), William Oswald (4.16), Philip Kloss (4.17, 4.18)
Production Designer: Edward Thomas
Director of Photography: Ernie Vincze BSC (4.14, 4.16), Rory Taylor (4.15, 4.17, 4.18)
Associate Producer: Catrin Lewis Defis (4.14*, 4.17, 4.18), Debbi Slater (4.15, 4.16)

Executive Producer: Russell T Davies, Julie Gardner

BBC Wales

PART FOUR
EPISODE GUIDE

The durations quoted in the episode guide below are for the complete versions of the episodes on the BBC's master tapes. The durations on transmission were generally a few seconds shorter, as each episode tended to be cut into slightly by the preceding and/or following continuity caption and announcement.

Readers who have yet to see the episodes may wish to bear in mind that this guide is a comprehensive one that contains many plot 'spoilers'.

4.14 – THE NEXT DOCTOR

Writer: Russell T Davies
Director: Andy Goddard

DEBUT TRANSMISSION DETAILS

BBC One
Date: 25 December 2008. Scheduled time: 6.00 pm. Actual time: 6.00 pm.

Duration: 60′ 30″[17]

CREDITED CAST

David Tennant (The Doctor[18]), David Morrissey (Jackson Lake), Dervla Kirwan (Miss Hartigan[19]), Velile Tshabalala (Rosita), Ruari Mears (Cybershade), Paul Kasey (Cyberleader), Edmund Kente (Mr Scoones), Michael Bertenshaw (Mr Cole), Jason Morell (Vicar), Neil McDermott (Jed), Ashley Horne (Lad), Tom Langford (Frederic[20]), Jordan Southwell (Urchin), Matthew Allick (Docker), Nicholas Briggs (Cyber Voices)

Cybermen originally created by Kit Pedler and Gerry Davis

PLOT

The Doctor arrives in London on Christmas Eve 1851. He meets a stranger who at first appears to be his own later incarnation, currently engaged in tracking a Cybershade – a creature of the Cybermen – with the aid of his companion Rosita. A group of Cybermen have recently arrived in London from the void when the divisions between parallel universes temporarily weakened as a result of the Daleks' thwarted scheme to deploy a reality bomb. The stranger is eventually revealed to be a maths teacher named Jackson Lake, whose mind was accidentally imprinted with a Dalek database of information about the Doctor recorded on a Cyberman info-stamp. This occurred during his first encounter with the Cybermen – an encounter that resulted in his wife Caroline being killed and his son Frederic kidnapped. Shock caused Lake's mind to enter a 'fugue state', and he came to believe that he was the Doctor. With the aid of a local workhouse matron, Miss Hartigan, the Cybermen have kidnapped many other young urchins and set them to work to activate the CyberKing – a giant, Cyberman-shaped robot ship with

---

[17] The version released on DVD/Blu-Ray, with extended closing credits, runs to 60′ 40″.
[18] Character named as 'Doctor Who' on DVD/Blu-Ray version.
[19] First name given in dialogue as 'Mercy'.
[20] Surname given in dialogue as 'Lake'.

which they intend to carry out mass cyber-conversions of the human population. Miss Hartigan is placed in the ship's 'throne' to become its operator. The Doctor frees the children, including Frederic, then takes to the air in Lake's TARDIS – a hot air balloon, the acronym standing for 'Tethered Aerial Release Developed in Style'. When Miss Hartigan refuses to capitulate, the Doctor uses more info-stamps to break the connection between her mind and the Cybermen's computers. Her eyes opened to the terrible things she has done, she destroys the Cybermen, and the CyberKing with them. The Doctor then uses an appropriated Dalek dimension vault to send the wreckage into the time vortex. The danger over, he agrees to join Lake for Christmas dinner.

QUOTE, UNQUOTE

- **Jackson Lake**: 'I'm the Doctor. Simply the Doctor. The one, the only and the best!'
- **Cybermen:** 'The CyberKing will rise!'
  Miss Hartigan: 'The CyberKing will rise. Indeed. How like a man.'

CONTINUITY POINTS

- The Doctor conjectures that the Cybershade is: 'Some sort of primitive conversion. Like they took the brain of a cat, or a dog'. It is left open to speculation what type of animal, or alien creature, has been used for the Cybershade's body.
- The Cybershade that the Doctor and Lake try to capture is referred to by the Cybermen as 'Cybershade 16', implying that there are at least that many at large in London. It is unclear what becomes of them at the end of the story.
- The Doctor initially suspects that Jackson Lake is his own future incarnation (and tries to shake his apparent amnesia by referring to the events of 'Blink' (2007)). This could be regarded as inconsistent with the convention established in the multi-Doctor stories of the classic series, whereby the Doctor always unerringly recognised his past and future incarnations. It is however in line with the fact that in Steven Moffat's 'Time Crash' (2007), the fifth Doctor at first fails to realise that he is meeting his tenth incarnation. Addressing this point in *Doctor Who Magazine*, Russell T Davies commented: 'Thank you Steven Moffat! Now we've established that Time Lords always recognise each other, unless it's another version of themselves! A "Blinovitch Limitation Effect" … or something!'
- In 'Army of Ghosts'/'Doomsday' (2006) it was stated that nothing could live in the void – hence the Daleks' need for a void ship to allow them to survive its ravages. This is called into question in 'The Next Doctor', however, as the group of Cybermen encountered in this story were consigned to the void at the end of 'Doomsday', and yet managed to survive and eventually escape back into the Doctor's universe due to the events depicted in 'The Stolen Earth'/'Journey's End' (2008), using a Dalek dimension vault to travel back in time. Given that they achieved this, it seems possible that other groups of Cybermen could also have escaped from the void – and perhaps even groups of Daleks as well, given that many of them too were sucked into the void at the

end of 'Doomsday'. This leaves the way open for further appearances by the Cybus Industries Cybermen, and perhaps the Daleks also, in later stories.

- The information about the Doctor in the Daleks' database, as recorded on the info-stamp found by Lake, includes an image of his ninth incarnation, although the only Daleks to encounter him on screen either self-destructed ('Dalek' (2005)) or were erased from time altogether by super-Rose ('The Parting of the Ways' (2005)). It would seem that the only way the Daleks from the void could have known about the ninth Doctor is if they encountered him during the Time War. This implies that the eighth Doctor regenerated into the ninth either before or during the Time War – although the exact circumstances remain a mystery.
- The deceased clergyman whose house the Doctor and Lake break into is named as Aubrey Fairchild. Curiously, this is also the name of the Prime Minister (presumably the successor to 'Harold Saxon') mentioned in the novel *Beautiful Chaos* and in Davies's draft script for 'The Stolen Earth' – although in the transmitted version of the latter episode the Prime Minister is not named.

PRODUCTION NOTES

- David Morrissey is credited in the opening titles after David Tennant.
- Production on this special carried straight on from the end of that on the Series Four finale 'Journey's End' (2008). 7 and 8 April 2008 saw the scenes inside the late Reverend Fairchild's house being taped at Fonmon Castle in Barry. The graveyard scenes were recorded on 9 and 10 April at St Woolos Cemetery in Newport, previously featured as the site of Kathy Nightingale's final resting place in 'Blink' (2007). 13 to 14 April saw the crew move to The Maltings in Cardiff for the scenes where the Doctor meets Jackson Lake and they pursue a Cybershade; this location had previously been used for the Pharmacy Alley in 'Gridlock' (2007) and the Shan Shen market in 'Turn Left' (2008). Tredegar House in Newport, seen in numerous earlier stories, was transformed into Lake's temporary base, including the courtyard where he keeps his 'TARDIS', for recording from 16 to 17 April. Moving further afield, director Andy Goddard and his team taped several scenes in Gloucester between 20 and 23 April. The first three days saw shots being captured in Millers Green, which was dressed with fake snow to become the square that the Doctor enters on his arrival in Victorian London; in College Green, which became the route of the funeral procession; and in the adjacent College Street. The last day in Gloucester then saw recording taking place in Berkeley Street for a street scene. On 24 April, Shire Hall in Monmouth was used for the scenes outside the Cybermen's base.
- Other titles considered for this special, before 'The Next Doctor' was decided upon, were 'The New Doctor' and 'Court of the CyberKing'.
- The black-and-white clips of all the Doctor's incarnations seen in the sequence of images from the Daleks' database were taken from the following stories: 'The Time Meddler' (1965), 'The Ice Warriors' (1967), 'Terror of the Autons' (1971), 'City of Death' (1979), 'Arc of Infinity' (1983), 'The Trial of a Time Lord' ('The Mysterious Planet' segment) (1986), 'Time and the Rani' (1987), the TV movie (1996), 'The Parting of the Ways' (2005) and 'The Family of Blood'

(2007). Other clips of David Tennant's Doctor featured in a subsequent sequence derive from 'Tooth and Claw' (2006), 'The Runaway Bride' (2006), 'The Lazarus Experiment' (2007), 'Blink' (2007) and 'Voyage of the Damned' (2007).

- After recording of the story had been completed, Russell T Davies regretted that he had not rewritten the climax to have Miss Hartigan teleport the wreckage of the destroyed CyberKing into the vortex, thus giving her a further moment of redemption and avoiding the need for the inclusion in the story of the Daleks' dimension vault, which he considered a rather contrived device.
- All DVD and Blu-ray releases of this special have closing titles that differ slightly from the transmitted version, being extended to include more credits.

OOPS!

- In the sequence where the CyberKing rises from the Thames, the close-ups of Rosita show her standing beside a wall, but in the long shots there is no wall in sight.
- Jackson Lake is wearing the shoulder-strap of info-stamps retrieved from his luggage trunk when he and the Doctor enter the Cybermen's lair to rescue the children, and discards it on the floor. Just minutes later, however, it is inexplicably back in the trunk, where the Doctor finds it after rummaging through the other contents.
- The version of this special included on the 'Complete Specials' DVD and Blu-Ray sets has some errors on the soundtrack. One line of the Doctor's dialogue is missing, another is a different take from that used in the transmitted version, some of the incidental music is different and – perhaps most noticeably – in the scenes featuring Miss Hartigan immediately after she is converted into the CyberKing controller, the electronic processing that should be heard on actress Dervla Kirwan's voice is missing (though it is present and correct in the later scenes, when the CyberKing is rampaging through the city). These errors were not present on the original, single-disc DVD release of the special, or on the version released with the *Doctor Who DVD Files* part-work magazine.

PRESS REACTION

- 'Of course, "The Next Doctor" has flaws. Davies is expert in pushing emotional buttons and does so ruthlessly, which can get a little wearing. There are some extraordinarily sentimental moments, far too many urchins [and] holes in the plot plugged with lumps of expositional dialogue, and then there's the overpowering music, which, lest you're unsure, tells you precisely What To Feel and When. Furthermore, as baddies go, I'm not terribly fond of the Cybermen. I know they predate the Borg but as hive-mind villains go, *Star Trek*'s are more terrifying, not least because they're uglier. That said, the sculptural Cybermen knock "Voyage of the Damned" [2007]'s Max Capricorn into a cocked hat and global domination certainly beats insurance fraud as an evil *raison d'etre*. Meanwhile, those familiar with *Buffy [The Vampire Slayer]* may be reminded of the climax of season six. (Make of the Hartigan/Hannigan interface what you will.) Those reservations notwithstanding, "The Next

Doctor" is the best *Doctor Who* Christmas special yet, or is at the least on a par with "The Christmas Invasion" [2005]. It doesn't have the emotional scope of the Doctor and Rose's farewell in "Doomsday" [2006] but it's moving, funny, impressive and has a big, beating heart. Possibly two, in fact.' Gareth McLean, guardian.co.uk, 18 December 2008.

- 'Much of the fun of Tennant's stint as the Doctor has come from his boundless enthusiasm for the wonders of the universe, both large and small. Here, he gets to delight in the thought of meeting a version of himself – and of getting a rare outside perspective on what it's like to encounter the Doctor – and that delight is there regardless of who (or Who) Morrissey turns out to be. The interplay between Tennant and Morrissey ... is the highlight of 1850s-set "The Next Doctor". Otherwise, the movie feels a bit of a trifle compared to some of the previous *Doctor Who* specials since the franchise itself was resurrected a few years ago by writer Russell T. Davies.' Alan Sepinwall, *New Jersey Star-Ledger*, 26 June 2009.

- 'Morrissey gives a performance that befits a Doctor. He goes about it quite differently from Tennant: he does much less of the boyish gaping and mugging and raised eyebrows. He's solid, sturdy, serious but with a soft side. And a voice oddly reminiscent of the prison warden Mr Mackay from the '70s sitcom *Porridge*: it's a rich, full-throated bark ... Viewers who have previously considered *Doctor Who* over-hyped (this reporter among them) may find themselves thawing. The episode is witty, compelling, and, perhaps most importantly, does not feature Catherine Tate and her ceaseless squawking. Tennant himself gives perhaps his most energetic performance in the role to date. Whether or not Morrissey is the next Time Lord, it's clear that Tennant will be a hard act to follow.' Michael Deacon, telegraph.co.uk, 18 December 2008.

- '"The Next Doctor" exemplifies just how right they're getting [the show]. It's a perfect amalgam of snappy drama, effortless comedy and great production values. The Doctor pops up in 1851 London where he bumps into Dervla Kirwan, playing a creepy proto-feminist who's using the Cybermen to advance her cause. Visually, it's glorious: the terrifying climactic scene, in which a steam-driven Cyberman the size of Big Ben rampages through the city, is something that today's eight-year-olds will one day be showing their own kids.' Maxton Walker, *Guardian*, 15 January 2010.

ANALYSIS

Russell T Davies always insisted on making his Christmas specials overtly and unashamedly 'Christmassy', and 'The Next Doctor' is no exception to the rule. This time, it is the idealised chocolate-box image of a wintry Victorian-era London that the writer calls upon, complete with bountiful snowfall, cheery carol singers and poor orphaned urchins, evoking the spirit of Dickens' *A Christmas Carol* and its many heirs – and in the process recalling 'The Unquiet Dead' (2005), Mark Gatiss's Christmas-set, but not in that instance Christmas-transmitted, Series One story featuring Dickens.

This is the third Christmas special in a row to start with the Doctor travelling alone; but whereas both 'The Runaway Bride' (2006) and 'Voyage of the Damned'

(2007) saw him quickly acquire a companion – Donna Noble and Astrid Peth respectively – during the course of the action, 'The Next Doctor' departs from that pattern, in that neither of the two new friends he makes here – Jackson Lake and Rosita – falls into the conventional companion mould. Rather, Rosita is the companion to Lake, in his assumed role of 'the Doctor', while Lake effectively shares the lead with the Doctor himself. This gives the story a quite different dynamic, and one arguably unprecedented in the whole history of *Doctor Who*. It also establishes what will turn out to be an important theme running through these final five David Tennant-era specials: the Doctor's aversion to taking on a new human companion in the wake of the loss of all his others – which culminated in his final separation from Rose (whose name is recalled in Rosita's) and unavoidable decision to wipe Donna's memory at the conclusion of Series Four in 'Journey's End' (2008). This is an issue explicitly raised in the closing moments of 'The Next Doctor', when Lake asks the Doctor why, unlike in the past, he is travelling without a companion, and the Doctor replies: 'They leave, because they should, or they find someone else; and some of them ... some of them forget me. I suppose, in the end, they break my heart.' The Doctor then agrees to join Lake for Christmas dinner, 'In memory of those we've lost.'

It was an astute move on Davies's part to come up with the title 'The Next Doctor' – first announced in the preview that closed 'Journey's End' – as this neatly set up an intriguing mystery surrounding the identity of the character in question and inevitably led to much advance speculation amongst fans and in the media as to whether or not this special would indeed see the debut of the man who would succeed Tennant as the Doctor. This could be viewed as essentially a repeat of the trick Davies pulled with the 'fake regeneration' cliff-hanger to Series Four's penultimate episode, 'The Stolen Earth' (2008), which led to astonishing levels of viewer and press excitement over the potential arrival of a new Doctor – and, by whipping up huge anticipation for 'Journey's End', helped to make that the number one rated programme in the week of its transmission. Davies himself, however, has asserted in interviews that he never anticipated the incredible intensity of public interest provoked by these two storylines – particularly given that, by the time 'The Next Doctor' was transmitted, it had already been confirmed that Tennant would be seeing out his tenure as the Doctor with a succession of further specials over the course of the following year. Perhaps, then, this was just a happy accident.

Prior to transmission, many fans speculated that 'The Next Doctor' might have been inspired to some extent by the *Doctor Who* audio play 'The One Doctor' (Big Finish, 2001), in which the sixth Doctor and his companion Mel come up against an impostor Doctor, actually a conman named Banto Zame, and his own companion, Sally-Anne. In the event, though, Jackson Lake's story turns out to be rather more reminiscent of another audio play, 'Minuet in Hell' (Big Finish, 2001), in which a character called Gideon Crane believes himself to be the Doctor after suffering a temporal accident.[21]

---

[21] Crane was portrayed by new series Dalek and Cyberman voice actor Nicholas Briggs, who had previously played the Doctor himself, most notably in the AudioVisuals audio plays that were the amateur forerunners of the Big Finish series, and whose likeness had been used as the model for a future Doctor in the *Doctor Who Magazine* comic strip.

One disadvantage of Lake being presented as, effectively, the co-lead in the special – as signalled both by the title itself, which places the focus squarely on his character, and by David Morrissey's co-star billing – is that it creates an expectation that he and his situation will be central to the story; and this is an expectation that, in the event, is not met. As things unfold, it transpires that his involvement is really only tangential to the main crisis precipitated by Miss Hartigan and the Cybermen. Davies tries hard to mesh these two aspects of the plot seamlessly together, but doesn't quite manage it. After the solution of the mystery surrounding his identity, about half way into the running time, Lake unfortunately becomes largely redundant. There is the business about him regaining his memory of his kidnapped son – who, implausibly, just happens to be the only child slave worker whose escape from the Cybermen's lair necessitates him being plucked off a high ledge in a daring rescue – but even then it is the Doctor rather than Lake who performs the rescue, and the latter is subsequently sidelined from the action, along with Rosita, while the former takes to the sky in the hot air balloon to save the day. It is actually hard to understand why Davies did not have Lake insist on accompanying the Doctor at this point – it was, after all, his balloon! To have shown the two men confronting the danger side by side would surely have afforded a more fitting and satisfying climax to the story than the one seen on screen, which is further marred by the rather lame idea of having the Doctor use an all-too-convenient dimension vault to send the destroyed CyberKing into the time vortex. Perhaps, though, Davies felt that by this stage in the proceedings there was a need to put the focus back on Tennant, in light of his status as the ongoing star of the show. This impression is reinforced when Lake is ultimately placed in the position of being merely a cheerleader to the Doctor, encouraging the assembled throng to give the Time Lord a rare show of appreciation for his efforts on their behalf – albeit in what is admittedly quite an affecting sequence.

The development of the touching friendship between Lake and the Doctor is undoubtedly one of the highlights of 'The Next Doctor', underpinned by the obvious chemistry between actors Morrissey and Tennant – who had previously co-starred in another BBC One drama, the six-part *Blackpool* (2004), along with Sarah Parish, who later played the Racnoss Empress in 'The Runaway Bride'. Things get off to a spirited start with a very amusing and well-staged action sequence in which, immediately after meeting, the two men try in vain to tether a Cybershade that drags them painfully up a wall and along the floor of what appears to be an abandoned warehouse. Also memorable is the scene shortly afterwards where they fight off a group of Cybermen who threaten to delete them as they investigate the late Reverend Aubrey Fairchild's house. The thrills here are again counterpointed by some great touches of humour, probably the best of which comes after the Doctor spots that Lake is wearing a fob watch and tells him, 'Legend has it that the memories of a Time Lord can be contained within a watch' – referencing a key plot element of the earlier episodes 'Human Nature'/'The Family of Blood' (2007) and 'Utopia' (2007). As Murray Gold's incidental music swells to a crescendo, it seems that the mystery of Lake's identity is about to be solved in highly dramatic fashion; but the bubble of anticipation is instantly burst when the Doctor opens the watch only to have its innards spill out, revealing that it is actually nothing more than an ordinary timepiece, and a broken one at that! This quickly leads on to another apparent homage to the past, as the Doctor's startling initial discovery of a Cyberman inside a closed cupboard recalls a similar incident in 'Terror of the Autons' (1971) where, in his third incarnation, he inadvertently released an Auton from inside a locked safe.

Another stand-out scene is the one where the Doctor finally explains to Lake the terrible truth of what has happened to him and his family. This is notable amongst other things for including a flashback sequence presenting clips not only of the tenth Doctor but also of his nine previous incarnations. There is a long tradition of such sequences in the show, stretching back to a still-photo montage of the first three Doctors in 'Day of the Daleks' (1972). This, though, is only the second instance of new-era *Doctor Who* explicitly acknowledging the classic-era Doctors – the first having come when some of them were depicted as sketches in John Smith's *A Journal of Impossible Things* in 'The Family of Blood'. It is worth reflecting here that only a few short years ago, it would have seemed like pure fantasy to think that images of all the past Doctors might be featured in this way in a flagship BBC One Christmas Night special; and the fact that it was actually done, in *Doctor Who*'s forty-fifth anniversary year, is testament to the incredible achievement of Davies and his colleagues in reviving the show with such respect for its traditions and, at the same time, to such huge popular acclaim. It is particularly pleasing to see such recognition being given to the first three Doctors, William Hartnell, Patrick Troughton and Jon Pertwee, so many years after their untimely deaths. How gratifying it must be for the families of those great actors to see their memories being honoured in this way. A very nice touch indeed, and all credit to executive producer Julie Gardner for suggesting it to Davies.

Morrissey himself has stated in interviews that his performance was to some extent influenced by his recollections of those early Doctors of the 1960s and 1970s. This, coupled with his Victorian costume, complete with frock coat, gives his take on 'the Doctor' a decidedly old-school quality, making for an effective contrast to Tennant's emphatically modern interpretation. At the same time, though, it shows why a retro-style Doctor like this would not really suit the show today on an ongoing basis. It works well as a one-off in an appropriate historical setting, but would seem simply too arch and old-fashioned if carried forward into other stories. That said, Morrissey certainly excels here, and manages to hold his own opposite Tennant, which is no mean feat given that the latter turns in his usual stellar portrayal of the Doctor.

The story's other main guest star, Dervla Kirwan, also gives an excellent performance in her role as the icily villainous Miss Mercy Hartigan. Although this character introduces herself as 'Matron of the St Joseph Workhouse', intriguing hints are dropped to the effect that she might actually have had a more scandalous profession as a prostitute, or perhaps the madam of a brothel – an unusual twist for *Doctor Who*, and arguably a rather brave one for any Christmas Night family drama. With her wonderful red costume and umbrella, she appears as a literal scarlet lady in the graveyard scene. When one of the mourners likens her to a harlot, she replies: 'Oh, and you should know, Mr Cole … You've walked past me so many times, all you good men of charity, never once asking my name.' When another mourner correctly identifies her, she taunts: 'Oh, *you* noticed. I saw you looking, you cheeky boy.' Much later in the story, when the Doctor challenges her from the hot air balloon, she describes him as: 'Yet another man come to assert himself against me in the night.' There is even a brief suggestion (intentional on

Davies's part) that Rosita too might be a lady of the night: at one point, Miss Hartigan dismissively silences her by telling her, in reference to the Doctor, 'I doubt he paid you to talk.' However, Rosita certainly does not take kindly to this, as she later punches her in the face, drawing the Doctor's not-entirely-convincing reproach, 'Can I say, I completely disapprove!'

One thing that isn't made clear is whether Miss Hartigan's villainy is entirely of her own doing, or whether it is partly due to the Cybermen having exerted an influence over her mind. In her initial confrontation with the Doctor, she asserts, 'No-one has ever been able to change my mind,' and it certainly seems that she is a very strong-willed and intelligent woman. This is further evidenced later on when, after the Cybermen force her into the CyberKing's 'throne', they find to their surprise that her mind is able to overpower their computers and control them. On the other hand, at the end of the story, when the Doctor breaks the Cyber-connection, leaving her mind, as he puts it, 'Open, I think, for the first time in far too many years,' she is aghast to see what she has done, and proceeds to destroy her former allies. Which begs the question, was she acting under her own free will to start with, or not? This all sits rather awkwardly with a strand of narrative subtext that seems to hold Miss Hartigan up as some kind of exemplar of early feminism – perhaps most obviously when she speaks repeatedly of seeking 'liberation' from abusive men. Unfortunately, one possible reading of the story's denouement is that this desire for liberation is really just a sort of mental aberration that the Doctor is able to 'cure' by opening her eyes to the truth. Perhaps, though, a fairer interpretation would be that it is only her chosen means that are to be adjudged misguided, not the basic end she seeks to attain.

This is the third story to feature the new-era version of the Cybermen, following their debut in 'Rise of the Cybermen'/'The Age of Steel' (2006) and their face-off with the Daleks in 'Army of Ghosts'/'Doomsday' (2006), both in Series Two.[22] Unlike the Daleks, the Cybermen have undergone a succession of significant design revisions over the decades, and this latest type works quite well as an *art deco*-influenced 21st Century reinterpretation of the basic look. The head thankfully retains the distinctive 'handle bar' attachments so associated with the Cybermen, but also has a slightly insect-like quality to it, emphasising the regimented, almost hive-like mindset of these monsters and recalling how their classic-era antecedents emerged from honeycomb-shaped cells in 'The Tomb of the Cybermen' (1967), hatched from what looked like huge eggs in 'The Wheel in Space' (1968) and broke out of cocoons in 'The Invasion' (1968). It does, though, fall some way short of the effectiveness of the very best of the previous designs: specifically, the blank, featureless, starkly functional mask used in 'The Moonbase' (1967) and 'The Tomb of the Cybermen', with its skull-like ringed eye sockets and slit mouth. These new-era Cybermen are not only a little too aesthetically pleasing in appearance for such a coldly logical race – the designers having drawn some of their inspiration from the beautiful architecture of the Chrysler building in New York – but also, disappointingly, lack the other key defining characteristic of their 1960s and 1970s

---

[22] There are some fans who maintain that these Cybermen, created by John Lumic and his Cybus Industries on a parallel universe version of Earth, ought more properly to be referred to as Cy*bus*men, to distinguish them from those created on the planet Mondas in the standard *Doctor Who* universe.

forerunners: an external chest unit. What makes this all the more frustrating is that some of the original concept sketches drawn up for 'Rise of the Cybermen'/'The Age of Steel', as reproduced in the book *Doctor Who: Aliens and Enemies* (BBC Books, 2006), did incorporate masks more closely akin to the blank-faced archetype of 'The Moonbase', and clearly-defined chest units as opposed to just a Cybus Industries logo on a raised chest as on the final versions. Admittedly some of the other published concept sketches departed even more radically from the classic Cyberman look, and one of them was arguably too horrific to have been suitable for a family show; but it does seem that in this instance some of the designers' initial ideas were rather better than what actually ended up on screen.

Another unfortunate feature of these new-style Cybermen is the loud 'Cyber-stomp' they make whenever they move. Not only is this rather silly and overly cartoonish but also it inevitably leads to them being depicted, *en masse*, as a phalanx of robotic figures marching in unison, like – to paraphrase a description coined by the fourth Doctor in 'Revenge of the Cybermen' (1975) – an army of tin soldiers. This is perhaps not altogether surprising, given that 'Rise of the Cybermen'/'The Age of Steel' is in many respects a homage to 'The Invasion', the only classic-era story in which the Cybermen were seen to operate primarily in that mode (although others such as 'Earthshock' (1982) and 'Silver Nemesis' (1988) gave nods to it as well); but it does have the notable downside that it renders implausible any scene in which the Cybermen are required to practise stealth. A good example is the incident in 'The Age of Steel' where a Cyberman somehow manages to creep up behind the Doctor and his ally Mrs Moore – a contrivance much derided by fan reviewers. In fact, 'The Next Doctor' contains what might be considered an in-joke allusion to – or possibly even a justification of – that earlier incident, as two Cybermen manage to approach the Doctor and Rosita undetected, and the Doctor protests: 'Oh, that's cheating, sneaking up! D'you have your legs on silent?' Could it be that the 'Cyber-stomp' is really just a ploy that the Cybermen have adopted simply in order to intimidate their opponents, and one that they can 'turn off' at will …?

All reservations aside, the Cybermen certainly make a very formidable impression in the aforementioned graveyard scene, as they emerge out of the driving snow to attack the mourners gathered at the late Reverend Fairchild's graveside. They have always seemed particularly well suited to being presented in snowy settings, not only because their very first appearance in *Doctor Who* came in the midst of a snowstorm in 'The Tenth Planet' (1966) – something that Russell T Davies has acknowledged was an influence on him – but also because the silver colour of their armour blends in well with the white of the snow. Here, they have an almost ghostly quality as they remorselessly stalk their victims amongst the gravestones.

The graveyard setting also serves to remind the viewer of another aspect of the Cybermen that is often overlooked: the debt these monsters owe to the iconography of vampire fiction. Just like vampires, their intent is to convert innocent victims into others of their kind, transforming them into an army of the undead. Just as vampires can be killed by daylight, burned by holy water and warded off by garlic, so Cybermen can be destroyed by radiation ('The Tenth Planet'), melted by plastic solvents ('The Moonbase') and repelled by gold ('Revenge of the Cybermen' and others). And just as vampires exhibit superhuman strength, so too do Cybermen.

A further appealing aspect of the Cybermen over the decades has been the occasional introduction of new 'variants' – the Cybermats in 'The Tomb of the Cybermen', the Controller in the same story, the Cyber-Planner in 'The Wheel in Space' and so on. 'The Next Doctor' presents two more such innovations. First there are the Cybershades, which are realised surprisingly cheaply, and only just well enough to avoid, narrowly, becoming a new-era equivalent of the most risible man-in-a-bear-suit monster ever featured in the show, the Taran Wood Beast from 'The Androids of Tara' (1978). Then there is the CyberKing, which is much better, but still less than fully convincing; this is one of those rare instances where the show seems to have bitten off rather more than it could chew in terms of the sheer scale and sophistication of CGI work required to create a completely successful effect.

In fictional terms, the CyberKing recalls other giant menaces such as *Doctor Who*'s own enlarged K1 robot in 'Robot' (1974/75), and the creature that inspired it, King Kong, as depicted in the 1933 movie of the same name. Then there is the whole *kaiju* strand of Japanese monster movies; most famously the Godzilla franchise. Then too there is the abundance of so-called mecha stories found in *anime*, involving walking machines controlled by a pilot. The Victorian setting of 'The Next Doctor' also lends it the trappings of the steampunk genre, most obviously in the smoke-wreathed scenes of the child slave workers toiling to activate the CyberKing. Another of the *Doctor Who* audio plays comes to mind here too: 'Human Resources' (Big Finish, 2007), involving office blocks that turn out to be giant, robot-like war machines, in this instance pitted in a battle *against* the Cybermen. And this is not the first time that Russell T Davies has climaxed one of his stories with the threat of a giant, human-piloted machine emerging: his *Doctor Who* novel 'Damaged Goods' (Virgin Publishing, 1996) features a Gallifreyan N-Form war machine gradually enveloping its operator, a young drug dealer known as the Capper; and the closing episodes of his BBC children's serial *Dark Season* (1991) see a huge war computer called Behemoth rising up from beneath the ground after the sinister Miss Pendragon occupies the 'throne' at its heart.

The idea of the Cybermen using forced child labour neatly positions them in the role usually occupied by 'wicked capitalists' in Dickensian fiction, and chimes with their use of huge factories to 'upgrade' lorry-loads of abducted homeless people in 'Rise of the Cybermen'/'The Age of Steel'. It also, though, highlights a number of plot issues. Assuming that the CyberKing did not arrive with the Cybermen via the void – which it might have done, although there is no clear indication to that effect in the script – then it must presumably have been constructed *in situ* beneath the Thames. This begs a number of questions, such as how the Cybermen have managed to remain undetected during the considerable period of time it must have taken them to accomplish such a project; why they did not choose a less heavily populated location to carry out this clandestine work; and why they need child labour to complete the final stages when they could presumably perform the same tasks themselves just as effectively and, given their formidable strength, with considerably greater ease. It is also a bit of a mystery how the Doctor immediately recognises the CyberKing as a 'Dreadnought-class' ship, given that it is a creation of the parallel universe Cybermen seen in only two previous stories, neither of which featured such a ship. Does this imply that he has actually had another prior encounter with these new-era Cybermen, unscreened and previously unmentioned, in which he first saw a CyberKing ...?[23]

A further conundrum – and, in this instance, one to which the script itself effectively draws attention – is how the terrifying rampage of the CyberKing, presumably witnessed by hundreds of people, can have failed to go down in recorded history. 'Yeah, funny that,' comments the Doctor when Lake suggests that the events will be 'spoken of for centuries to come'. Certainly Dickens, who in December 1851 would have just taken up residence in Tavistock House in central London, seemed completely unaware of the incident when the Doctor and Rose met him in 1869 in 'The Unquiet Dead'; and Queen Victoria similarly made no mention of it when they encountered her in 1879 in 'Tooth and Claw'. The most plausible explanation would seem to be that this is one of those points in time and space where history is 'in flux' – to adopt a phrase used by the Doctor in 'The Fires of Pompeii' – and is subsequently rewritten.[24] Possibly if the Doctor were to encounter Dickens or Queen Victoria again, they would now recall the CyberKing incident, and it would henceforth be recorded in all the history books.[25]

In the end, though, it really doesn't matter that the script leaves a few plot points unaddressed or up in the air. Like 'The Christmas Invasion', 'The Runaway Bride' and 'Voyage of the Damned' before it, 'The Next Doctor' has to be considered in the context in which it was originally intended to be seen: as an enjoyable slice of festive family entertainment for a probably less-than-fully-attentive audience settling into their armchairs after indulging, or in some cases overindulging, in their Christmas food and drink. In the final assessment, it fulfils that remit admirably. It has pace, fun, thrills, emotion and spectacle aplenty and, on balance, probably just about pips 'The Christmas Invasion' to become the best of the Christmas specials to date.

---

[23] An alternative possibility is that the Mondas-originated Cybermen in the Doctor's universe were the first to create CyberKings, and the Cybus Industries versions learned about this from the Daleks in the void, along with all the other information they stole from them. This would allow for the possibility that the Doctor previously saw a CyberKing in an untelevised encounter with the Cybermen in one of his earlier incarnations, before the Time War.

[24] The Series Five episode 'Flesh and Stone' later essentially confirms this.

[25] The most obvious prior example of a scenario requiring such an explanation is van Statten's ignorance of the Daleks in the Series One episode 'Dalek', set in 2012. Clearly, at the point when the Doctor and Rose meet him, history in his timeline has yet to be rewritten to incorporate the events of subsequent stories such as 'Army of Ghosts'/'Doomsday', set in 2007, or 'The Stolen Earth'/'Journey's End', set in 2009, when the whole world becomes aware of the Daleks.

4.15 – PLANET OF THE DEAD

Writer: Russell T Davies, Gareth Roberts
Director: James Strong

DEBUT TRANSMISSION DETAILS

BBC One/BBC HD
Date: 11 April 2009. Scheduled time: 6.45 pm. Actual time: 6.44 pm.

Duration: 58′ 58″

CREDITED CAST

David Tennant (The Doctor), Michelle Ryan (Christina[26]), Lee Evans (Malcolm[27]), Noma Dumezweni (Capt Magambo[28]), Adam James (DI McMillan), Glenn Doherty (Sgt Dennison), Victoria Alcock (Angela[29]), David Ames (Nathan), Ellen Thomas (Carmen), Reginald Tsiboe (Lou[30]), Daniel Kaluuya (Barclay), Keith Parry (Bus Driver), James Layton (Sgt Ian Jenner), Paul Kasey (Sorvin), Ruari Mears (Praygat)

PLOT

The Doctor and aristocratic jewel thief Lady Christina de Souza are amongst the passengers on a London double-decker bus that accidentally enters a wormhole in space and is transported to the planet San Helios. There they encounter two Tritovores, fly-like aliens whose ship has also crash-landed on the planet. Together they discover that the wormhole has been created by a swarm of metallic-shelled flying creatures resembling stingrays, which have completely devoured the planet's populace, reducing them to sand. The creatures are now about to travel to Earth via the wormhole and resume feeding there. The Tritovores are killed by the stingray creatures, but the Doctor, aided by Lady Christina and the other passengers, manages to take the bus back to London through the wormhole ahead of the swarm. UNIT scientific adviser Dr Malcolm Taylor, with whom the Doctor has been communicating via mobile phone, manages to close the wormhole, while UNIT troops dispose of the few stingray creatures that have managed to get through.

---

[26] Full name given in dialogue as 'Lady Christina de Souza'.
[27] Full name given in dialogue as 'Dr Malcolm Taylor'.
[28] First name given in dialogue as 'Erisa'.
[29] Surname given in dialogue as 'Whitaker'.
[30] Said in dialogue to be short for 'Louis'.

QUOTE, UNQUOTE

- **The Doctor:** 'Call it a hunch, but I think we've gone a little bit further than Brixton.'
- **The Doctor:** 'People have travelled with me, and I've lost them. Lost them all. Never again.'
- **Carmen:** 'You be careful, because your song is ending, sir.'
  The Doctor: 'What do you mean?'
  Carmen: 'It is returning. It is returning through the dark. And then, Doctor. Oh, but then ... He will knock four times.'

CONTINUITY POINTS

- The Doctor traces the time wormhole using a 'rhondium sensor'. He was previously seen to use such a device (although of a different design) in 'The Time Warrior' (1973/74).
- When the bus passengers see that there are three suns in the sky on San Helios, Nathan says, 'Like when all those planets were up in the sky' and Barclay replies, 'But it was the Earth that moved back then, wasn't it?' These are references to the events of 'The Stolen Earth'/'Journey's End' (2008). This means that the Easter seen in 'Planet of the Dead' is probably Easter 2010, and certainly no earlier than that, as 'The Stolen Earth'/'Journey's End' was set in summer 2009.
- The Doctor mentions UNIT's involvement in the incident involving the giant robot, as seen in 'Robot' (1974/75).
- Using the equipment aboard the Tritovores' ship, the Doctor determines that the planet San Helios is in the 'Scorpion Nebula ... on the other side of the universe [from Earth]'.
- The Doctor states that he has previously visited 'World War I, creation of the universe, end of the universe, the war between China and Japan, and the Court of King Athelstan in 924 AD'. King Athelstan lived between circa 895 and 939 AD and reigned England for the last 15 years of his life. The Doctor's statement that Athelstan was 'the first King of Britain' is arguably erroneous, given that Britain as a nation did not exist at that time – although Athelstan may well have had ambitions to rule the whole of the British Isles.
- The Doctor also says that he remembers 'the original' Easter. He tells Lady Christina, 'What really happened was ...' but is then distracted.
- The underground traffic tunnel through which the 200 bus passes on its route from Victoria to Brixton – identified as 'the Gladwell Road tunnel' in dialogue – has no direct equivalent in the real world. The on-screen UNIT map pinpoints the epicentre of the wormhole – and therefore the location of the tunnel – as being north of the Thames, near Fleet Street. This would suggest that the bus takes a very circuitous route – particularly as it is said to be travelling north through the tunnel.
- The advertising posters on the side of the bus refer to the 'Neon by Naismith' telecommunications company – the significance of which will become clear in the final tenth Doctor story, 'The End of Time'.

- The Doctor reveals that he is able to speak 'every' alien language – apparently, even without the aid of the translation circuits in the TARDIS, which is left behind on Earth when the bus is transported to San Helios. This may be due to the 'Time Lord gift' that, in 'The Masque of Mandragora' (1976), he tells Sarah Jane Smith that he allows her to share with him.
- Malcolm mentions Bernard Quatermass of the British Rocket Group – who in the real world is a character created by Nigel Kneale and featured in the seminal TV science fiction serial *The Quatermass Experiment* (1953) and its celebrated sequels *Quatermass II* (1955), *Quatermass and the Pit* (1958/59) and *Quatermass* (1979). A 'Bernard' previously referred to in 'Remembrance of the Daleks' (1988) was widely assumed by fans to be Quatermass, but 'Planet of the Dead' gives the first explicit confirmation that he is a real person in the *Doctor Who* universe. A British Rocket Group facility was previously seen as the venue for a press conference in 'The Christmas Invasion' (2005), implying that the organisation was responsible for the Guinevere space probe mission featured in that story.
- Captain Magambo says that the TARDIS was found in the gardens of Buckingham Palace. Obviously referring to the Queen, the Doctor says, 'She doesn't mind.'

PRODUCTION NOTES

- Michelle Ryan is credited in the opening titles after David Tennant.
- Recording for this special got under way in Cardiff on 19 January 2009, when the National Museum of Wales and the adjacent Gorsedd Gardens Road were used as the location for the International Gallery. The tunnel scenes were recorded at the Grangetown/Butetown tunnel link on 20 to 21 January and 27 to 28 January. Some fans who attended this location to watch and take photographs of the proceedings can be glimpsed in the background of one shot in the transmitted programme. In between the two tunnel sessions, recording on 22 January comprised the scene of Lady Christina escaping from the Gallery via an alley in The Friary, and that of the Doctor and Lady Christina talking on the bus in Lloyd George Avenue. On 26 January, St Mary Street was used as the location where Lady Christina and the Doctor board the bus. The scenes of the interior of the Tritovore spaceship were taped from 3 to 5 February in the Mir Steel works in Newport. The overseas location shoot in Dubai took place on 12 and 13 February, the first day's work being severely hampered by a sand storm. The bus interiors were then recorded in the regular *Doctor Who* studios at Upper Boat in Cardiff.
- 'Planet of the Dead' concludes with a trailer for the next special, the title of which is revealed as 'The Waters of Mars'.
- This is the first *Doctor Who* story to be recorded in high definition. It is also the first since the series returned in 2005 to have two credited writers, although Russell T Davies, as showrunner, had a significant input into almost all previous scripts by other contributors.
- Two Bristol VR double-decker buses were used during recording. The first became badly damaged in transit to Dubai for the desert location work. The damage was hastily written into the script by Russell T Davies as being due to

the journey through the wormhole.

- The number of the bus route, 200, was chosen to mark the fact that 'Planet of the Dead' was the two-hundredth live-action *Doctor Who* story to be transmitted on TV. In reality, the 200 bus route runs between Wimbledon and Mitcham in Surrey, not between Victoria and Brixton in London as indicated in the story. The numerical code, 754, used by one of the guards at the International Gallery to activate the security system around the Cup of Athelstan's plinth is one more than the number of individual *Doctor Who* episodes transmitted up to and including 'Planet of the Dead'. It is unknown why this was used rather than 753; possibly it was a counting error.
- 'Mais pas si nous allons vers un cauchmar', the French phrase spoken by Lady Christina in response to the Doctor's 'Allons-y', translates as 'But not if we go towards a nightmare'.
- Unusually, no press launch was held for this special. This was because final post-production work was not completed until shortly before transmission.

OOPS!

- The number plate of the bus changes during the course of the action: initially it gives the registration as 'W974 GHM' – as actually read out by Detective Inspector McMillan during the chase through London – but later, most obviously when the bus rises into the air as Lady Christina makes her escape at the end, it reads 'RUA 461W'.
- The entrance to the wormhole is part-way along the underground traffic tunnel when the bus enters it, but then for no apparent reason moves to the end of the tunnel.
- There are a huge number of stingray creatures seen following close behind the bus when it enters the wormhole for its return trip to Earth, but despite the fact that there is some delay before Malcolm is able to close the wormhole – partly because the Doctor inexplicably waits for a couple of minutes before even telling him to do so via mobile phone – only three of the creatures get through.

PRESS REACTION

- 'As hollow as a big chocolate Easter egg, "Planet of the Dead" is a major disappointment from the *Doctor Who* camp. Lacking in the enthralling drama and compelling characterisation that has been the lynchpin of the Russell T Davies era, it says a great deal that some of the more credible dialogue comes from the mouths of creatures who can only communicate via clicks.' Ben Rawson-Jones, Digital Spy website, 11 April 2009.
- 'The only thing remotely Eastery about the latest *Doctor Who* special was the Doctor scoffing a chocolate egg and the fact that it seemed to reference a whole host of Bank Holiday film favourites – *Indiana Jones*, *Mission Impossible*, *Harry Potter*, *The Italian Job* and *Carry On Abroad*. Not to mention *Holiday on the Buses*. "Planet of the Dead", despite the crew's jolly to Dubai, didn't feel like the slightly over-rich five-course banquets we've come to expect from *Doctor Who* Christmas specials. It felt more like a light lunch. But sometimes, a nourishing snack is better than a gut-busting gorge-fest, and while "Dead" felt a little

flimsy and inconsequential, what it did offer was pretty damned tasty. And we don't just mean Michelle Ryan.' Dave Golder, *SFX* website, 13 April 2009.

ANALYSIS

'Planet of the Dead' was the first of the new-era *Doctor Who* specials not to be made for transmission at Christmas. Consequently, freed of the perceived need to include various festive elements, Russell T Davies and co-writer Gareth Roberts had a blank canvas to work on; although there is one token reference to Easter early on, thankfully they avoided any temptation to come up with a tale about evil Easter bunnies or the like. Despite this, 'Planet of the Dead' still feels very different from a regular *Doctor Who* episode, eschewing detailed, multi-layered plotting in favour of pseudo-blockbuster-style action and grand spectacle. In this respect, it has a lot in common with earlier specials such as 'The Runaway Bride' (2006) and 'Voyage of the Damned' (2007). Certainly Roberts' two previous episodes, 'The Shakespeare Code' (2007) and 'The Unicorn and the Wasp' (2008), had far more intricate, involved storylines than this essentially one-dimensional romp.

The spectacle here derives principally from the impressive desert-set scenes, for the taping of which the crew made their much-publicised trip to Dubai. The shots they captured are quite stunning – there is no way anyone could mistakenly believe that this recording was done on a beach somewhere in Wales, although there are sand dunes elsewhere in the UK that could possibly have formed an acceptable backdrop – and it is good to see *Doctor Who* being afforded a visit to a more far-flung location than usual. The downside is that this apect of the production obviously ate up a fair bit of the available budget, necessitating savings elsewhere. This is most readily apparent in the realisation of the Tritovores, which – like the Cybershades in 'The Next Doctor' – are visibly cut-price aliens, recalling the somewhat crude man-in-a-boilersuit horrors of 1950s B-movies such as, inevitably, *The Fly* (20th Century Fox, 1958). As such, they only just avoid being laughably unconvincing. It doesn't help that the script surrounds them with some glaring implausibilities, most notably that their ship has internal communications equipment with earpieces designed for humanoid ears, which they clearly lack, and anti-gravity clamps that are, rather too conveniently, exactly the right size and shape to fit onto the wheels of a London bus! Equally contrived is the way they are quickly killed off just as soon as their usefulness to the plot is exhausted. The stingray-type monsters, on the other hand, are quite convincing CGI creations, with a credible feeding cycle – migrating from one planet to another, ravaging each in turn – very similar to that of the Nimon in the fourth Doctor story 'The Horns of Nimon' (1979/80); and the fact that they are acting simply on instinct rather than out of any malicious intent makes them quite unusual as *Doctor Who* monsters.

The roots of the basic story can be traced back to Davies's initial ideas for the opening episode of Series Four. As recounted in his and Benjamin Cook's book *The Writer's Tale* (BBC Books, 2008), he thought up a tale in which an alien world with big, desert-like vistas had been overrun by monsters called the Vorlax – envisaged at that stage as resembling wild dogs – who had eaten most of the population and now threatened to burst through a wormhole to Earth and do the same thing there. Although this notion had been dropped in favour of the story that became 'Partners in Crime' (2008), Davies revived it for 'Planet of the Dead' after a number of other ideas – including making the story a semi-spoof space-opera and setting part of the action in a plush hotel – had been considered and abandoned. It was Roberts who suggested the stingray-like creatures in place of the Vorlax.

The element of the London bus and its passengers being transported through the wormhole was meanwhile derived from a similar notion in Roberts' *Doctor Who* novel *The Highest Science*, a 1993 entry in Virgin Publishing's New Adventures range, although in that case the humans who unexpectedly found themselves on a far-flung world were a group of commuters aboard a London tube train – which itself recalled the plot of the *Doctor Who Magazine* comic strip story *Train-Flight* from 1990[31]. The substitution of a red London double-decker bus in 'Planet of the Dead' makes for some suitably quirky imagery in the desert scenes and may have been inspired in part by the use of such a vehicle as the habitual disguise of the TARDIS belonging to Iris Wildthyme, a Time Lady character featured in the BBC's range of original *Doctor Who* novels in the 1990s and subsequently given her own independently produced series of spin-off novels, audio plays and short story collections. Particularly in the scenes at the end where it takes to the air, it is also slightly reminiscent of the Knight Bus from J K Rowling's *Harry Potter* novels and their movie adaptations.

At one point, it was intended that the Chelonians, the race of turtle-like aliens created by Roberts for *The Highest Science* and featured in a number of other *Doctor Who* novels, would make their TV debut in 'Planet of the Dead', but the Tritovores ultimately took their place in the narrative, partly because they were much cheaper to realise.

Other influences actually acknowledged by Davies are the movies *The Flight of the Phoenix* (20th Century Fox, 1965 and 2004), involving the crash of a transporter aircraft in the middle of a desert; *Pitch Black* (Universal, 2002), in which a spaceship crashes on a desert planet and the survivors are attacked by predatory flying creatures; and *Raiders of the Lost Ark* (Paramount Pictures, 1981), the opening sequence of which has Indiana Jones stealing a golden idol and replacing it with an object of equal weight on its plinth. The initial International Gallery sequence of 'Planet of the Dead' also recalls jewellery heist scenes from numerous other films, perhaps most notably the one that opens the fourth entry in the *Pink Panther* franchise, *The Return of the Pink Panther* (United Artists, 1975). The scenario of a group of people cut off from civilisation aboard a public transport vehicle threatened by alien attack was previously featured in the Series Four episode 'Midnight' (2008) – as actually alluded to in a line of the Doctor's dialogue here – while Lady Christina's background as an aristocratic cat burglar echoes the basis of the new companion character that script editor Andrew Cartmel and writer Ben Aaronovitch had devised for inclusion in Season 27 of the classic-era *Doctor Who* in 1990 – an idea thwarted by the BBC's failure to renew the series after Season 26.

Lady Christina essentially acts as a stand-in companion figure in this special, although the Doctor's refusal to allow her to join him aboard the TARDIS at the end explicitly confirms the indications given in 'The Next Doctor' of his resolve to continue travelling solo for the time being. She is an interesting character, of a type not really seen in the show before, and played with feisty charm by the well-cast

[31] *Doctor Who Magazine* had also featured a comic strip story entitled *Planet of the Dead* in 1988.

Michelle Ryan, previously best known for her roles in *EastEnders* and the US series *Bionic Woman*. The verbal sparring between the Doctor and Lady Christina works very well – certainly far better than that between the Doctor and Donna in the latter's introductory story, 'The Runaway Bride' (2006) – and one is left almost wishing that this *had* become an ongoing partnership. The circumstances in which the pair meet are particularly amusing as, already on the run from the police, Lady Christina finds her troubles compounded by being apparently sat next to a talkative nutter on the bus – a classic awkward situation dreaded by every commuter, and one previously featured in the tenth Doctor comic strip story *Bus Stop!*, published in Issue 385 of *Doctor Who Magazine* in August 2007.

As the story unfolds, the readiness with which Lady Christina accepts that the bus has been transported to another planet and that the Doctor is an alien does perhaps undermine the character's believability; but this is really unavoidable, as the special's relatively short running time does not allow for the kind of gradual coming to terms with the situation that would normally be seen with a new companion over the course of her first few episodes. Some viewers may raise an eyebrow at the realisation that the Doctor helps a self-confessed thief to escape from the police at the end; but Lady Christina has, after all, assisted in saving the Earth from a potential catastrophe, and so is probably owed a break; and her requisition of the flying bus as a getaway vehicle is perhaps not a million miles removed from the Doctor's own appropriation of the TARDIS from the Time Lords when he first set out on his travels through space and time – as he himself recalls after initially expressing disapproval of Lady Christina's theft of the Cup of Athelstan.

Of the other guest characters, the most comment-worthy are probably Captain Magambo, with Noma Dumezweni reprising her role from 'Turn Left' (2008), and UNIT's new scientific adviser, Dr Malcolm Taylor, played by comedian Lee Evans. While it is good to see Magambo becoming a recurring character, and Dumezweni again does the part justice, it seems strange – as indeed it did in 'Turn Left' – that such an important UNIT operation is not commanded by a more senior officer. This of course contrasts with the situation back in the 1970s, when all British UNIT activities were overseen by Brigadier Lethbridge-Stewart, while his Captain, Mike Yates, took very much a supporting role. Malcolm, portrayed by Evans as a sort of cross between Jerry Lewis's Nutty Professor and Norman Wisdom's bumbling Norman Pitkin, is another character that would have seemed distinctly out of place in the 1970s UNIT set-up. In fact, it is difficult to think of a more overtly comedic character being featured in *Doctor Who* at any time in its 46-year history; and while he seems to have been popular with many fans – of whom it has been speculated that he may have been intended as an affectionate send-up, with his geeky manner and wide-eyed adulation of the Doctor – it almost seems at times as if he has been mistakenly transplanted from another production altogether. While it is entirely believable that he should admire and respect the Doctor, based on what he has read about him in the UNIT files, his worshipful adoration of him is distinctly over the top – ridiculously so in the scene towards the end where he repeatedly tells him that he loves him. The cod Welsh accent that Evans chose to adopt for the role has also divided opinion – it has even been suggested by some fan critics that the dialogue about Malcolm having a sore throat may have been added at a late stage to try to excuse his exaggerated delivery – and although Davies reportedly vetoed a suggestion by the actor that he should wear a set of comedy buck-teeth dentures, it would hardly have made the character any more outlandish had this idea been approved. This again puts one in mind of the format of family action-adventure blockbusters, which often tend to include a (hopefully) endearing comedy-relief character to provide an occasional interlude from the more serious thrills and spills.

The disjunction in style between this character and the rest of the production is perhaps most tellingly apparent in the scene where Captain Magambo demands that Malcolm close the rift, even though this will inevitably lead to the demise of the Doctor and the other bus passengers, and Malcolm steadfastly refuses to do so. This confrontation is really jarring – not only because of the awkward contrast between the sternly serious Magambo and the absurdly goofy Malcolm, but also because it seems inherently implausible that this relatively lowly UNIT officer would be prepared, or have the authority, to sacrifice the Doctor so summarily. While it could perhaps be said that such unsentimental pragmatism is in keeping with the depiction of a harsher, more uncompromising UNIT in new-era *Doctor Who* – and even more so in the *Torchwood* spin-off – it ignores the obvious value to the Earth of ensuring that the Doctor, so often its saviour in the past, is kept alive to aid in averting any future crises. Admittedly Magambo has never met the Doctor, and so has had no opportunity to build up a friendship with him in the way that previous UNIT regulars have, but she must surely recognise his status within and importance to the organisation – indeed, her dialogue at other points clearly indicates that she does, albeit that she stops short of idolising him in quite the way that Malcolm does – so her sudden willingness to let him be killed comes across as contrived and contradictory.

This is not the only oddity in the script – even leaving aside the already-mentioned incongruities regarding the Tritovores and their technology. There is also a degree of strangeness about the way Lady Christina behaves when she steals the Cup of Athelstan at the start of the action. Having lowered herself down from the roof and raised herself back up again on wires in order to pluck the Cup from its plinth without being seen by the armed security men, she is then, strangely, seen back on the ground floor in another part of the Gallery, and seems surprised and exasperated when the alarm is raised – despite the fact that she must have realised this would happen, as she left behind on the Cup's plinth a toy cat with a squeaky waving arm! How the security men failed to hear her when she was performing her aerial acrobatics, given that they were standing so close by, is a mystery in itself, as is the reason why such exceptional security measures were felt to be required in the first place, given that the Cup's stated £18 million value is very modest by museum standards. Perhaps even more puzzling is why, when Lady Christina is making her getaway on the bus, the pursuing police cars fail to catch up with it, despite the fact that they must obviously be capable of far higher speeds, and indeed why the bus driver fails to pull over when he hears their sirens and sees their lights behind him (unless this is a humorous allusion to the fact that bus drivers can notoriously refuse to let *anyone* on once they have left their stop). Also curious is the fact that, after the bus is transported to San Helios, the Doctor appears to overlook an obvious solution to the predicament in which he and his fellow passengers find themselves: if being inside a metal shell – the bus – was sufficient to protect them when they travelled from Earth to the planet, why does he not simply ask UNIT to send a tank or some other armoured vehicle through the wormhole to rescue them? Or even, perhaps, throw one end of a metal tow-rope through, to pull them back on the bus? Then there is the fact that, at the end, the Doctor tries to fix up the two young men, Barclay and Nathan, with new jobs in UNIT, seemingly at odds with his stance in 'The Sontaran Stratagem'/'The Poison Sky' (2008), when he disapproved of his former companion Martha Jones having gone to work for the organisation (although possibly his experiences in that story and 'The Stolen Earth'/'Journey's End' (2008) caused him to adopt a more favourable view of it).

These are all fairly minor reservations, however, which do not detract greatly from the viewer's overall enjoyment of the action. And that is really what this special is all about: enjoyment of a fun, lightweight action-adventure story, before the show's mood turns considerably darker in 'The Waters of Mars', as the end approaches for David Tennant's time as the Doctor.

4.16 – THE WATERS OF MARS

Writer: Russell T Davies and Phil Ford
Director: Graeme Harper

DEBUT TRANSMISSION DETAILS

BBC One/BBC HD
Date: 15 November 2009. Scheduled time: 19.00 pm. Actual time: 18.59 pm.

Duration: 62' 04"[32]

CREDITED CAST

David Tennant (The Doctor), Lindsay Duncan (Adelaide Brooke), Peter O'Brien (Ed Gold), Aleksandar Mikic (Yuri Kerenski), Gemma Chan (Mia Bennett), Sharon Duncan-Brewster (Maggie Cain), Chook Sibtain (Tarak Ital), Alan Ruscoe (Andy Stone), Cosima Shaw (Steffi Ehrlich), Michael Goldsmith (Roman Groom), Lily Bevan (Emily), Max Bollinger (Mikhail), Charlie De'Ath (Adelaide's Father), Rachel Fewell (Young Adelaide), Anouska Strahnz (Ulrika Ehrlich), Zofia Strahnz (Lisette Ehrlich), Paul Kasey (Ood Sigma)[33]

Daleks Created by Terry Nation

PLOT

The Doctor arrives on Mars, where Captain Adelaide Brooke and her crew have established Bowie Base One, intended to be the first permanent Earth colony on another planet. On learning the date, 21 November 2059, the Time Lord realises that the Base is about to be destroyed in mysterious circumstances and its human occupants killed – an event that will ultimately inspire Adelaide's grand-daughter to follow in her pioneering footsteps by piloting the first light-speed ship to Proxima Centauri. As this is a fixed point in time, the Doctor is forbidden to interfere. He determines to leave as quickly as possible, but before he can do so, he becomes embroiled in the crisis overtaking the Base. One by one, the crew members start to become infected by an alien virus that inhabits the water on Mars, turning them into zombie-like creatures. This menace, which the Doctor dubs the Flood, wants to use the humans' rocket ship to get to Earth. The surviving humans blow up the ship, and Adelaide sets the Base to self-destruct. Contravening the Laws of Time, the Doctor rescues Adelaide and two of her colleagues and takes them back to Earth in the TARDIS. However, realising that her survival would

---

[32] The version released on DVD/Blu-Ray, with extended closing credits, runs to 62' 07".
[33] Not credited in *Radio Times*.

change the course of history, Adelaide kills herself, and the Doctor realises that he has gone too far.

QUOTE, UNQUOTE

- **Adelaide:** 'State your name, rank and intention.'
  The Doctor: 'The Doctor. Doctor. Fun.'
- **The Doctor:** 'Water is patient, Adelaide. Water just waits. It wears down the cliff-tops, the mountains, the whole of the world. Water always wins.'
- **The Doctor:** 'But you were saving Earth. That's what inspires your grand-daughter. She takes your people out into the galaxy because you die on Mars. You die today. She flies out there, like she's trying to meet you.'
  Adelaide: 'I won't die. I will not.'
  The Doctor: 'But your death creates the future.'
- **The Doctor:** 'There are Laws of Time, and once upon a time there were people in charge of those Laws. But they died. They all died. D'you know who that leaves? Me! It's taken me all these years to realise: the Laws of Time are mine. And they will obey me!'
- **The Doctor:** 'For a long time now, I've thought I was just a survivor, but I'm not. I'm the winner. That's who I am. The Time Lord Victorious.'

CONTINUITY POINTS

- The news articles seen on screen during the course of the story, apparently originating from some unidentified website or similar, disclose a number of facts and biographical notes not otherwise revealed through the dialogue or action – although they should perhaps be treated with caution, as they contain some obvious contradictions and errors (see 'Oops' below), along with a number of spelling and grammatical mistakes, and are also seen to change their wording after the Doctor changes the course of history. Amongst the more notable details, they indicate that Captain Adelaide Brooke and her team – Deputy Edward Gold, Dr Tarak Ital MD, Nurse Yuri Kerenski, Senior Technician Steffi Ehrlich, Junior Technician Roman Groom, Geologist Mia Bennett, Officer Margaret Cain and Officer Andrew Stone – made a two-year-long journey to Mars aboard a shuttle designated Apollo 34 before establishing Bowie Base One in the Gusev Crater. Their mission is to spend five years there, carrying out research and scientific studies, taking soil samples and assessing whether or not the planet can be made habitable. The expedition has been mounted by the American space agency NASA. Adelaide has made at least one previous journey to Mars, when she became the first woman to land on the planet, as part of a three-strong team. She had earlier been the first British woman to land on the Moon. She campaigned for Mars rather than the Moon to be chosen as the site for the first off-Earth human colony. Before developing an interest in space, Dr Tarak Ital was an athlete, winning a gold medal for Pakistan in the 400 metres race in the 2044 Olympics in Havana, Cuba. Germany had mounted ten Moon missions by 2050, the last of which had Steffi Ehrlich as one of its prime crew. Mia Bennett's father was named Peter (an in-joke reference to sometime *Torchwood* and *Doctor Who* assistant director and latterly producer Peter Bennett).

- 'The Ambassadors of Death' (1970), probably set around the year of its transmission, tells of the first manned missions to Mars. That is not contradicted by 'The Waters of Mars', as although Bowie Base One is the first human colony to be established on the planet, it has clearly been preceded by other expeditions. (More difficult to reconcile with 'The Ambassadors of Death' is 'The Christmas Invasion' (2005), in which the unmanned Guinevere One probe is said to be the first that Britain has launched to Mars. It seems unlikely that the Mars Probe missions of 'The Ambassadors of Death' could have been completely hushed up since, even with UNIT's involvement, so perhaps something has occurred to change the history of human exploration of Mars – an intriguing possibility, given the Doctor's comments in 'The Waters of Mars' about Adelaide's death being a fixed point in history.)
- In reality, the respective orbits of Mars and Earth will place them on almost opposite sides of the solar system on 21 November 2059, about 200 million miles distant from each other. The *Doctor Who* universe must be different in this respect, as on first arriving in Bowie Base One, the Doctor – albeit without knowing the exact date at that point – states that the distance between them is only 40 million miles, and this figure is later confirmed by Yuri. Another difference is that the Martian moon seen in the final shot of the planet is rotating, whereas in the real world, both of the moons always show the same face towards it.
- The Doctor can speak the Ancient North Martian language.
- Bowie Base One was constructed above an underground glacier for ease of access to a plentiful water supply. It is implied that the Flood has been frozen there for 10,000 years.
- The Doctor recounts to Adelaide that the legends of Mars tell of 'a fine and noble race who built an empire out of snow – the Ice Warriors.' He speculates that it may have been the Ice Warriors who originally found the Flood and froze it in the glacier, although this remains unconfirmed. Later, when he decides to use heat as a weapon against the Flood, he says 'Works against the Ice Warriors; works against the Flood'. The Ice Warriors have appeared in four *Doctor Who* stories on TV – 'The Ice Warriors' (1967), 'The Seeds of Death' (1969), 'The Curse of Peladon' (1972) and 'The Monster of Peladon' (1974) – and in numerous others is tie-in novels, audio plays and comic strips. On many occasions in these stories, the Ice Warriors have been shown to be susceptible to high temperatures.
- The Doctor tells Adelaide that her grand-daughter, Suzie Fontana Brooke, will later learn what happened to her 50 years earlier, on 'the day the Earth was stolen and moved across the universe' – a reference to the events of 'The Stolen Earth'/'Journey's End' (2008). Adelaide recalls that on that day, one of the invading Daleks hovered outside her bedroom window, looked in at her, but spared her life and went away. It was this that inspired her to become an astronaut, and that in turn will ultimately inspire Suzie to – as the Doctor puts it – '[take] the human race all the way out to the stars'. Since the Doctor had no prior knowledge of the Daleks' plans in 'The Stolen Earth'/'Journey's End', he must have learned of the history of Adelaide and her family only after the events of that story – a history that may actually have been created by those

very events, changing the whole course of human progress. Alternatively, had the Dalek invasion of 'The Stolen Earth'/'Journey's End' never happened, it is conceivable that some other incident may have inspired Adelaide to become a space pioneer, and that her life and that of her family may have been largely unchanged – consistent with the fact that her death on Mars is a fixed point in time. At any rate, the fact that the Doctor is now so familiar with the new timeline in which Adelaide saw a Dalek suggests that he may have been travelling alone in the TARDIS for quite some time since he deposited Donna on Earth.

- The Doctor later says to Adelaide: 'You've wondered all your life why that Dalek spared you. I think it knew. Your death is fixed in time, forever. And that's right.' Although this is just speculation on the Doctor's part, it implies that the Dalek may have sensed that Adelaide's life was important to the timeline and that it should not, or could not, harm her. If so, this may indicate that the Daleks – a time-travelling race like the Time Lords – are bound by the same or similar Laws of Time. It would also, however, suggest that the Dalek's actions were instinctive rather than reasoned, as otherwise it would have realised in advance that Davros's plan to deploy a reality bomb must fail.
- The Doctor tells Adelaide it was recently prophesied that his death would be preceded by someone knocking four times – a reference to the warning that Carmen gave him at the end of 'Planet of the Dead'.

PRODUCTION NOTES

- Lindsay Duncan is credited in the opening titles after David Tennant.
- The Cemex quarry in Pentyrch, Cardiff, was the location used for the Mars surface exteriors, recording taking place there on 23 and 24 February 2009. On 25 and 26 February, the National Botanic Garden of Wales in Carmarthenshire was used for the botanic dome interiors and air lock of Bowie Base One. 27 February saw the crew moving to Victoria Place in Newport, where the scenes outside Adelaide's London residence were taped. The premises of a company called Next Generation Data in Celtic Way, Newport, were used for the Base's connecting tunnels and infrastructure, recording there being done from 2 to 4 March. Studio recording took place, as usual, in the show's Upper Boat base.
- 'The Waters of Mars' concludes with a 'Coming Soon' trailer for 'The End of Time', and a caption reading: 'In Memory of Barry Letts 1925 – 2009'. Letts, who had produced *Doctor Who* during the third Doctor's era in the early 1970s and made a number of other contributions to the show, had died on 9 October 2009, little over a month before the debut transmission of 'The Waters of Mars'.
- As originally conceived, this story was to have been the 2009 Christmas special, and had the working titles 'A Midwinter's Tale', 'Red Christmas' and 'Christmas on Mars'. (This was before the decision was taken to transmit the tenth Doctor's two-part swansong over the festive season.) A number of 'Christmassy' elements were mooted for inclusion, including the Doctor improvising the construction of a TARDIS homing device out of a metallic Christmas tree, but these were dropped when it became clear that the special would actually be transmitted close to Halloween – although the snowy conditions outside Adelaide's home in the climactic scene at the end can be

seen as a hang-over from the earlier version, and there is also a reference to the crew members growing vegetables in anticipation of eating them for Christmas dinner.

- The name of the base, Bowie Base One, is a homage to the rock musician David Bowie, one of whose best-known hits was 'Life on Mars?' (1971) and who for a time performed under the guise Ziggy Stardust and the Spiders from Mars.
- The date of the action, 21 November 2059, was chosen as it was exactly 50 years after 21 November 2009, tentatively planned as the debut transmission date of the special at the time when Russell T Davies was writing it. In the event, it went out six days earlier.
- In the special as transmitted, the crew members infected by the water do not speak once their transformation is complete – partly for the practical reason that the actors could not talk properly when they had water constantly trickling out of their mouths from concealed pipes. Originally, however, there was to have been some dialogue in which the fully transformed Margaret Cain identified the attacking entity as 'the Flood'. The decision to drop this at the editing stage made it appear in the final version as if it is the Doctor who coins that name. The deleted scene is amongst those included in an extra on 'The Complete Specials' DVD and Blu-ray set.
- Chook Sibtain, who plays Tarak Ital in 'The Waters of Mars', previously appeared as Mark Grantham in 'Warriors of Kudlak' (2007), a Series One episode of *The Sarah Jane Adventures* – a rare example in post-2005 *Doctor Who* and its spin-offs of the same actor recognisably playing two different guest roles.
- All DVD and Blu-ray releases of this special have closing titles that differ slightly from those of the transmitted version, being extended to include more credits.

OOPS!

- In the pre-credits sequence, blue sky and white clouds can be seen reflected in the visor of Yuri's spacesuit, rather than the red sky of Mars.
- All the characters on Mars move as if the gravity is exactly the same as on Earth, whereas it should actually be less than half as strong (although stronger than on the Moon).
- It is never explained why Adelaide and her crew have guns. This would seem unnecessary, given that they are not expecting anyone else to be present on Mars – although brief mention is made of possible rival expeditions being mounted by the Philippines or Spain or 'the Branson inheritance lot' (and conceivably there could be some known or anticipated alien threat to the solar system in 2059).
- In the first of the news articles flashed up on screen, it is stated that the human expedition took two years to reach Mars. Adelaide then tells the Doctor that they have been on the planet for 17 months, enabling him to pinpoint the date as 2059. Thus the total length of time that Adelaide and her crew have been away from Earth should be around three-and-a-half years. However, in the recorded message that Adelaide is seen watching in the very first scene of the

story, her daughter mentions that she has been away for 'two years'.

- This first news article also refers to Adelaide having a 'seven strong team' on Mars, but there are in fact eight crew members, whom it proceeds to name. (A typing error, or a case of journalistic incompetence?)

- In another of the news articles, it is stated that Adelaide was born on 12 May 1999 and was aged 10 when her parents were pronounced missing and presumed dead after the Dalek invasion – i.e. the invasion seen in 'The Stolen Earth'/'Journey's End' (2008). This would mean that the pronouncement in question was made sometime after 12 May 2009, her tenth birthday, which is consistent with the summer 2009 timing of the Dalek invasion as established by implication in previous stories. However, the article inconsistently dates the invasion as having occurred in '2008'. (Possibly another typing or journalistic error?)

- Adelaide says that bicycles were not brought on the mission to Mars because of weight restrictions. However, the weight of a few bicycles would surely have been insignificant compared with that of the huge, and very thick, steel sections used to construct the domes and tunnels of the base.

- Steffi's children speak German with strong Welsh accents!

- The picture of the Lithuanian flag seen on the wall of the central dome's command centre – one of an array of such pictures, representing the crew members' different nationalities – is upside-down.

- No explanation is given as to why, once he has decided he is no longer going to be bound by the Laws of Time, the Doctor does not simply walk to the TARDIS and rescue Adelaide and her crew by travelling back in time a few minutes (but not so far back as to meet himself in the base, which might cause a paradox attracting the attention of the Reapers, as seen in 'Father's Day' (2005)). This would surely be a much neater plan than returning to the base and trying to contain the situation there while sending Gadget to fetch the ship. (Or is the law that prevents him from crossing his own timeline more in the nature of a physical law that it is impossible to break, rather than simply a prohibition?)

- There is an editing error in the London scene at the end: Yuri is seen to exit the TARDIS, with the door closing behind him, twice. Gadget, on the other hand, is not seen to exit the TARDIS at all, and there would seem to be no opportunity for it to do so, so it is a mystery how it comes to be outside in the snow.

PRESS REACTION

- '[David] Tennant is electrifying in his defiant portrayal of an angry god, complemented by the understated fervour and strength of [Lindsay] Duncan as Adelaide. Her sacrifice to protect the world that could be is one of the most wrenching and profound moments *Doctor Who* has ever produced and forces the Doctor to taste the bitterness of humility. Over recent years, Russell T Davies has sought scale and convolution over substance, and a return to character pieces like this is a welcome change of pace. Running away from his fate and the blood that stains his hands, the Doctor is treading water and time is ticking down.' Paul Leake, Screengeek website, 17 November 2009.

- 'Stone sinks to his knees, and spasms pass through him as the alien life-form takes over. His pupils contract, his mouth turns black, cracks appear in his skin and the water from his body pours out. Ouch. Dude, you need to moisturise more, because you're worth it. This will give anyone with dry skin nightmares. Others, too – it's a scary one, though maybe children don't get scared any more. It's making me thirsty and itchy, and I want to hide behind the sofa.' Sam Wollaston, *Guardian*, 16 November 2009.
- 'The Doctor has a terrible dilemma … He dithers, walks away, comes back, interferes with history, changes his mind again. It's a side to the Doctor, who has always known what to do in a crisis, that we haven't really seen before – indecisive, confused, at times simply plain wrong.' Sam Wollaston, *Guardian*, 16 November 2009.
- 'With David Tennant opening his long farewell from *Doctor Who*, no-one could accuse writers Russell T Davies and Phil Ford of taking the soft option as the two-hearted Time Lord began the process of morphing into Matt Smith. "The Waters of Mars" was an episode that overflowed with ambition.' Keith Watson, *Metro*, 16 November 2009.

ANALYSIS

'The Fires of Pompeii' (2008) established an important point of *Doctor Who* continuity, developing ideas touched on in earlier stories such as 'Pyramids of Mars' (1975) and 'The Unquiet Dead' (2005) and finally providing a fictional explanation as to why the Doctor sometimes resolutely avoids interfering in the course of history, while on other occasions he shows no hesitation in intervening to bring about quite radical changes in events. 'Some things are fixed,' he tells Donna, 'some things are in flux.' When Donna asks how he knows the difference, he replies: 'Because that's how I see the universe. Every waking second, I can see what is, what was, what could be, what must not. It's the burden of a Time Lord, Donna.' So now we know why, for instance, he is unable to oppose the Aztecs' practice of human sacrifice in 'The Aztecs' (1964), but by contrast has no qualms about helping to overthrow the early-21st Century despot Salamander in 'The Enemy of the World' (1968). This dichotomy actually turns out to be the crux of 'The Fires of Pompeii', when the Doctor realises that the alien Pyroviles are holding back the eruption of Mount Vesuvius and he has to intervene in order to ensure that history takes what he knows to be its proper course – even though this means condemning thousands of innocent citizens of Pompeii to death.

A very similar dilemma lies at the heart of 'The Waters of Mars', although given a neat twist, in that the events depicted here lie in the future, and so to the viewer are completely unfamiliar, whereas to the Doctor they are still just as much a part of established human history as those in Pompeii. In the Time Lord's eyes, Captain Adelaide Brooke and her team are equally famous and significant historical figures as earlier space pioneers such as Neil Armstrong and his fellow Apollo astronauts. And Adelaide's death in the destruction of Bowie Base One is a fixed point in time, meaning that, as with, say, the slaughter foreshadowed in 'The Massacre of St Bartholomew's Eve' (1966), the Doctor ought to allow the tragedy to unfold as it is predestined to do. Except that, in this instance, he finds himself unable simply to walk away and leave the human crew members to their fate; a momentous change of heart that leads on to a shocking conclusion.

If there is a certain sense of *déjà vu* about the story's theme, coming in the wake of 'The Fires of Pompeii' (the circumstances of which are explicitly referred to by the Doctor at one point), then even more familiar is its format. This follows closely the 'base under seige' template exploited to great effect in many classic-era stories, particularly during the second Doctor's tenure in the late 1960s. All the archetypal elements are present and correct: the self-contained base, cut off from the outside world; the multinational crew of experts; the strong-willed commander, initially distrustful of the Doctor but ultimately turning to him for help as the situation spirals out of control; and the terrifying alien menace attacking and infiltrating the base. 'The Tenth Planet' (1966), 'The Power of the Daleks' (1966), 'The Moonbase' (1967), 'Fury from the Deep' (1968) and 'The Wheel in Space' (1968) are just some of the most obvious examples of earlier stories that fit this pattern. 'The Moonbase' is a particularly striking precedent, with a domed base comprising a human outpost on one of Earth's closest solar system neighbours; the Doctor donning a spacesuit to cross between the TARDIS and the base; and the base crew gradually succumbing to an infection from contaminated drinks, turning them into hapless drones. Also of note, 'Fury from the Deep' featured seaweed-possessed characters emitting streams of toxic gas from their wide-open mouths – a possible inspiration for the idea of the infected crew members on Bowie Base One spewing forth gouts of poisonous water. 'The Impossible Planet'/'The Satan Pit' (2006) and '42' (2007) are the only previous Russell T Davies-era stories to have adopted the 'base under seige' approach, and 'The Waters of Mars' bears a certain similarity in tone to them, as emphasised – whether deliberately or not – by the fact that the Doctor's spacesuit here is of the same design as they presented. And the fact that it is such a scary story – as highlighted, albeit perhaps slightly exagerrated, in the advance publicity – demonstrates that this scenario has lost none of its potency over the years.

The alien menace in this case, the Flood, is a very unusal and effective one, although the idea of an entity inhabiting water is not entirely original, having previously featured most notably in the *Doctor Who* audio drama 'The Genocide Machine' (Big Finish, 2000). Given that the story is set on Mars, it is actually rather a pity that the opportunity was not taken to bring back its established indigenous race, the Ice Warriors, who are surely long overdue a return appearance in the show and whose first two stories back in the 1960s were both of the 'base under seige' type – the latter of them, 'The Seeds of Death' (1969), involving a Martian virus that is destroyed by water rather than carried by it.[34] At least, however, they do receive a couple of welcome mentions in the dialogue. The people infected by the Flood are not actually killed by it, and so do not become zombies in the literal sense, but in terms of appearance are nevertheless arguably the most zombie-like creatures ever to have been featured in *Doctor Who* (at least on TV). Scientifically-

---

[34] Also notable is that the first Ice Warrior story, 'The Ice Warriors' (1967), features a scene in which the second Doctor is trapped inside an airlock and threatened with the pressure being lowered to the point where he explodes – a scenario strongly recalled by the scene in 'The Waters of Mars' where Adelaide traps the tenth Doctor inside an airlock and threatens to increase the pressure to the point where he is crushed.

minded viewers may perhaps question how they are able to create the water that they shoot from their hands and mouths, given that it can't come from nowhere (and although the human body consists mainly of water, as the Doctor points out, they hardly seem to become dehydrated); but this is not the first time a *Doctor Who* monster has used a scientifically-implausible attack method, and from a dramatic standpoint, it serves its purpose very well.[35]

One notable difference between 'The Waters of Mars' and other new-era stories such as 'The Impossible Planet'/'The Satan Pit' is that the featured base in this instance has a clean, pristine, high-tech appearance – a 'NASA look', as Davies has described it – as opposed to the grimy, industrial interiors that have come to typify such settings in the show. The use of the National Botanic Garden of Wales as a location makes for a pleasing contrast to the usual disused factory and warehouse sites, and lends a tremendous sense of scale to the proceedings. The other settings are also superbly realised, from the highly convincing Mars surface exteriors – seamlessly mixing quarry-taped location material with CGI visuals – to the base interiors and, finally, to the beautifully-shot snowy London street scene at the end. In fact, the production as a whole is a visual treat, featuring also some typically superb effects work from Any Effects and some brilliant prosthetic make-up design from the Millennium FX team for the infected crew members, whose gruesome appearance surely tests the limits of what is deemed acceptable these days in terms of horror content in an early-evening family-viewing show. Aurally, too, 'The Waters of Mars' is very pleasing, with a particularly good score from Murray Gold. Critics of Gold's music often complain that it tends to be over-the-top and intrusive, but there is really only one scene here where that could perhaps be said to be the case, specifically the one where Adelaide and the Doctor flee down the tunnel from the bio-dome back to the central dome, pursued by the infected Andy and Tarak. Otherwise, the music fittingly complements the story throughout.

Director Graeme Harper is on top form here, too, handling the action scenes and character scenes with equal aplomb. Aside from David Tennant, the acting honours this time go principally to Lindsay Duncan, who gives a fine, multi-layered performance as Adelaide. Although in advance promotion for the story the production team characterised her, rather unchivalrously, as the Doctor's oldest companion to date, she is – even more so than Jackson Lake in 'The Next Doctor' – not really a companion at all, by any reasonable definition of that term, but simply a leading guest star character. As with Lady Christina in 'Planet of the Dead', the ease and rapidity with which she comes to trust the Doctor and accept that he is an alien time traveller is not really credible, but can be forgiven due to the obvious need to get on with telling the story. And her part in proceedings turns out to be absolutely crucial, as it is the Doctor's decision to change history by rescuing her, along with her colleagues Mia and Yuri, that places him in direct contravention of the Laws of Time – the momentous development to which events have been building up, and which really constitutes the main *raison d'etre* of the story.

The Doctor's loss of moral compass here as he succumbs to hubris and

---

[35] In their script, the writers sought to address the point about the source of the water in the following stage direction for a scene involving Margaret Cain: 'NB. The room doesn't slowly flood, despite the flow; it's as if the water goes round her in a cycle, into her clothes, absorbed back up.'

arrogance, declaring himself to be the Time Lord Victorious, takes *Doctor Who* into new dramatic territory and packs a considerable emotional punch. It is in many ways the culmination of a strand of characterisation that has run throughout the tenth Doctor's tenure, from his description of himself in 'The Christmas Invasion'(2005) as a 'no second chances' sort of man, through his declaration in 'New Earth' (2006) that there is no higher authority than him, to Donna's realisation in 'The Christmas Invasion' that he needs someone – a human companion – to keep him grounded and stop him from going too far. Actually, it could be said that this latter fact has been apparent right since the very start of the show in 1963, when over the course of the first three stories the Doctor was seen to grow gradually less arrogant and self-centred as he became affected by his contact with his first two human travelling companions, Ian and Barbara. At any rate, this is a major development within the theme running through the final five Tennant-era specials, of the Doctor travelling alone for virtually the first time in the show's history, and of the effect this lack of human companionship has on him. A large part of the credit for the tremendous impact of these closing scenes must go to Tennant himself, who rises to the acting challenges presented by the script, co-written on this occasion by Davies and Phil Ford, and is utterly convincing as a Doctor initially wracked by indecision and self-doubt and ultimately turning much darker.

Yet, as dramatically effective as this extraordinary twist is, it is hard not to have serious reservations about it. For younger viewers of *Doctor Who* in particular, the Doctor represents a figure of trust and reassurance, an incorruptible hero, who can always be depended upon to do the right thing. For this image to be undermined, as it is at the conclusion of 'The Waters of Mars', arguably risks striking a blow to the heart of what *Doctor Who* is really all about, and one of the main sources of its enormous appeal. Admittedly, the Doctor has always been a *flawed* hero. Even leaving aside the fact that 'The Trial of a Time Lord' (1986) showed him to have the potential to become the villainous Valeyard – a distillation of his darker qualities, somehow brought into existence between his twelfth and thirteenth incarnations – there have been a number of occasions in the past when his actions have appeared highly questionable, such as when he co-operated with the Daleks in testing his companion Jamie in 'The Evil of the Daleks' (1967) and when he collaborated with the Vardans in their infiltration of Gallifrey in 'The Invasion of Time' (1978). More recent examples include his killing of the Racnoss young in 'The Runaway Bride' (2006) and his meting out of harsh punishments to the Family of Blood in the 2007 episode named after them. (There have been other instances in the tie-in novels and audio dramas as well.) On all those previous occasions, however, his apparently suspect actions have always turned out to be a necessary part of his overall strategy to defeat his vicious adversaries. While it could be said that his motivation for breaking the Laws of Time in 'The Waters of Mars' is also a compassionate one – specifically, to save Adelaide and her crew members from their predestined deaths – never before has he been shown to have made such a serious error of judgment, and never before have his actions so calamitously backfired as to cause one of his friends to take the shockingly drastic step of commiting suicide.

Moreover, the Doctor's compassion here seems tainted by selfishness, as there is more than a hint that he sees in Adelaide's situation a parallel to his own. The ending of his 'song' has been similarly foretold, both by Ood Sigma in 'Planet of the Ood' (2008) and by Carmen in 'Planet of the Dead', and it seems that he hopes his defiance of historical imperative will enable him to save not only Adelaide but also himself. This suggestion is reinforced when, immediately after Adelaide shoots herself, he receives a mysterious visitation from Ood Sigma, a silent reminder of those earlier portents of doom, as if pressing home to him the point that Time cannot be denied and that his death (or regeneration at least) remains as inevitable as hers; a reality that, even as the cloister bell tolls within the TARDIS, he determines to continue resisting.

'If you could decide who lives and who dies,' Mr Copper told the Doctor at the conclusion of 'Voyage of the Damned' (2007), 'that would make you a monster' – a prescient comment, suggesting that Davies may have envisaged this development even as far back as that. Tellingly, Davies and Ford chose to have Adelaide, Mia and Yuri react to the TARDIS and its rapid transporation of them to Earth not with wonder or excitement, as is usually the case with any newcomers boarding the ship, but with confusion and alarm. Mia seems particularly shocked, asking the Doctor 'Who the hell *are* you?' before running off in fear, Yuri following close behind. While this undoubtedly supports the writers' aim of casting the Time Lord in a new, more sinister light, and also gives a novel twist to what has become a fairly familiar scenario in the show, it again risks undermining one of the key elements of *Doctor Who*'s perennial appeal: namely, the thrill and pleasure of travelling in the TARDIS, and the sense of security the ship affords not only for the Doctor and his travelling companions, as a sanctuary from the dangers they face in their adventures, but also for the audience at home.

There are other problems with the resolution to the story, as well. It is clearly established that the significance of Adelaide's death on Mars is the inspirational effect it will have on future generations, and in particular on her own grand-daughter. This is why it is such an important event in human history, and why it is wrong for the Doctor to interfere with it. And yet, he seems to have overlooked an obvious way in which he could have rescued Adelaide and her crew while still leaving human history undisturbed: he could have simply used the TARDIS to take them all off to another civilised world, perhaps on the far side of the galaxy somewhere, where they could have happily lived out the rest of their lives while leaving everyone on Earth still under the impression that they had died in the destruction of Bowie Base One. Perhaps the writers' intention here was to suggest that the Doctor was so overcome with his newfound sense of universal superiority that he simply no longer cared about the effect of his actions on human history. However, that was clearly not the case earlier on, when he initially walked away from the Base intending to leave the crew to their fates, his face etched with pained emotion as he wrestled with his conscience; so why did he not think of that alternative approach then?

Equally, there is something distinctly amiss, and even rather distasteful, about the clearly-intended implication that Adelaide's suicide will restore history to its proper course. Although it can certainly be said to be a selfless sacrifice on her part once she realises the folly of the Doctor's actions, will it really have the same inspirational effect on future generations as her death on Bowie Base One would have done? This seems especially doubtful given that presumably no-one will ever know the true reason why she killed herself. Most viewers will also, no doubt, have been left wondering how the people of Earth will react to or even be able to comprehend the mysterious reappearance of Adelaide, Mia and Yuri back in London, when they are supposed to be on Mars. Only dedicated fans will have taken the trouble to freeze-frame their recordings of the episode to read the full text of the news articles flashed up on screen (a clever device that unfortunately becomes rather overdone), and thus seen the answer: 'The surviving couple explained how the almost mythical "Doctor" was on the planet Mars at the time of this terrifying episode and aided the crew in their attempted escape …'.

The downbeat nature of the story's conclusion is only the most obvious manifestation of a more general characteristic of 'The Waters of Mars': specifically, that it is almost unremittingly dark in tone. Davies and Ford have seemingly recognised this and tried to address it by adding in some comic relief in the form of Gadget. The 'cute robot' idea is rather passé now, though, having been a stock ingredient of science-fiction films and TV shows for at least the last 30-odd years since the advent of R2-D2 in *Star Wars* (1977), and Gadget's lack of originality is only emphasised by its visual similarity to the titular subject of the Disney/Pixar movie *Wall-E* (2008) – a similarity that the script itself makes no bones about, one stage direction actually describing Gadget as 'a Wall-E-type … robot probe on tracks'. Consequently, as admirably well-realised as Gadget is in production terms, it fails to generate any real amusement and simply comes across as a rather tired and hackneyed inclusion. The writers even make the mistake of having the Doctor himself pour scorn on 'funny robots' – dogs excepted, of course! – and thus give voice to the very scepticism that many viewers will have been feeling. The scene toward the end where Gadget 'heroically' zooms across the planet's treacherous surface to fetch the TARDIS is no doubt intended to be seen as winning its redemption in the Doctor's eyes, but this doesn't really work, and still leaves the story almost devoid of humour.

While it gained an excellent Audience Appreciation figure and has drawn high praise from many adult fans, the overall bleakness of this special seems likely to have made it rather less appealing to younger viewers – the *Guardian*'s TV reviewer, Sam Wollaston, was even moved to ask, 'This isn't really for [children] anyway, is it?' It is certainly starkly at odds with the wonderful sense of fun that has permeated the Russell T Davies version of *Doctor Who* prior to this point. Although undeniably well written, expertly directed and superbly produced, 'The Waters of Mars' is one of the most downbeat *Doctor Who* stories ever to have been presented on TV, and one that comes perilously close to compromising the essential heroic integrity of the show's lead character. It consequently has to be considered something of a mixed blessing.

4.17 – THE END OF TIME – PART ONE

Writer: Russell T Davies
Director: Euros Lyn

<u>DEBUT TRANSMISSION DETAILS</u>

BBC One/BBC HD
Date: 25 December 2009. Scheduled time: 6.00 pm. Actual time: 5.59 pm.

Duration: 59′ 38″ [36]

<u>CREDITED CAST</u>

David Tennant (The Doctor), John Simm (The Master), Bernard Cribbins (Wilfred Mott), Timothy Dalton (The Narrator), Catherine Tate (Donna Noble), Jacqueline King (Sylvia Noble), Claire Bloom (The Woman), June Whitfield (Minnie Hooper), David Harewood (Joshua Naismith), Tracy Ifeachor (Abigail Naismith), Sinead Keenan (Addams), Lawry Lewin (Rossiter), Alexandra Moen (Lucy Saxon), Karl Collins (Sean Temple), Teresa Banham (Governor), Barry Howard (Oliver Barnes), Allister Bain (Winston Katusi), Simon Thomas (Mr Danes)[37], Sylvia Seymour (Miss Trefusis), Pete Lee-Wilson (Tommo), Dwayne Scantlebury (Ginger), Lacey Bond (Serving Woman) [38], Lachele Carl (Trinity Wells), Paul Kasey (Ood Sigma), Ruari Mears (Elder Ood), Max Benjamin (Teenager) [39], Silas Carson (Voice of Ood Sigma)[40], Brian Cox (Voice of Elder Ood).

<u>PLOT</u>

Heeding a warning by the Ood, the Doctor travels to early 21st Century Earth, where he finds that his old Time Lord nemesis the Master has not only cheated death but also acquired strange new powers as a result of his former wife, Lucy Saxon, having tried to prevent his resurrection. Accompanied by Wilf Mott, who has managed to track him down with the aid of a group of elderly friends calling themselves the Silver Cloak, the Doctor follows the Master's trail to the mansion home of billionaire entrepreneur Joshua Naismith. Naismith wants to give his daughter Abigail immortality using a device known as the Immortality Gate,

---

[36] The version released on DVD/Blu-Ray had the same duration. Although it had extended credits, this was compensated for by a briefer 'TO BE CONTINUED' caption (see Production Notes).

[37] Not credited in *Radio Times*.

[38] Not credited in *Radio Times*.

[39] Not credited in *Radio Times*.

[40] Not credited on DVD/Blu-Ray release.

originally constructed by the alien Vinvocci – two of whom are secretly present at the mansion to try to salvage it – and obtained from the now-defunct Torchwood. However, the device is not working properly, and Naismith, still believing the Master to be Harold Saxon, has kidnapped him in the hope that he can repair it. The Master instead takes control of the Gate and uses it to transform every human being on Earth – bar Wilf and his granddaughter Donna – into a copy of himself. An even greater crisis is looming, however, as an impressively-robed figure declaims to serried ranks of his people: 'This was the day the Time Lords returned! For Gallifrey! For victory! For the end of time itself!'

QUOTE, UNQUOTE

- **Wilf:** 'I thought, when I saw you before, you said your people could change, like, your whole body.'
  The Doctor: 'I can still die. If I'm killed before regeneration, then I'm dead. Even then, even if I change, it feels like dying. Everything I am dies. Some new man goes sauntering away. And I'm dead.'
- **The Master:** 'The human race was always your favourite, Doctor. But now, there is no human race. There is only the Master race.'

CONTINUITY POINTS

- Since the contemporary Earth scenes of this special seem to take place not long after the events of 'Journey's End' (2008), which was set in summer 2009, the date is probably Christmas 2009 – the same as the debut transmission date. (This would be prior to 'Planet of the Dead', which takes place no earlier than Easter 2010.) It could however be Christmas 2010, or just possibly a later year, as there is nothing said that would absolutely rule that out.
- There is an image of the TARDIS in the stained glass window of the church where Wilf first encounters the mysterious woman in white. The woman tells him: 'They call it the legend of the blue box … This was the site of a convent back in the 1300s. It's said a demon fell from the sky. Then a man appeared; a man in a blue box. They called him the Sainted Physician. He smote the demon, and then disappeared.' This is an incident that has not (yet) been recounted in any televised or tie-in *Doctor Who* story, and that appears to have no bearing on the events of 'The End of Time' itself. (The image may have been inspired by a similar one referred to, and pictured on the inlay artwork of, the audio CD drama 'Jubilee' (Big Finish, 2003).)
- On arriving on the Ood-Sphere, the Doctor recalls being 'summoned' by Ood Sigma at the end of 'The Waters of Mars'. He says that he has made numerous other trips in the TARDIS in the interim: 'I saw the Phosphorous Carousel of the Great Magellan Gestadt. Saved a planet from the Red Carnivorous Maw. Named a galaxy Alison. Got married; that was a mistake. Good Queen Bess. And let me tell you, her nickname is no longer – anyway!' Assuming he is not simply joking, it would seem from this that, possibly while still in 'Time Lord Victorious' mode, the Doctor has changed Earth history by marrying Queen Elizabeth I – although it is possible that his 'Got married' comment refers to some other incident; perhaps even his getting hitched to River Song as hinted

at in 'Silence in the Library'/'Forest of the Dead' (2008) – and does not directly relate to the 'Good Queen Bess'. If the 'nickname' to which he refers is 'the Virgin Queen', it would seem to be implied that he at least had sex with Queen Elizabeth I.[41] At any rate, this meeting between them seems likely to account for the Queen's previously-mysterious antipathy toward the Doctor, as seen at the end of the Series Three episode 'The Shakespeare Code' (2007).

- The Elder Ood tells the Doctor that his race has gained the power to see through time, 'Because time is bleeding. Shapes of things once lost are moving through the veil, and these events from years ago threaten to destroy this future, and the present and the past … The darkness heralds only one thing: the end of time itself.' Once the Doctor has left to hurry back to the TARDIS, he adds: 'Events that have happened are happening now.' This idea of the 'convergence' of past, present and future may perhaps explain the ostensibly strange perspective of the Time Lord narrator: at times he seems to be recounting a legend ('It is said that in the final days of planet Earth, everyone had bad dreams'), and to be referring to events in the past tense ('This was the day the Time Lords returned!'), and yet in Part Two it will be revealed that he is speaking from just before the end of the Time War, before any of these things have actually happened – and of course these will turn out *not* to be the final days of planet Earth. Possibly the Time Lords' unusual relationship to time – as a time-travelling race sitting somewhat outside the normal flow of history – may also help to account for this apparent oddity.

- Lucy Saxon has been imprisoned following a trial that the new Governor of Broadfell Prison recalls was 'held in secret, with no jury'. It is not stated what she was charged with at this trial, but presumably it was murder, following the shooting of her husband, the Master, in his guise as Prime Minister Harold Saxon, at the end of 'Last of the Time Lords' (2007). The Governor says: 'No-one knows who Harold Saxon was, where he came from, why you killed him.' Presumably however it is at least public knowledge that she did kill him, and that prior to that he killed US President Arthur Coleman Winters; Ginger, one of the down-and-outs that the Master later encounters in the wasteland, states that Saxon 'went mad'.

- The Governor and her prison warder colleague Miss Trefusis are amongst a group of 'disciples' who have been working toward Harold Saxon's return, following a plan set out in 'the secret books of Saxon'. It is now revealed to have been Miss Trefusis who took his ring from his funeral pyre at the end of 'Last of the Time Lords' (2007). The 'final biometrical signature' needed to revive Saxon is his 'imprint' – a 'widow's kiss' – left on Lucy Saxon's lips. This recalls the way that the Doctor performed a 'genetic transfer' by kissing Martha Jones in 'Smith and Jones' (2007). It seems that the effect of such transfers must be long-lasting, given that Lucy has been in prison for some time. (The idea of a genetic imprint being transferred via a kiss was first used in a *Doctor Who* context in the audio CD drama 'Seasons of Fear' by Paul Cornell and Caroline Symcox, released by Big Finish in 2002.)

- The Master makes his hair blond in an attempt to disguise himself, so that he

---

[41] This is an implication that will be picked up on and essentially confirmed in the Series Five episode 'The Beast Below'.

will not be recognised as Harold Saxon. It is unclear how he does this – whether by simply dying his hair or by effecting some more permanent change. It is notable that all the Master duplicates at the end of the special also have blond hair.

- The Master is 'burning up [his] own life force' following Lucy Saxon's only-partially-successful attempt to interfere with his resurrection. He now has the ability to make huge leaps through the air and shoot bolts of energy from his hands. However, this is at the cost of him having a ravenous hunger and his body 'ripping open', intermittently revealing the skeletal form within.

- The mention by Minnie Hooper of an unseen Silver Cloak member named Netty may be a reference to the character Netty Goodheart, who was Wilf's lady friend in script editor Gary Russell's earlier *Doctor Who* novel *Beautiful Chaos* (BBC Books, 2008).

- As the Doctor and Wilf enter the café where they have their heartfelt discussion, they pass a sign for the London Credit Bank. This (fictional) financial institution has been referenced in a number of previous episodes, most notably in the scene in 'The Runaway Bride' (2006) where the Doctor uses the sonic screwdriver to obtain money from one of its ATMs.

- Wilf refers to 'those Atmos things', as seen in 'The Sontaran Stratagem'/'The Poison Sky' (2008), and 'planets in the sky' and 'me with that paint gun', incidents from 'The Stolen Earth'/'Journey's End' (2008).

- The Doctor tells Wilf, 'People have waited hundreds of years to find me, and then you manage it in a couple of hours'. The 'hundreds of years' may be a reference to the period of time Captain Jack Harkness waited in Cardiff to catch up with 'his' Doctor while working for Torchwood Three. The Doctor adds: 'We keep on meeting, Wilf, over and over again, like something's still connecting us … Why you?'

- Donna still doesn't recall her time travelling with the Doctor, following his wiping of those memories to save her life at the conclusion of 'Journey's End' (2008). She is now engaged to be married to a man named Shaun Temple, following which she is intending to take the surname 'Temple-Noble'. The wedding is due to take place 'in the spring', presumably meaning the spring immediately after the Christmas at which the main events of the story take place.

- The Master recalls his and the Doctor's youth on their home planet, Gallifrey: 'I had estates. Do you remember my father's land back home? Pastures of red grass, stretching far across the slopes of Mount Perdition. We used to run across those fields all day, calling up at the sky.'

- When Wilf asks the Doctor why he cannot simply travel back in time in the TARDIS to catch the Master, the Doctor replies: 'I can't go back inside my own timeline. I have to stay relative to the Master within the causal nexus.' This accords with what has been established in previous stories.

- In the *Sarah Jane Adventures* episode 'The Wedding of Sarah Jane Smith' (2009), the Trickster told the Doctor, 'The Gate is waiting for you'. This foreshadowed the revelation of the Immortality Gate in 'The End of Time'.

- Joshua Naismith says, 'The Gate was found inside a spaceship buried at the foot of Mount Snowdon. It was moved to an institute known as Torchwood.

But when Torchwood fell ... let's just say, I acquired it.' It is uncertain whether the fall of Torchwood referred to here is the destruction of Torchwood One as seen in 'Doomsday' (2006) or the downfall of Torchwood Three as depicted in the *Torchwood* mini-series 'Children of Earth' (2009) The latter is arguably more likely, given that Mount Snowdon is in Wales, Torchwood Three's area of responsibility.

- On arriving at the Naismiths' mansion, the Doctor hides the TARDIS by putting it 'a second out of sync', rendering it invisible. This is the same way the Daleks hid their stolen planets in the Medusa Cascade in 'The Stolen Earth'/'Journey's End' (2008), which may be when the Doctor picked up the trick, given that he has never employed it before.

- The two Vinvocci, Addams and Rossiter, are hiding their true alien physiognomy using what the Doctor refers to as a 'shimmer', making them appear human. They explain that the Immortality Gate is really a Vinvocci-made device designed to 'mend' whole planets by transmitting a medical template across the entire population.

- Prior to the transmission of 'The End of Time' Part One, it seemed that the succession of US Presidents in the *Doctor Who* universe – taking into account evidence from the novel and audio CD tie-in stories as well as from the TV show – was as follows (with the elections taking place in different years than in our universe)[42]:

> Jan 1994 – Jan 1998: President Bill Clinton
> Jan 1998 – Jan 2002: President Tom Dering
> Jan 2002 – Jan 2004: President Bruce Springsteen
> Jan 2004 – Jan 2008: President George W Bush
> Jan 2008: President Arthur Coleman Winters
> Jan 2008 – Jan 2013: President Chuck Norris
> Jan 2013 – Jan 2017: President Mather

In the light of events in this special, however, it now appears that Chuck Norris must have served as President for only a short period, probably from January 2008 to January 2009, with Barak Obama then holding the office for the four year term from January 2009 to January 2013. This would accord with the fact that Norris was assumed to have been Arthur Coleman Winters' Republican running mate in the 2007 election and to have taken over from him on a pro-tem basis after Winters was assassinated by the Master using the Tocalfane.

- As Donna starts to regain her memories, clips are seen from 'Journey's End' (2008) (Davros, Dalek Caan and the Supreme Dalek), 'The Runaway Bride' (2006) (the Empress of the Racnoss), 'The Unicorn and the Wasp' (2008) (the Vespiform), 'The Poison Sky' (2008) (the Sontarans), 'Forest of the Dead' (2008)

---

[42] See the entry on 'The Sound of Drums' in *Third Dimension: The Unofficial and Unauthorised Guide to Doctor Who 2007* (Telos Publishing, 2007) for an explanation of how this list was arrived at. The novel *Option Lock* also indicates that Ronald Reagan was President some time before Tom Dering – presumably, as in the real world, in the 1980s.

(the Vashta Nerada-animated spacesuit), 'Partners in Crime' (2008) (an Adipose baby), 'The Fires of Pompeii' (2008) (the Pyrovile form of the High Priestess) and 'Planet of the Ood' (2008) (the red-eyed Ood).

- All the Time Lords seen in the scene at the end of this special are wearing scarlet and orange robes. In 'The Deadly Assassin' (1976) it was stated that these were the colours of the Prydonian Chapter – the Chapter to which the Doctor belongs. This could possibly imply that only members of that Chapter have survived to the end of the Time War. There are however other possible explanations: for instance, it could be that the tradition of having separate Chapters has been abandoned during the Time War (or at some point prior to that) as a measure to unify Time Lord society.

PRODUCTION NOTES

- John Simm and Bernard Cribbins are both credited in the opening titles after David Tennant. In Simm's case, this is the first time an actor playing one of the Doctor's adversaries has been credited in this way. Catherine Tate's name, however, appears only in the closing credits.
- The main location recording for both parts of 'The End of Time' was carried out between the end of March and the middle of May 2009. The venues used for this were almost all in South Wales, and for Part One included the following. Tredegar House in Newport was used for the exteriors and some of the interiors of the Naismiths' opulent home, with recording taking place there between 30 March and 3 April. As in Series Four, 11 Nant-Fawr Road in Cardiff doubled for the Nobles' house, scenes there being taped between 6 and 8 April. The interiors and exteriors of the café where the Doctor and Wilf talk were all recorded on 13 April at the Kardomah Café on Portland Street, Swansea. The location used for the area where the Silver Cloak catch up with the Doctor as he is hunting the Master was Cardiff docks; this work was carried out on 14 April. Mir Steel, a disused smelting works in Newport Docks, was the venue for the scene where the Doctor confronts the Master on the wasteland, taping taking place on 15, 21 and 22 April. The Taffs Well quarry in Pentyrch was dressed with fake snow to become the Ood-Sphere, the shots of which were done on 16 April. The scene of the Doctor meeting the Ood Council was recorded in difficult conditions underground at Wookey Hole Caves in Wells, Somerset on 17 April. 20 April saw brief recording taking place in three separate locations: Wharton Street in Cardiff for the opening sequence of Wilf wandering amongst other Christmas shoppers; Paget Road in Penarth for the shots of the Doctor seeing the debris from the explosion at Broadfell Prison; and St Augustine's Church in Penarth for the scene of Wilf talking with the mysterious woman in white. Caerphilly Castle in Caerphilly was the venue for recording on 27 April, for the Broadfell Prison interiors. Two days later, City Hall in Cardiff was the location used for the shots of the press conference by US President Obama, including the green-screen effects work needed to show most of the audience members being transformed into multiple copies of the Master (latex masks moulded from John Simm's face being used for others in the deep background). 14 May saw the crew make a rare trip outside Wales, to Jesson House on Rodney Estate in Southwark, London, for the scene of the

multiple Masters emerging from their flats on a housing estate. Studio recording for the two-parter was carried out, as usual, at the show's Upper Boat base, on various dates between 23 April and 3 June.

- This special had the working title 'The Final Days of Planet Earth'. The eventual decision to use 'The End of Time' for both this and the following instalment made it the first multi-part *Doctor Who* story since 'Survival' (1989) to have a single overall title.

- Executive producer Julie Gardner effectively co-produced 'The End of Time' with Tracie Simpson, although only the latter received a credit in this capacity. This was because Simpson was appointed as one of the producers of Series Five and had to start work on setting that up. Gardner also directed the scene in the White House press room where the representatives of the media transform into duplicates of the Master.

- Clips from 'The Sound of Drums'/'Last of the Time Lords' (2007) are shown as the Doctor tells the Ood about the Master and Lucy Saxon.

- The music track heard as Wilf opens his Christmas present from Donna is 'Merry Xmas Everybody' by Slade (1973). This was previously featured in Christmas scenes in 'The Christmas Invasion' (2005), 'The Runaway Bride' (2006) and 'Turn Left' (2008).

- As recorded, the scenes featuring the two Vinvocci, Addams and Rossiter, in their undisguised alien forms had the actors' normal Caucasian skin tones visible on their faces: only the spiny head prosthetics attached over their hair were green. Reviewing the rushes of these scenes subsequently, Russell T Davies and his team decided that this did not look very good. Consequently he had all the shots of these characters' faces altered in post-production to make them green. Publicity photographs taken on set were also retouched to reflect this. Unfortunately the results are patchy and the characters' normal skin tones can often be seen.

- In the transmitted version of this special, the closing credits are preceded by the words 'TO', 'BE' and 'CONTINUED', in large silver letters, which loom toward the viewer in succession. In the DVD and Blu-Ray versions, which have extended credits, there is simply a caption stating 'TO BE CONTINUED …' in the same font as the credits themselves.

- The closing credits are followed by a trailer for 'The End of Time' Part Two.

- The cliff-hanger scene with the Time Lords and the trailer for the second instalment were both cut from the version of this special shown at the advance press screening, so as to preserve the surprise of the Time Lords' return.

OOPS!

- The CGI image immediately following the opening titles shows the TARDIS materialising on a relatively flat area of the Ood-Sphere landscape, completely different from the rocky quarry location seen in the subsequent shots of the Doctor emerging from the ship and meeting Ood Sigma.

- In the scenes on the Ood-Sphere, the camera crew can be briefly glimpsed in the reflection in the Doctor's sunglasses.

PRESS REACTION

- 'Though Donna Noble was in and out of the episode, always just around the corner from the Doctor, it was Wilf who became his final travelling companion. Like Donna, and pretty much everyone else the Doctor gets close to, his presence is not accidental; the universe has thrust him upon the Doctor like a magician forcing a card. Destiny is a powerful narrative device – it says that life has purpose and strikes the place in us that wants that to be so – and Davies has used it again and again. Just so, it's the web of special relationships that surround the Doctor that makes tolerable, and navigable, the awful vastness of space and time. He's a Time Lord who needs people, and he needs those people back around him for his death to have the proper effect and meaning.' Robert Lloyd, *Los Angeles Times*, 28 December 2009.

- 'A powerful episode, successfully balancing the needed whimsy of a Christmas episode with drama the end of the series calls for. The most delightful surprise is the amount that Bernard Cribbins had to play. He delivers some sold acting, something people only knowing him from his comedy might not expect. His scene with Tennant in the café is a prizewinner, both in the acting from the pair as well as the writing.' Vinnie Bartilucci, Newsarama website, 28 December 2009.

- 'The Master's plan for world domination was pretty evil, even by his standards. By commandeering the Immortality Gate (don't ask), he managed to literally take over the bodies of everyone on Earth. This sounds a little silly when written down, but the moment the camera panned back to reveal a crowd of people with the Master's cackling head on each of their torsos was genuinely chilling. It also led to the episode's best line as the Master's head hijacked the body of a female newsreader and then announced to camera, "Breaking news: I'm everyone." It was at this point ... that I had my revelation. It came thanks to the seven year-old who was sitting next to me. Every time the Master appeared on screen, he had instinctively grabbed my arm in terror. But as the credits rolled and I started to think my curmudgeonly thoughts about the series' dramatic shortcomings, my sofa companion turned to me with a calm, blissful expression. "That was the best TV ever," he said. And that's where I'd been going wrong: the true brilliance of *Doctor Who* can only be felt if you're experiencing it in the company of wide-eyed seven year-olds. A bit like Christmas, in fact.' Andrew Pettie, *Daily Telegraph*, 29 December 2009.

ANALYSIS

'The End of Time' Part One represents quite a big departure from the tone of *Doctor Who*'s previous Christmas specials. The latter could all be categorised as essentially lightweight, undemanding fare. Replete with overt festive elements and quasi-blockbuster-style action sequences, they were clearly designed to appeal to a relaxed, probably less-than-fully-attentive Christmas evening audience unlikely to be in the mood for anything overly serious or taxing. The 2009 entry, by contrast, is dark, brooding and intense, with an involved plot – even including flashbacks to previous episodes – and an air of impending doom reflecting the imminent end of the tenth Doctor's era. It has touches of humour, certainly, and is by no means as grim and depressing as 'The Waters of Mars', but overall it is a far more powerful and challenging slice of *Doctor Who* than would normally be served up as a seasonal offering. It is all the better for it, too, and actually ends up being arguably the most dramatically effective of all the five gap year specials (albeit obviously not the most self-standing, being only the first of a two-parter).

A major talking point is the return of the Master as played by John Simm, whose bravura debut performance in the role at the end of Series Three was one of the highlights of that year's run of episodes. The sequence of him being brought back to life at Broadfell Prison has a nicely gothic, almost Hammer Horror feel to it, recalling other villainous resurrections in movies such as *Taste the Blood of Dracula* (1970). The use of what are, in effect, magic potions meanwhile puts the viewer in mind of more modern cinematic fables such as the *Harry Potter* franchise. Although some fan commentators have criticised these prison scenes as being too fantastical, few could deny that it is at least good to have some explanation for the Master's revival, in contrast to the situation in the 1980s, when the means by which the character survived a succession of apparently fatal defeats were left a complete mystery. Another bonus is the opportunity these scenes afford for another appearance, albeit all too brief, by Alexandra Moen as the Master's understandably vengeful wife Lucy Saxon, who is again excellent.

Simm's Master, hair bleached blond as a disguise, chin covered in stubble (perhaps a nod to the bearded countenance of his earlier incarnations?) and initially reduced to a feral, ravenously-hungry scavenger prowling a dockside wasteland near the prison, is even more terrifyingly manic than before. His killing and implied eating of the burger van attendants and down-and-outs on the wasteland, and later his gnawing apart and wolfing down of an entire roast turkey at the Naismiths' mansion, are stomach-churning incidents – and particularly surprising inclusions for a Christmas special, as an explicit parallel is drawn between these disgusting displays of gluttony and the conspicuous over-consumption in which many people indulge during the festive season.

The idea of the Master being able to shoot bolts of energy from his hands and make flying leaps through the air – a consequence of Lucy having thrown a metaphorical spanner in the works of his resurrection – stretches credibility to the limit, but makes for some very exciting visuals; and, besides, this is by no means the first time the character has undergone an unexpected transformation, previous examples being his corruption by the Cheetah planet in 'Survival' (1989) and his metamorphosis into a serpent-like morphant creature at the beginning of the TV movie (1996). It is pleasing too, albeit possibly coincidental, that the skeletal inner form that becomes briefly visible whenever he uses his newfound powers somewhat resembles the bulging-eyed, cadaverous version of the Master seen in both 'The Deadly Assassin' (1976) and 'The Keeper of Traken' (1981).

Possibly the best scene of the entire episode is the one where the Doctor confronts the Master on the wasteland and discovers, to both their astonishment, that the sound of drums in the latter's head is actually real, and not just a symptom of his madness. One of the problems with 'The Sound of Drums'/'Last of the Time Lords' (2007) was that David Tennant and John Simm were afforded insufficient screen time together, but that is thankfully rectified here, and both deliver absolutely brilliant performances. As on numerous occasions in the past, going right back to the days of Jon Pertwee's Doctor and Roger Delgado's Master in the early 1970s, one gets a real sense of the deep bond these two renegade Time Lords share, despite their great enmity. It is almost as if it is only with each other that they can be truly themselves, without putting on any kind of front for the benefit of others. This is particularly well conveyed by Tennant's sincere, understated delivery of his lines here, demonstrating – as on a number of previous occasions, such as when River Song whispers his real name in his ear in 'Forest of the Dead' (2008) – that the tenth Doctor's usual chirpy, fast-talking, energetic persona is to a large extent a carefree façade that he elects to present to his companions and adversaries.

One of the other stand-out scenes of the episode is another two-hander, specifically the earlier conversation between the Doctor and Wilf in the café, where Bernard Cribbins, also making a very welcome return to the show, again demonstrates his wonderful ability to convey pathos and bring a tear to the viewer's eye. Like the aforementioned scene with the Master, this too sees David Tennant giving an unusually low-key and emotional performance; and appropriately so, as it involves the Doctor mournfully contemplating his foretold demise, pondering the ominous significance of his repeated meetings with Wilf and reflecting on the terrible loneliness of his current life travelling without human companions. The only downside to this is that, particularly in the plaintively-delivered line 'I'm going to die', it risks bringing an unattractive note of self-pity to the character. It could perhaps be said that this is simply the latest evidence of a gradual shift away from the classic series norm of presenting the Doctor as an unambiguously heroic figure – a shift that really began as far back as in the groundbreaking New Adventures novels published by Virgin between 1991 and 1999. On the other hand, it is arguable that the Doctor has never before, in any medium, seemed quite so spineless as he does here. There is a strong hint of this, too, in his very first scene in the special, when his painfully forced and exaggerated jollity on arriving on the Ood-Sphere seems not so much a carefree façade as a defensive mask to hide an abject fear of facing up to what the future has in store for him, and possibly even a sense of embarrassment that he has put off for so long his momentous rendezvous with Ood Sigma. The clear implication is that he has, in short, been running scared from his fate – which, as in a classical tragedy, is what will ultimately lead him to it.

Of course it is not only Wilf who makes a return appearance in 'The End of Time' but also his daughter Sylvia and granddaughter Donna. Readers of my previous books in this series may perhaps recall that I am not the biggest fan of Catherine Tate's portrayal of Donna. She does seem to be something of a love-her-or-hate-her companion. Nevertheless, she is definitely at her best when placed in an ordinary domestic setting and not called upon to react (or, as is all too often the case, over-react) to some fantastical situation or alien monster. That is very much the case here and – surprised though I am to find myself saying so – it is actually good to see her back under these circumstances. The same goes for Sylvia, too. Together, they provide some welcome moments of amusement, affording a respite from the more serious action that predominates. Writer Russell T Davies cleverly keeps Donna flitting about on the periphery of events, being her usual bolshy self but always narrowly avoiding bumping into the Doctor and fatally regaining her memory of her adventures with him.

The other main source of humour comes in the form of Wilf's elderly Silver Cloak friends, who remarkably succeed in helping him to track down the Doctor. Particularly funny is the scene where they persuade him to pose for photographs with them, and Minnie 'The Menace' Hooper – a nice guest role for veteran comic actress June Whitfield – takes the opportunity to goose him.

The only other characters of any real significance introduced in this special are the Naismiths – unscruplous telecommunications entrepreneur Joshua and his daughter Abigail, for whom he is seeking the key to immortality – and the Vinvocci salvage team – Addams and Rossiter. The latter pair, when they drop their human disguises, are seen to be somewhat similar in appearance to Bannakaffalatta from the 2007 Christmas special 'Voyage of the Damned', although they claim that his race, now named as the Zocci, is 'completely different' from theirs. That is more or less the only thing that is learned about them, though, and both they and the Naismiths come across as rather generic types. That said, they fulfil well enough their joint plot function, which is essentially just to provide the Master with a ready-made scheme to usurp and twist to his own purpose: a scheme centring around the so-called Immortality Gate, a piece of crashed Vinvocci technology recovered by Torchwood and subsequently 'acquired' by the Naismiths.

Whereas in the past the Master has always laid his plans meticulously, sometimes even months in advance of when they come to fruition, here he takes a leaf out of the Doctor's book and opportunistically improvises a breathtakingly audacious strategy on the hoof, using the Gate to replace every human being on Earth – bar Donna, whose mind is still part Time Lord, and Wilf, who is protected inside one of the control booths of the device's 'nuclear bolt' power supply – with a version of himself. As unlikely as it seemed that Davies would be able to come up another piece of villainy for the Master that was as grand, imaginative and downright evil as the one depicted in 'The Sound of Drums'/'Last of the Time Lords', he has actually managed to equal and possibly even surpass that here. The shots of the multiple Masters, all still wearing the clothes of the men and women they have supplanted, are superb in their execution and gloriously barmy. The Master's manic laughter here, in all his different forms, is even more incessant than the evil chuckling of his 1980s counterpart as played by Anthony Ainley, but far more chilling, as it thankfully avoids the potential pitfall of taking the character into Christmas panto territory. And Davies's decision to show the effect of the transformation on *Doctor Who*'s resident US newsreader Trinity Wells, played as usual by Lachele Carl, and even on a mid-press-conference President Barak Obama – this year's version of the now-traditional end-of-series (or equivalent) celebrity cameo appearance, albeit in this instance obviously achieved with a look-alike rather than the real individual – neatly emphasises the world-encompassing nature of the Master's takeover.

This ingenious and completely unexpected turn of events would have been sufficiently climactic in itself to serve as an effective ending, but it is followed by a still bigger surprise. The mysterious narrator, played by none other than A-list movie star and one-time James Bond Timothy Dalton, whose pronouncements have punctuated the action of the special (an unusual device for *Doctor Who*), finally spits out – literally – the secret of his identity: he is a Time Lord, and his people are returning! In the context of Davies's version of *Doctor Who*, which has been built upon the premise of the Doctor being the last of the Time Lords following the terrible events of the Time War, this is a truly earth-shattering development, and raises to fever-pitch the sense of excited anticipation that the viewer feels for the second half of this landmark two-part story.

This stunning cliff-hanger is really the icing on the cake of a fantastic, expectation-defying special; and one that, judging from its excellent Audience Appreciation figure[43], seems, remarkably, to have carried the general Christmas Night audience with it too, despite its grimness and intensity. As always with a two-parter, however, any assessment of the overall effectiveness of the story has to await and take into account the second instalment as well. 'The End of Time' Part One does its job admirably in setting up a series of tantalising questions: why has everyone been having 'bad dreams' of the Master?; who is the mysterious woman in white, played by the wonderful Claire Bloom, who keeps appearing to Wilf?; what will happen to Donna now that her memories of the Doctor are being reawakened?; how can the Time Lords have survived the Time War?; what does their return portend?; how does all this relate to the Master's conquest of the Earth?; what role will the Naismiths and the Vinvocci have to play in proceedings?; what is the meaning of the 'He will knock four times' prophecy?; and, of course, what are the fateful circumstances that will lead to the Doctor's heavily-foreshadowed regeneration? Perhaps the most crucial issue of all, though, is: just how successful will Part Two be in delivering satisfying pay-offs to all these many questions?

---

[43] See Appendix D for details.

4.18 – THE END OF TIME – PART TWO

Writer: Russell T Davies
Director: Euros Lyn

DEBUT TRANSMISSION DETAILS

BBC One/BBC HD
Date: 1 January 2010. Scheduled time: 6.40 pm. Actual time: 6.40 pm.

Duration: 72' 36"[44]

CREDITED CAST

David Tennant (The Doctor), John Simm (The Master), Bernard Cribbins (Wilfred Mott), Timothy Dalton (Lord President), Catherine Tate (Donna Noble), Jacqueline King (Sylvia Noble), Billie Piper (Rose Tyler)[45], Camille Coduri (Jackie Tyler)[46], John Barrowman (Captain Jack Harkness)[47], Freema Agyeman (Martha Smith-Jones)[48], Noel Clarke (Mickey Smith)[49], Elisabeth Sladen (Sarah Jane Smith)[50], Jessica Hynes (Verity Newman)[51], June Whitfield (Minnie Hooper), Claire Bloom (The Woman), Thomas Knight (Luke Smith)[52], Russell Tovey (Midshipman Frame)[53], David Harewood (Joshua Naismith), Tracy Ifeachor (Abigail Naismith), Lawry Lewin (Rossiter), Sinead Keenan (Addams), Joe Dixon (Chancellor)[54], Julie Legrand (The Partisan), Brid Brennan (The Visionary), Karl Collins (Sean Temple), Krystal Archer (Nerys), Lachele Carl (Trinity Wells), Paul Kasey (Ood Sigma), Ruari Mears (Elder Ood), Silas Carson (Voice of Ood Sigma)[55], Nicholas Briggs (Voice of the Judoon), Dan Starkey (Sontaran)[56] and introducing Matt Smith (The Doctor)[57].

---

[44] The version released on DVD/Blu-Ray, with extended closing credits, runs to 72' 40".
[45] Not credited in *Radio Times*.
[46] Not credited in *Radio Times*.
[47] Not credited in *Radio Times*.
[48] Not credited in *Radio Times*.
[49] Not credited in *Radio Times*.
[50] Not credited in *Radio Times*.
[51] Not credited in *Radio Times*.
[52] Not credited in *Radio Times*.
[53] Not credited in *Radio Times*.
[54] Character credited in *Radio Times* as 'The Second'.
[55] Not credited on DVD/Blu-Ray version.
[56] Not credited on DVD/Blu-Ray version or in *Radio Times*.
[57] Not credited in *Radio Times*.

PLOT

The Time Lord President, Rassilon, formulates a plan to enable his race to escape from the Time War. He has a regular sequence of four beats implanted in the Master's mind from childhood as a signal, allowing for the renegade's location to be determined at the point when the War ends. He then sends a diamond-like white point star out of the time lock in which the War is held, to create a physical connection. The white point star falls to Earth on Christmas Day, and the Master collects it, using the signal in his head, duplicated across the world's population, to determine its position. He then links the white point star to the Immortality Gate equipment, allowing Rassilon and some of his fellow Time Lords to materialise in the Naismiths' mansion. The Doctor and Wilf, having previously been rescued from the mansion by the Vinvocci in their spaceship, return when the Doctor learns what is happening. Rassilon reverses the Master's earlier supplanting of the Earth's population with copies of himself, thwarting his intention to do the same to the Time Lords as well. Rassilon's ultimate plan is to bring about the end of time, transforming the Time Lords into beings of pure consciousness and destroying the whole of creation – which is why the Doctor had to destroy the Time Lords as well as the Daleks at the end of the War. Gallifrey starts to materialise in the sky above Earth, but the Doctor uses Wilf's service revolver to shoot the Immortality Gate equipment, breaking the connection and sending Rassilon, the Time Lords and Gallifrey all back into the War. The Master is apparently carried off with them. In order to rescue Wilf from one of the control booths of the Immortality Gate's nuclear bolt power source, which is about to go critical, the Doctor is forced to expose himself to a powerful burst of radiation. This triggers the start of a regeneration. After paying brief final visits to a number of his past companions and friends, the Doctor returns to the TARDIS and is transformed into his eleventh incarnation.

QUOTE, UNQUOTE

- **The Doctor:** 'You're a genius. You're stone cold brilliant, you are. I swear, you really are. But you could be so much more. You could be beautiful. With a mind like that. We could travel the stars. It would be my honour. 'Cause you don't need to own the universe. Just see it. Have the privilege of seeing the whole of time and space. That's ownership enough.'
  The Master: 'Would it stop then, the noise in my head?'
  The Doctor: 'I can help.'
  The Master: 'I don't know what I'd be without that noise.'
  The Doctor: 'I wonder what I'd be without you.'
- **The Doctor:** 'I'm older than you.'
  Wilf: 'Get away.'
  The Doctor: 'I'm 906.'
  Wilf: 'What, really though?'
  The Doctor: 'Yeah.'
  Wilf: '900 years! We must look like insects to you.'
  The Doctor: 'I think you look like giants.'
- **The Doctor:** 'It's not like I'm an innocent. I've taken lives. And I got worse; I

got clever. Manipulated people into taking their own. Sometimes I think a Time Lord lives too long.'

- **The Doctor:** 'What year is this?'
  Rose: 'Blimey, how much have you had? 2005, January the first.'
  The Doctor: '2005. Tell you what, I bet you're gonna have a really great year.'
  Rose: 'Yeah? See ya.'

CONTINUITY POINTS

- In the scenes immediately after the opening credits, the Time Lords are seen conferring on the final day of the Time War. A female Time Lord (credited as 'The Partisan') states that the Doctor has 'disappeared' but that he still possesses 'the Moment' and will 'use it to destroy Time Lords and Daleks alike'. No further details are given as to what 'the Moment' is. The same Time Lord adds that Gallifrey is on the 'furthest edge' of the Time War, and that at the War's heart, 'millions die every second, lost in bloodlust and insanity, with time itself resurrecting them to find new ways of dying, over and over again; a travesty of life'.
- Rassilon refers to 'a billion years of Time Lord history riding on our backs'. This may be an indication of the age of the race at the time of the Time War.
- One of the Master duplicates states that there are '6,727,949,338 versions' of him. This is presumably therefore the exact size of Earth's human population at this point, in the *Doctor Who* universe, excluding Donna and Wilf. Although all physically identical, the Master duplicates seem to defer to and take orders from the original, implying that he is a kind of 'alpha Master'. This may explain why they do not seem to do anything significant or even to change position without being instructed to do so by him; the duplicate who was previously Barak Obama, for instance, remains standing at his press conference lectern even though it is clearly implied that some considerable time has passed since the worldwide transformation occurred.
- Although previously it was stated that Donna would die if her memories of the Doctor returned, this does not in fact happen. The Doctor tells the Master, 'Do you think I'd leave my best friend without a defence mechanism?' He then reassures Wilf that Donna will just sleep. When she later wakes up, it is seen that she has returned to her normal self, presumably still with no memories of the Doctor.
- When the Doctor realises that the Immortality Gate has failed to remedy the gradual break down of the Master's body, the Master tells him, 'This body was born out of death. All it can do is die.'
- Rassilon states that the 'rhythm of four' that has tormented the Master all his life corresponds to 'the heartbeat of a Time Lord'. Later, another Time Lord tells him, 'The signal has been sent. A simple task of four beats, transmitted back through time and implanted in the Master's mind as a child.' It now becomes clear, therefore, that the sound of drums in the Master's head has been put there by the Time Lords themselves, and that they have caused his lifelong derangement. Rassilon comments, 'Then we have a link to where the Master is right now.' The other Time Lord replies, 'But we're still trapped inside the time lock, sir.' It was previously established in 'Journey's End'

(2008) that the Time War was time locked, so that neither the Daleks nor the Time Lords could use time travel technology to escape from it. The Time Lord's comment here indicates that the time lock was put in place at some point before the destruction of both races at the end of the War. The 'right now' part of Rassilon's comment would seem to imply that the last day of the Time War is, on Earth, Christmas Day 2009 (assuming that this is when the Earth scenes are set – see Continuity Points on Part One). As the sound of drums is 'nothing more than a thought, an idea', Rassilon concludes that something is needed to make the contact with the Master 'physical'. Prompted by the Visionary – a cryptic female seer whose prophesies seem to have been informing the Time Lords' actions – he removes from the end of his staff a large diamond, later described as 'a white point star' found only on Gallifrey, and throws it at what appears to be a hologram of Earth. It is not explained how this results in the diamond falling to Earth in a place close to the location of the 'alpha Master' on Christmas Day, ready for him to retrieve. Presumably, though, the diamond is something small enough to escape the time lock and be sent through time and space (or just space?) to arrive at the correct point for Rassilon's purposes. The Master later states that he can use the white point star to boost the signal in his head and create a 'lifeline', allowing the Time Lords to return.

- On the Vinvocci ship, orbiting 105,000 miles above Earth, the mysterious woman in white tells Wilf, 'Events are closing. The day is almost upon us.' This would seem to accord with the suggestion that the Christmas Day seen here is the last day of the Time War. She adds, 'This is the Doctor's final battle. At the end of his life, he must stand at arms, or lose himself and all this world, to the end of time.' When Wilf asks who she is, she merely replies, 'I was lost, so very long ago.' It later transpires that she is one of two members of the Time Lord High Council who have voted against Rassilon's plan to escape the Time War. This presumably means that she is a Time Lord. If so, however, it is unclear how she has been able to appear to Wilf and talk to him, given that she must be within the time lock.

- Wilf recounts that in 1948, as Private Mott, he was stationed in Palestine for 'the end of the Mandate'. This Mandate was a legal instrument drawn up in 1922 to formalise British rule of Palestine. It did indeed end in 1948, when the Jewish leadership of the country declared independence.

- When Wilf points out that the Doctor has previously spoken about the Time Lords as if they were wonderful, the Doctor explains that this is how he prefers to remember them, 'the Time Lords of old', but that fighting the Time War 'changed them, right to the core'.

- Rassilon describes the two Time Lord objectors to his plan as being 'like the Weeping Angels of old'. Presumably this does not mean that there is some literal connection between the Time Lords and the statue-like creatures introduced in Steven Moffat's 'Blink' (2007) but is merely a metaphorical likening, based on the fact that the two objectors have been made to stand with their hands raised to cover their eyes in a ritual gesture of shame.

- The Doctor tells the Master: 'You weren't there, in the final days of the War. You never saw what was born. But if the time lock's broken, then everything's coming through. Not just the Daleks, but the Skaro Degredations, the Horde of

Travesties, the Nightmare Child, the Could-Have-Been King with his army of Meanwhiles and Never-Weres. The War turned into hell, and that's what you've opened, right above the Earth.' No further details are given of any of the things the Doctor mentions. However, it was previously stated in 'Journey's End' (2008) that he saw Davros's command ship 'fly into the jaws of the Nightmare Child.'

- Rassilon explains that he plans to bring about the end of time: 'The rupture will continue until it rips the time vortex apart ... We will ascend to become creatures of consciousness alone, free of these bodies, free of time and cause and effect, while creation itself ceases to be.' This strongly recalls the idea of the Celestis from Lawrence Miles' *Doctor Who* novel *Alien Bodies* (BBC Books, 1997). The Celestis were a group of Time Lords, previously known as the Celestial Intervention Agency, who foresaw a Time War approaching and removed themselves from history, becoming creatures of pure consciousness.

- The scene with Mickey Smith and Martha Jones (now Martha Smith-Jones) reveals that they have married each other since last seen in 'Journey's End' (2008) and that Mickey has persuaded Martha to 'go freelance', implying that she no longer works for UNIT. There is no indication as to the dating of this scene. However, in the *Torchwood* mini-series 'Children of Earth' (2009), the main action of which is probably set somewhere between autumn 2009 and spring 2010, Captain Jack mentions that Martha is on honeymoon. Unless Mickey is not Martha's first husband (which seems unlikely, although she was previously engaged to Tom Milligan, as first revealed in 'The Sontaran Stratagem' (2008), set around spring 2009), this would seem to suggest that they got married at that time.

- Luke Smith, speaking on his mobile phone, tells his friend Clyde that in order to explain away the Master's Christmas takeover of the Earth, his mother Sarah Jane got her alien computer, Mr Smith, 'to put out this story saying that Wi-Fi went mad all across the world, giving everyone hallucinations'. This implies that the scene with Luke takes place very shortly after the Christmas seen in the main action of 'The End of Time'. It is not explained how Mr Smith was able to square this cover story with CCTV and other recordings of the events at Christmas, which would presumably have captured images of the multiple Masters.

- Wilf states that Joshua Naismith and his daughter Abigail have been arrested and locked up for 'crimes undisclosed'. It is likely that these crimes relate in some way to the events of Christmas Day, despite Mr Smith's Wi-Fi cover story having attempted to convince the Earth's population that those events never occurred. What exactly they were charged with, however, is unknown.

- In the bar scene with Captain Jack and Alonso Frame, a number of familiar *Doctor Who* creatures are seen – a Slitheen, two Hath, a Judoon, a Sycorax, a Graske and an Adipose – along with some new ones. No date is specified for this scene, although as Frame looks little older than he did in 'Voyage of the Damned' (2007), set at Christmas 2008, it is probably not long after that.

PRODUCTION NOTES

- 'The End of Time' Part Two superseded 'Voyage of the Damned' (2007) as the longest episode of *Doctor Who* since the show returned in 2005.

- John Simm and Bernard Cribbins are both credited in the opening titles after David Tennant.
- In addition to those also seen in Part One, Part Two used the following locations. The Cardiff University branch of Blackwell's Bookshop on Senghennydd Road, Cardiff, saw recording on 'The End of Time' get underway on 21 March 2009, with the Doctor attending a book signing by author Verity Newman. Some of the Vinvocci spaceship interiors and the sequence of the Doctor saving Martha and Mickey from being shot by a Sontaran were taped on 4 April at the Corus Strip Products premises in Newport. St Mary's Church in Marshfield, Newport, was used for the exterior of the church where Donna and Shaun get married, this material being recorded on 9 April. The scene of the Master duplicates retrieving the white point star from the crater where it has fallen to Earth was taped on the same day, around the back of the church. On 10 April, an alley adjoining Clinton Road in Penarth was used as the venue for Donna's confrontation with the multiple Masters. The same day, and just around the corner, the crew also taped the Bannerman Road scene of the Doctor's encounter with Luke and Sarah Jane Smith. The Tiger, Tiger bar in The Friary, Cardiff, was the venue for Captain Jack's meeting with Midshipman Alonso Frame, taped on 29 April. Finally, on 15 May, the Brandon Estate in Kennington, London, once more doubled as the exterior of the flats where Rose and Jackie Tyler live. The studio scene of the Time Lords' round-table meeting at the beginning of the episode was shot in the HTV Wales Studios in Cardiff on 21 May. This was because the show's usual Upper Boat studios were full of other sets and did not have the same facility for surrounding the scene with black drapes.
- The returning companion characters who make cameo appearances in 'The End of Time' Part Two were not listed in the *Radio Times* billing (which was just a single billing for both parts, printed with the 1 January listing). This was because the production team wanted to preserve the surprise of their return.
- This was the sixtieth and last episode on which Russell T Davies and Julie Gardner worked as executive producers.
- Other titles considered for this special by Russell T Davies as he formulated ideas for his script included 'The Final Reckoning' and 'Death of the Doctor'.
- Russell T Davies initially considered involving the Daleks in 'The End of Time', possibly implying an alliance between them and the Time Lords in the last days of the Time War, but dropped this element after he learned from Steven Moffat that they were to feature in Series Five.
- In the scene where Donna's memories are returning, clips are seen from 'The Fires of Pompeii' (2008) (a Pyrovile), 'Journey's End' (2008) (Dalek Caan), 'The Unicorn and the Wasp' (2008) (the Vespiform), 'The Runaway Bride' (2006) (the Racnoss Empress), 'Planet of the Ood' (2008) (a red-eyed Ood) and again 'The Runaway Bride' (the Doctor).
- When the Master recalls being taken at the age of eight to stare into the untempered schism on Gallifrey, a clip is shown of the flashback to these events seen in 'The Sound of Drums' (2007).
- David Tennant, who had not long recovered from having an operation on his

back, found it uncomfortable to record the 'worst rescue ever' scene where the male Vinvocci, Rossiter, bumps the Doctor down a flight of stairs on a trolley. A latex dummy was substituted for the actor in a couple of shots.

- Wilf's description of his military service in Palestine in 1948 was based on Bernard Cribbins' own experiences in the Parachute Regiment, which he had recounted to Russell T Davies.

- Verity Newman's name was drawn from those of Verity Lambert, *Doctor Who*'s first producer, and Sydney Newman, the show's principal creator. (Previously, in 'Human Nature'/'The Family of Blood' (2007), the Doctor's human *alter ego* John Smith told Verity Newman's great-grandmother, Joan Redfern, that his parents were named Sydney and Verity.)

- The final recording that David Tennant did for this special was the green screen shot of the Doctor falling from the Vinvocci ship. This was not his last performance as the Doctor, however, as he subsequently recorded his appearance for 'The Wedding of Sarah Jane Smith' (2009) in *The Sarah Jane Adventures*.

- The song heard playing in the bar where Captain Jack is seen drinking is 'My Angel Put the Devil in Me', first composed by Murray Gold for the Series Three episode 'Daleks in Manhattan' (2007).

- The final moments of the special with Matt Smith's Doctor were written, uncredited, by Steven Moffat, and overseen by him and his fellow incoming executive producer Piers Wenger.

- On its original BBC One transmission, 'The End of Time' Part Two was preceded by a specially-recorded voiceover continuity announcement by David Tennant in character as the Doctor, over the end of the *Doctor Who*-themed Christmas channel ident: 'This is the Doctor. And now, the end of time is nigh. The Master's in control, the Time Lords are returning, and it's time to face the final battle.' This narration was not heard nationwide, however, with at least BBC Wales not transmitting it. Immediately after the special ended, there was a short teaser for the next series, consisting of the TARDIS-shaped DW logo for Series Five with the light flashing on top, followed by the caption 'Spring 2010'. A full trailer for Series Five was shown later the same evening.

OOPS!

- The Doctor realises that one of the masked guards at the Naismith mansion is not a Master duplicate – he is, in fact, the male Vinvocci, Rossiter, planning to rescue the Doctor and Wilf – because he is 'an inch too tall'. However, it is obvious in various other shots – such as the one where, later, Joshua Naismith and his daughter Abigail revert to their normal forms – that the Master duplicates are not all the same height.

- There are clearly-visible gaps between the glass doors and walls of the Immortality Gate's supposedly sealed nuclear bolt control booths, including in the very scene where the Doctor is telling Wilf that the 'Vinvocci glass' will keep radiation in. It is also unclear how the Doctor knows the properties of Vinvocci glass and the functioning of their equipment, as earlier he appeared not to be familiar with the Vinvocci.

- In the scene where the Doctor is agonising over whether to shoot Rassilon or the Master, he is heard to cock the revolver several times without uncocking it in between.
- When Verity Newman supposedly signs a copy of her book for the Doctor, it can be seen that the pen is not actually touching the page.

PRESS REACTION

- 'Russell T Davies wasn't big on throwing in references to non-*Who* pop culture during his run, but this one had a few really obvious nods to some big guns of sci-fi, with Wilf's stint as an asteroid laser gunner obviously modeled on Luke Skywalker and Han Solo in the Millennium Falcon's turret guns in the original *Star Wars*, Captain Jack's space cantina modelled on a similar sequence also in *Star Wars*, and the Doctor's fate in the radiation chamber looked quite a bit like Mr Spock's sacrifice in *Star Trek II: The Wrath of Khan*. For that matter, the scene where the Doctor shut off all the systems on the salvage ship so the Master couldn't find it felt very much like a silent running sequence from any number of classic submarine movies.' Alan Sepinwall, *New Jersey Star-Ledger*, 3 January 2010.
- 'A celebration not just of the tenth Doctor, "The End of Time" was a fitting finale to the Russell T Davies era of *Doctor Who*, epitomising everything that has come to represent the show over the last five years.' Peter Quentin, Total Sci-Fi Online website, 4 January 2010.
- 'This was David Tennant's show, and a near-80-minute exercise in just how much he's going to be missed. Tennant was always at his best in these more sombre episodes – inevitably "The End of Time" Part Two was darker *Who* – and he was magnetically brilliant here. None of the running around like a loon of old. This was a character being taken apart bit by bit over the course of the episode, and Tennant's eyes alone told the story. It was an amazing performance. The Doctor was torn apart long before the regeneration started, and the broken Time Lord that we first got to see properly in "The Waters of Mars" (although he was hinted at many times beforehand) was fully exposed here. Credit too for the introduction of the Ood to sing the Doctor out. "The universe will sing you to your sleep", they said. That's just great writing.' Simon Brew, Den of Geek website, 1 January 2010.
- 'Everything that wasn't in Part One of the *Doctor Who* special "The End of Time" was in the part Two. Action, drama, sadness, emotional, excitement, memories and rebirth. Name an emotion, this one had it, and Russell T Davies knows how to go out with a bang, delivering one hell of a finale to the end of his and Tennant's tenure in the show.' Emerson Parker, iF Magazine website, 4 January 2010.
- 'Despite some misgivings with the stretched-out storyline and the mangled plot exposition, it's only fair to accentuate the positives of the second part of "The End Of Time", given the nature and significance of the episode. An array of fine performances certainly helped to bolster events and ensure the Russell T Davies era was wrapped up in style. It wasn't an easy journey at times during the swansong, but ultimately the sheer spectacle, humour and heightened emotion of the events were hopefully enough to win viewers over.

After all, if the Doctor can still extend his hand of friendship to the Master despite all of his flaws, let's try to do the same for "The End of Time". The outgoing *Doctor Who* team deserve a happy ending.' Ben Rawson-Jones, Den of Geek website, 2 January 2010.

- 'You probably had to be a Time Lord yourself to make sense of the dizzyingly complicated plot, which had something to do with ancient prophecies, time vortices and a guest appearance from Timothy Dalton. But this barely mattered: the episode charged forward with such apocalyptic brio it was hard to be unduly worried about what, precisely, was going on.Witty, infectious and wearing its heart on its sleeve, this was a barnstorming hour of family entertainment. And the death of the Doctor, who sacrificed his life in place of Wilf's, was so tenderly acted and sad I half expected the phone number of a *Doctor Who* helpline to flash on screen to help a nation of heartbroken eight-year-olds get over the shock … Such has been Tennant's nonchalant mastery of the role it is hard, for the moment at least, to imagine an episode without him. His last words as the Doctor were "I don't want to go". No doubt 10 million viewers felt the same.' Andrew Pettie, *Daily Telegraph*, 1 January 2010.

ANALYSIS

After a superb opening instalment that seemed to promise so much for the tenth Doctor's long-heralded swansong, unfortunately things rather fall apart in 'The End of Time' Part Two.

One of the biggest frustrations is that most of the intriguing questions and tantalising plot points set up in the first half of the story turn out to have either a highly unsatisfactory resolution or, worse still, no resolution at all. Nothing more is said of the Ood's unnaturally accelerated development. No real explanation is given as to why everyone on Earth – or, if the Elder Ood's suggestion was correct, everyone in the universe – was having bad dreams of the Master prior to his resurrection. Joshua Naismith's book *Fighting the Future*, which seemed to have such significance attached to it, proves to be a complete red herring. The Naismiths themselves virtually disappear from the story – their ultimate downfall, to be arrested and locked up for 'crimes undisclosed', is covered in a throwaway line of dialogue from Wilf toward the end – making the casting of an actor of David Harewood's stature and ability in the role of Joshua a bit of a waste. The two Vinvocci also vanish just over half way through, fleeing Earth in their spaceship – although it is left to the viewer's imagination how they are able to do that when at least one of the exterior windows has been shattered in the excellent *Star Wars*-influenced dogfight scene of the shooting down of the missiles launched at them by the Master. The Master's wonderfully bold and inventive supplanting of the human race is all too quickly and easily reversed by Rassilon, who effectively takes over as the lead villain – although the Master does at least get to thwart him by firing bolts of energy at him in the end, in what seems likely to be the superb John Simm's last scene as the character. And then there's the business about Donna regaining her memories of her time with the Doctor. Previously it has been stated quite unequivocally that if this were ever to happen, it would be the end of her – even in Part One, the Doctor tells Wilf, 'If she ever remembers me, her mind will burn, and she will die.' Now, though, it turns out that she doesn't die at all; she is simply rendered unconscious and has her memories of the Doctor erased once more, in the process releasing a burst of energy that very conveniently knocks out (or even kills? – this isn't made clear) all of the Master duplicates who are menacing her. This, not to put too fine a point on it, is a cheat, a cop-out, and a desperately underwhelming outcome to that element of the Part One cliff-hanger. As much as I disliked the way Donna was written out in 'Journey's End' (2008), it did at least have a dramatic integrity to it, and that has now been undermined and cheapened almost as badly as 'Journey's End' itself undermined and cheapened the Doctor's heartbreaking farewell to Rose at the end of 'Doomsday' (2006).

One mystery that writer Russell T Davies was quite right to leave hanging is the identity of the woman in white who periodically communicates with Wilf and who is later seen to be a Time Lord dissenter from Rassilon's plan. Perhaps the most obvious interpretation is that she is the Doctor's mother – and it is clear from what he says in the second edition of his and Benjamin Cook's book *The Writer's Tale* (BBC Books, 2010) that this was what Davies intended, and indeed what Claire Bloom was told when she was cast in the part – although I personally prefer to believe that she is actually an older form of one-time companion Romana.[58] This, though, demonstrates precisely why it was right for Davies to leave the question unanswered on screen: it is just the sort of point that fans ought to be allowed to theorise about and debate amongst themselves, rather than being given a 'on the nose' explanation that might potentially cause continuity problems and limit future story development by other writers.[59] The difference between this and all the other unresolved points mentioned above is that it was clearly a deliberate and reasoned choice on Davies's part not to reveal the woman's identity, whereas in those other cases the viewer is left with the distinct impression that he has either forgotten to address the issues or simply lost interest in them and decided to take the story off in a different direction. Even then, he has failed to give a satisfactory explanation as to how the woman in white has been managing to communicate with Wilf even prior to the Time Lords' return, and how she knows what the Doctor will have to do in his final confrontation with Rassilon and the Master.

Another problem with this special is its overall treatment of the Time Lords. Davies always insisted in interviews that it would be wrong to attempt any on-screen depiction of the Time War, as it could never hope to live up to the images that viewers had conjured up in their own imaginations. The wisdom of those words is borne out here as, although the script is at pains to establish that Gallifrey is only on the 'furthest edge' of the War (which seems odd in itself, given that it is the Time Lords' home planet), the momentous events of the final day of the conflict are essentially reduced to a few CGI shots of a shattered citadel and some corridors, and a meeting around a table in a kind of black void. Things are made a little more dramatic by Rassilon's use of a death-dealing gauntlet to silence, permanently, a Time Lord whose opinion displeases him, and also by the inclusion

---

[58] It has long been established in the tie-in novels and audio CD plays that Romana returned to Gallifrey and became the Time Lord President some time after parting company with the Doctor in E-Space at the end of 'Warriors' Gate' (1980).

[59] In the 1996 TV movie, the Doctor stated that he was half-human on his mother's side. Although fans who dislike that notion have since put forward numerous theories to disprove it, it has never been directly contradicted in the TV show itself.

of a witch-like female soothsayer – perhaps a nod by Davies to the idea of the Pythias, the mystical seers who were matriarchs of Gallifrey prior to the rise of the Time Lords, originally created by Marc Platt for his New Adventures novel *Cat's Cradle: Time's Crucible* (Virgin Books, 1992). All in all, though, this is a rather disappointing portrayal of such a key point in Time Lord history. Davies has even missed an opportunity to create a real 'wow' moment by including a clip of the ninth Doctor – or, perhaps better still, the eighth – when the Time Lords are talking about his role in proceedings. In fact, if ever there was an ideal opportunity for Paul McGann to have been invited back to the TV show for a fitting cameo reprise of his eighth Doctor role, then surely this was it.

There is a certain appeal to the idea that the drumbeat in the Master's head corresponds to the heartbeat of a Time Lord, and that his lifelong derangement has been just a kind of side-effect of their plan to escape the Time War. Again, though, this raises some awkward questions – has it really never occurred to the Master that the incessant noise that has so tormented him is in the same rhythm as his own heartbeat? – and the added complication of the Time Lords needing to create a physical link by sending to Earth a diamond-like white point star makes the whole thing a bit too contrived and confusing. It is also rather too similar to the device of the diamond-like warp star with which Sarah Jane Smith threatened to destroy the Dalek Crucible in 'Journey's End', which was a silly enough idea in the first place. Much the same can be said of the images of Gallifrey appearing in the sky above the Earth, which recall the array of stolen planets in the latter episode and definitely engender a 'seen it all before' feeling.

The anticlimax continues as the Time Lords finally materialise in the Naismiths' mansion and, aside from Rassilon, there are merely four of them – including, bizarrely, the two High Council members who voted against Rassilon's plan. The fact that there is a bright white void in the background where previously the Immortality Gate could be seen makes it seem almost as if the production team intended to use CGI to add in some further ranks of Time Lords behind them, but were prevented from doing so by lack of money or some other production problem.

The scene where the Doctor is presented with the seemingly intractable dilemma of needing to shoot either Rassilon or the Master in order to prevent the Time Lords' full return is built up to be an absolutely key moment of the story. The earlier discussion between the Doctor and Wilf in which the latter tried, initially in vain, to persuade the former to take his service revolver – another beautifully played two-hander between David Tennant and Bernard Cribbins – has already raised the stakes by emphasising how unusual it is for the Doctor to carry arms. Now the Doctor is faced with the terrible prospect of actually having to use the gun. However, as the Doctor stands agonising over what to do, strangely neither Rassilon nor the Master makes any attempt to intervene, other than through verbal persuasion. The fact having been clearly established earlier on that the gauntlet Rassilon wears is capable of vaporising a Time Lord on the spot, it seems astonishing that he does not lift a finger – literally – to prevent the Doctor thwarting his plans. Perhaps the intended implication is that neither Rassilon nor the Master believes that the Doctor will really be able to bring himself to shoot. If so, this is somewhat akin to the game of brinkmanship that the Dalek Emperor played with the ninth Doctor in 'The Parting of the Ways' (2005). That, though, proved rather more dramatically satisfying, as it ended with the Doctor taking a positive decision that he would rather be seen as a coward than a killer.

So, as things transpire, the momentous return of the Time Lords boils down to just Rassilon and four others materialising in the Naismiths' mansion, a few planet-in-the-sky shots that are similar to but less spectacular than those in 'Journey's End', and the Doctor quickly sending them all back to the Time War by firing a revolver at a bit of electronic equipment. This falls some way short of the epic, mythic quality for which Davies was obviously aiming, and is really a bit of a let-down.

It is hard not to feel ambivalent, too, about the whole idea of Rassilon and the Time Lords being depicted in 'The End of Time' as a force for evil rather than for good. Admittedly it does chime well with the familiar notion of the two sides in a conflict tending to become just as bad as each other, regardless of the respective moral standpoints from which they started out. It also makes more sense of the fact that the Time Lords resurrected the Master to fight on their behalf in the Time War, as stated in 'The Sound of Drums' (2007). In addition, although it will doubtless have meant little or nothing to the great majority of viewers, the Doctor's identification of the Time Lord President as Rassilon provides a welcome *frisson* of excitement for fans, who will recognise the name as that of the legendary founder of Time Lord society. Furthermore, the portrayal of Rassilon in a sinister light pleasingly accords with the way the character has been developed over the years in the tie-in novels, such as *Lungbarrow* (Virgin Books, 1997), and audio CD dramas, such as *Zagreus* (Big Finish, 2003). Even in the TV show itself, 'The Five Doctors' (1983) makes mention of rumours that Rassilon was really a cruel despot; and although much of the action of that story centres around his supposed tomb, it is arguably obvious that he is not actually dead, not least because at one point he – or, at least, a projected image of his head – manages to engage in conversation with the assembled Doctors.

Against all these plus points, though, there is the significant drawback that the revelation of the Time Lords' wickedness casts an unwelcome new light on the desperate, albeit at present still unspecified, actions that the Doctor took, in either his eighth or his ninth incarnation, to end the Time War. Previously the implication seemed to be that he was forced into sacrificing his own race as the terrible price he had to pay to put a stop to the evil of the Daleks. Now, though, with the disclosure that the Time Lords had become just as much of a menace to the universe as the monsters they were fighting against, it seems clear that the Doctor did not so much feel forced to sacrifice them as positively determine to consign them to the same fate. This robs the scenario of much of its tragic quality. It suggests that the Time Lords had become just another evil race that the Doctor had to deal with, rather than the cruel victims of a horribly drastic solution that he felt he had no option but to implement.

The partial saving grace here is the consideration that, in destroying the Time Lords, the Doctor had to kill not only the bad ones but also the good, not to mention all the members of his own family. Perhaps this is why Davies decided to include the character of the woman in white, clearly shown to be an objector to Rassilon's plan and to have some special, possibly familial, relationship to the Doctor. Through this character, the writer effectively reassures the viewer that not all of the Time Lords were evil, and that the Doctor's ending of the Time War still had a great cost to him in terms of his own personal sacrifice, and that of his loved ones on Gallifrey. But the effectiveness of this is somewhat diminished by the fact that Davies has chosen to show those resisting Rassilon's tyranny to be very much in the minority rather than a significant faction of Time Lord society. In the end, one has to ask, is this really enough to compensate for what amounts to a dilution of the tragedy of the Doctor's role in ending the Time War? Probably not.

And so we come to what is, for this author, the biggest shortcoming of all in 'The End of Time' Part Two: its characterisation of the tenth Doctor himself, in this his final outing. Considering what a wonderful job Russell T Davies did in reviving *Doctor Who* for a 21st Century audience, and how much of the show's content he got absolutely spot-on during his hugely successful five year tenure in charge, it is ironic that the one key area in which he repeatedly made mistakes is this: the depiction of the show's central character. This is not to say that his treatment of the Doctor was off-beam throughout. On the contrary, for the most part it was just as adept as his handling of every other aspect of the scripting and production; and certainly during Christopher Eccleston's brief era he really didn't put a foot wrong in this regard. Every so often during David Tennant's era, however, he made a serious misstep. At one extreme, he seems to have had a strange inclination to see the Doctor presented as a Messiah-like figure: the highest authority in the universe ('New Earth' (2006)), meting out harsh, Old Testament-style punishments to his adversaries ('The Family of Blood' (2007)), saving the Earth in response to its people's prayers ('Last of the Time Lords' (2007)) and being metaphorically carried aloft by angels ('Voyage of the Damned' (2007)). At the other extreme, though, Davies occasionally had the character portrayed in a decidedly cowed and unheroic light. Probably the biggest offender in this regard is 'Last of the Time Lords', in which the Doctor is transformed into a helpless old man, treated like a dog, punched, taunted, deprived of his ability to regenerate, aged still further, turned into a withered homunculus, kept in a birdcage and, in short, utterly humiliated.

Both of these extremes of characterisation are again in evidence in 'The End of Time' Part Two. Back in 'Logopolis' (1980), falling from a great height onto a grassy bank was injurious enough to cause the fourth Doctor to have to regenerate. Now, though, it seems that leaping out of a fast-moving spaceship, smashing through a glass dome and crashing down onto a hard, marble-tiled floor causes the tenth Doctor to suffer nothing more serious than a few scratches! This Doctor-as-superhero approach is just all wrong, and damages the credibility of the story. Then, at the other end of the scale, there is the Doctor's continued abject fear of facing up to his foretold fate, which is equally strange – has he ever before been so credulous of cryptically-worded prophecies? – and inappropriate.

This is all a great pity as, setting aside these jarring extremes, Davies is actually to be commended on one aspect of his characterisation of the Doctor: the way he has managed to weave a consistent strand of development through all five years' worth of his stories. In Series One, it was clearly implied that the ninth Doctor, as the only Time Lord to have escaped the Time War, was experiencing a form of survivor's guilt – an aspect of post-traumatic stress disorder in which the sufferer typically has a self-punishing belief that he or she could have done more to try to save the victims of a disastrous event, and sometimes even feels unworthy to have lived through it. This was picked up on in the following three series, when the tenth Doctor was shown at times to exhibit a degree of recklessness that bordered on a death-wish – particularly when faced with his Time War adversaries, the Daleks. Perhaps the most notable example of this comes in 'Evolution of the Daleks' (2007), when he almost begs the Daleks attacking Hooverville to exterminate him, shouting: 'Then do it! Do it! Just do it! Do it!' How his attitude has changed by 'The End of Time'! The nub of this change comes at the end of 'The Waters of Mars', when he quite explicitly ceases to view himself as the Time War's sole survivor and instead proclaims himself to be the Time Lord Victorious. Although he quickly comes to see that he has gone too far, it would seem that his survivor's guilt has been expunged for good, and from that point on, he is effectively running scared for his life.

Fourth Doctor actor Tom Baker always used to assert in interviews that the character was a highly predictable one to play, because he never really changed or developed. That has certainly not been the case with the ninth and tenth Doctors, however, and Davies must take considerable credit for that. While it is difficult to believe that he intentionally set out to give the Doctor a five-year character arc that constituted, in effect, a sustained examination of the theme of survivor's guilt, that is essentially how things turned out, and it is a significant and often-overlooked achievement of his time in charge of the show.

Also helping to give a satisfying feeling of closure to Davies's tenure is the fact that, just as his first episode, 'Rose' (2005), drew heavy inspiration from the third Doctor's debut adventure, 'Spearhead from Space' (1970), most obviously in its reuse of the Nestenes and Autons, so his last episode, 'The End of Time' Part Two, bears some strong similarities to the third Doctor's swansong, 'Planet of the Spiders' (1974).[60] On one level, 'Planet of the Spiders' can be seen as a considered critique of the third Doctor's character. It ends with him coming to recognise his flaws – principally his arrogance and his greed for knowledge – and accepting that he must go to face his fear in the cave of the Great One on Metebelis III, even though he is fully aware that this will result in him being exposed to an intense bombardment of radiation that he will be unable to survive. Similarly, in 'The End of Time' Part Two, the tenth Doctor finally has to face his fear and subject himself to a burst of powerful radiation that he knows will bring about his regeneration. The difference here is that, far from recognising his character flaws and accepting that he must change, the tenth Doctor continues to rail against the hand that fate

---

[60] There are also echoes of all of the other previous regeneration stories: Gallifrey appearing in the sky above Earth is reminiscent of the approach of Mondas in 'The Tenth Planet' (1966), which also has the first Doctor traversing snowy ground to return to the TARDIS to regenerate; the unexpected arrival of the Time Lords parallels the end of 'The War Games' (1969); the tenth Doctor's fall from the Vinvocci spaceship recalls the fourth Doctor's fall from the radio telescope in 'Logopolis' (1981), which also features the Master and has the Doctor seeing past companions (albeit only through the use of clips) just before his regeneration; the Doctor sacrificing himself to save the life of a companion is featured in both 'The Caves of Androzani' (1984) and 'The Parting of the Ways', the former of which also has cameo appearances by past companions just prior to the regeneration; and the Master's involvement, and killing of his human wife, were elements of the TV movie (1996).

has dealt him. Again, this is desperately unheroic, and a rather ignominious way for him to bow out.

The worst manifestation of this comes immediately after the dramatic revelation that the 'He' of the 'He will knock four times' prophecy is actually Wilf, innocently tapping on the door of one of the Immortality Gate's nuclear bolt control booths – a rather contrived device, obviously serving no real purpose in the story but to provide a reason for the Doctor's regeneration, which consequently ends up seeming a bit tacked on. Rather than courageously and unhesitatingly giving up his own life to save that of his friend – as the fifth Doctor did in 'The Caves of Androzani' (1984) and as the ninth Doctor did in 'The Parting of the Ways' (2005) – the tenth Doctor, astonishingly, has a petulant rant first, tearfully lamenting the fact that he is going to have to sacrifice himself to prevent the death of an insignificant human. Of course he still goes ahead and does so anyway, but the clear implication is that this is not because he really wants to, but only because his conscience and his affection for Wilf will not allow him to do otherwise. It is hard to imagine a more reluctant self-sacrifice than this, and despite David Tennant's superb playing of the whole scene, it rings pretty hollow when the Doctor tells Wilf, 'It's my honour'. One almost expects Wilf to reply, 'Then why did you just throw that tantrum?' This takes the tenth Doctor's occasional unattractive hubris to a whole new level and is, in my opinion, probably the single most ill-judged scene in Russell T Davies's entire time in charge of *Doctor Who*.

The questionable characterisation does not end there, either, as the Doctor then proceeds to state that, before his regeneration runs its course, he is going to go off in the TARDIS and get his 'reward'. The idea that the Doctor actually feels that he deserves a reward for his actions is totally at odds with the essential nature of the character, at least as it has been written for the previous 46 years, and frankly rather distasteful. Sadly, it also indelibly taints the closing scenes of the special, where the Doctor revisits all his Davies-era companions in what should have been a satisfying valedictory curtain-call for these much-loved characters – notwithstanding that they already seemed to have been given one the previous year in 'Journey's End'.

There is nothing inherently wrong with the idea that the process of regeneration takes some time to complete – in fact, this again mirrors what happened in 'Planet of the Spiders', as the TARDIS brought the third Doctor back to his friends on Earth for his regeneration after he got 'lost in the time vortex' for an unspecified period following his departure from Metebelis III (and who knows what other journeys he might potentially have made during that period?) There is, though, something a little off-kilter about some of the brief companion vignettes that Davies has written in here. I am not as bothered as some other commentators seem to have been by the fact that the Doctor thinks it worthwhile to spend some of his precious last few minutes setting up Captain Jack on a date with Alonso Frame from 'Voyage of the Damned' (2007). There is, after all, no reason to suppose that this is going to be merely a one night stand, rather than a lasting relationship of greater significance; and arguably Captain Jack deserves some kind of validation from the Doctor after the traumatic events he went through in the *Torchwood* mini-series 'Children of Earth' (2009). Rather more troubling, though, is the idea that the Doctor saves Mickey Smith and Martha Jones (or Martha Smith-Jones, as she is now credited) from being shot by a Sontaran, and Sarah Jane Smith's adopted son

Luke from being run over by a car. These sequences seem to suggest that when the Doctor spoke of getting his 'reward' he actually meant that he intended to take one last opportunity to act in Time Lord Victorious mode, saving the lives of people whose deaths – like those of Captain Adelaide Brooke and her crew in 'The Waters of Mars' – were supposed to be fixed points in history. Otherwise, if he knew that Martha, Mickey and Luke were going to be in deadly peril at these particular points in time, why did he not intervene before – instead of messing about prior to his arrival on the Ood-Sphere in Part One, for instance? The idea that Martha and Mickey have got married to each other since last seen in 'Journey's End' doesn't quite ring true, either, and seems to have been included simply to try to give a sense of a neat 'happy ending' to these great characters' respective journeys in the show. Another issue is that the Doctor's meeting with the previously unseen Verity Newman, great-granddaughter of Joan Redfern from 'Human Nature'/'The Family of Blood' (2007), sticks out like a bit of a sore thumb amongst all these former companion appearances, and won't have been fully understood by casual viewers who had not seen, or did not recall, that earlier story. In fact, it might have been better for this scene to have been omitted (as director Euros Lyn tried in his first edit), emotionally affecting though it undoubtedly is, if only to shorten a little what threatens to become an overly long and self-indulgent goodbye.

Fortunately, though, two of the former companion vignettes do work extremely well: the one with Donna at her wedding, and the one with Rose and her mum Jackie. After her abandoned marriage in 'The Runaway Bride' (2006) and her virtual one in 'Forest of the Dead' (2008), it seems entirely right and proper that Donna should finally succeed in getting hitched in what seems likely to be her last appearance in the show. The Doctor's wedding gift, a (presumably winning) lottery ticket bought with a pound borrowed from her now-deceased father Geoff and passed on via Wilf, is a lovely touch – and all the more tear-jerking for fans who know that Howard Attfield, the actor who played Geoff in 'The Runaway Bride', sadly passed away just as he was on the point of reprising the role for Series Four; the behind-the-scenes development that led to Wilf being introduced as a replacement character. This beautifully-written, well-shot and superbly-acted sequence outside the church makes for a very fitting farewell not only for Donna and Sylvia but also for Wilf himself, who has essentially served as the Doctor's companion for 'The End of Time', and very commendably too.

The scene with Rose and Jackie is just as good. Setting this on New Year's Day 2005, before Rose even met the ninth Doctor, was a brilliant idea on Davies's part. Not only does it allow the viewer one last chance to see arguably the best of all the Doctor's companions, without having to disturb the mythology of her being left in the parallel universe at the close of 'Journey's End', but also it brings Davies's era as showrunner full circle and again gives a satisfying sense of closure. We see Rose as she was back when we first met her, an ordinary shop girl living with her mum on a London housing estate, and can happily reflect on the fact that in just a few months' time she will be setting out on her wondrous new adventures in the TARDIS, just as we did when 'Rose' was first transmitted on 26 March 2005. A poignant moment indeed.

There is just time after this for a final fleeting appearance by the Ood before the Doctor staggers into the TARDIS for his regeneration. Sadly, things go somewhat awry again here, as the Doctor once more succumbs to timid whining with his final line, 'I don't wanna go'. In the accompanying episode of *Doctor Who Confidential*, there is a segment where David Tennant is seen experimenting with various different ways of delivering this line and expressing his concern to the director that it could seem out of character for the Doctor if he were to sound too distraught. But the problem is not really with the delivery of the line, it's with the line itself, and it *is* out of character.

Then, to cap it all, the regeneration itself takes to the ultimate extreme an increasingly irritating trend during the tenth Doctor's era: specifically, the tendency for the TARDIS control console to erupt with ever-bigger displays of pyrotechnic bangs and flashes whenever the ship makes any sort of journey, however routine – the aim presumably being to add a spurious sense of excitement to these scenes. So this time, for no apparent reason, the Doctor's regeneration releases such a huge amount of energy that it almost completely wrecks not only the control console but also the whole room around it, causing the ship to start to crash!

Despite all the problems with 'The End of Time' Part Two, which is certainly one of the most flawed episodes since the show returned in 2005, it is hard not to feel very mixed emotions as David Tennant's features fade away to be replaced by those of Matt Smith. On the one hand, there is the exciting prospect of the advent of a new Doctor, who seems on the basis of his first scene (in which he has rather more dialogue than one might have expected) to hold a great deal of promise for the future. On the other hand, though, the loss of an actor of Tennant's exceptional quality, not to mention charm, decency, dedication and life-long love of the show, is a bitter pill to have to swallow. Notwithstanding the rather unfortunate turn the characterisation of the part has taken in these last few specials, which does leave his legacy just a little tarnished, the tenth Doctor still stands as the best the show has ever had.

SPECIALS OVERVIEW

The BBC were, as Russell T Davies himself has conceded, 'desperate' to have a full new series of *Doctor Who* for transmission in 2009, to follow on from the 2008 Christmas special already planned to go before the cameras immediately after the Series Four finale 'Journey's End' (2008). This is hardly surprising: the show was, after all, reaching an unprecedented level of public popularity and critical acclaim, and coming to rival *EastEnders* as the BBC's top ongoing drama. So it seems, on the face of it, utterly perplexing that a decision was taken to produce just a small number of one-off specials instead, and postpone the next full series until 2010.

Two reasons for this decision have been cited by Davies and his colleagues, and it is worth considering the validity of each of them in turn.

Reason 1: Time was needed for a new production team to be put in place

Davies, by all accounts, decided quite far in advance that he did not want to remain in charge of *Doctor Who* for more than four full series. In the first week of July 2006, just before recording got under way on 'The Runaway Bride' (2006), he had a meeting in Woods Restaurant in Cardiff Bay with his fellow executive producer, Julie Gardner, and lead actor, David Tennant, at which they discussed their respective futures on the show. It was out of this meeting that the plan was hatched for them all to leave together in the summer of 2009, following completion of a number of specials to be transmitted in a 'gap year' after Series Four. They would then make way for a new team and a new Doctor to be brought in for the 2010 series. Exactly how many specials would be made was an issue that remained unresolved for some time, due to budgetary and other considerations, before the number was eventually fixed at four, in addition to the 2008 Christmas special. However, although attempts were subsequently made by the BBC's senior management to persuade Davies to remain in charge for Series Five – and for a time they even contemplated ending the show altogether if he left, so crucial did they consider his involvement to be – it seems that he never wavered from the basic plan that had been agreed following his meeting with Gardner and Tennant.

It would appear, then, disingenuous at best to assert that the making of a full series for 2009 was precluded by the time needed to put a new production team in place. It was not until 17 July 2007, a full year after the Woods Restaurant meeting, that Davies first e-mailed Steven Moffat to ask if he would be interested in becoming the new showrunner. Had he contacted him straight away rather than delaying a year, there would seem to have been no reason in principle why Moffat could not have taken over the reins in time for Series Five to begin transmission in spring 2009 rather than spring 2010. That, however, would obviously have meant Davies, Gardner and Tennant bowing out after completion of work on the 2008 Christmas special, rather than staying on to make four further specials to round off their time on the show.

It is, of course, possible that Moffat would not have been available, or even willing, to take over as showrunner a year earlier than he actually did; but given that he was not asked at that time, this can only be a matter for conjecture. Had he been unavailable, it is possible that another suitable candidate could have been found instead. The fact remains that it was the agreement of Davies, Gardner and Tennant to stay on to make some post-Series Four specials, far more than the time needed to get a new production team on board, that ruled out having a full series in 2009.

Reason 2: Making the viewing public wait for the next full series would help to keep them excited about the show and secure its long-term future

In an e-mail of 31 May 2007, reproduced in their book *The Writer's Tale* (BBC Books, 2009), Russell T Davies told Benjamin Cook that the main rationale for the gap year was as follows: 'The show, by 2009, will simply need a rest. We need to starve people a bit. We're producing 14 movie-sized episodes a year, which are then repeated *ad infinitum*, and ratings are bound to decline, even just a little. *Doctor Who* is a phenomenon right now, but nothing stays a phenomenon. Not without careful management. People need to be begging for new *Doctor Who*, instead of just expecting it. That's fine for kids, too. They can wait for a few years between *Harry Potter* books and *Star Wars* films. If anything, the wait *increases* the legend.' Davies also asserted in a number of interviews that establishing this transmission pattern – of having a longer-than-usual break between series every few years – would help to ensure the show's longevity.

One hesitates to take issue with a man as astute as Davies, but it has to be said that this reasoning is highly questionable. *Doctor Who*'s ratings showed no signs of declining, 'even just a little', toward the end of his time as showrunner; on the contrary, they continued to climb during Series Four, and remained at a phenomenal level for the gap year specials themselves.[61] Furthermore, it seemed that the lack of a full new series was not really 'fine for kids', as despite the high ratings for the specials, the show's status as a playground favourite took a severe dent during 2009 – as evidenced by tumbling circulation figures for BBC Magazines' *Doctor Who Adventures* comic, declining sales for licensed toys and games, and a comparative dearth of new *Doctor Who*-related products coming onto the market.

It is obviously easy to be wise after the event, but even a cursory consideration of *Doctor Who*'s classic-era history should have been enough to cast doubt on Davies's strategy. A number of times in the past, the show had been successfully revamped, and a popular new Doctor introduced, without the need for any unduly long break between series. Perhaps the foremost example of this is the reformatting of the show to make it Earth-based when Jon Pertwee debuted as the Doctor in 1970, which saw the ratings rise significantly. By contrast, the one time there had been a lengthy between-series hiatus in classic-era *Doctor Who*, when the then BBC One Controller Michael Grade had decided to take it off the air temporarily following the 1985 run, the ratings were much lower when it came back than they had been before.

All things considered, then, it would seem that the normal between-series break

---

[61] See Appendix D for full details.

is quite sufficient to maintain a high level of public anticipation for the show's return, and that a longer-term hiatus can actually be detrimental to maintaining interest, particularly amongst children.

The conclusion one has to draw from all this is that neither of the two justifications put forward for the 2009 gap year really holds water. One thing that can be said for certain, though, is that had Davies, Gardner and Tennant not formulated the plan they did, and been able to dissuade their BBC superiors from overruling them and imposing a new team in their place (which was apparently a distinct possibility at one point), then viewers would have been deprived of the chance to see those last four specials with Tennant in the lead role. Barring any change of heart on the actor's part about staying on for another full series (which would have prevented him from taking on other work, including his starring role in the RSC's production of *Hamlet*), his final appearance would have come not on New Year's Day 2010 but on Christmas Day 2008, in a special with a script no doubt quite different from any of those that were ultimately produced.[62] This would in many ways have been a great shame: any additional opportunity to see Tennant's wonderful Doctor in action is to be seized with both hands and relished. Having said that, though, these extra four specials did have the unfortunate effect of making his exit seem a very protracted one – particularly as it was heavily trailed in the scripts by way of devices such as cryptic prophecies and ominous Ood appearances. The last of the specials, 'The End of Time' Part Two, drew things out still further by having a number of 'false endings', where the Doctor seems to be on the point of regenerating, only to dust himself off and carry on; and in the end, he even gets the chance to have one last encounter with each of his former companions before he finally transforms into his eleventh incarnation.

By the time that regeneration scene was transmitted, over 14 months had elapsed since Tennant had made the shock October 2008 announcement of his departure. Never before had there been such a long gap between the public learning of a Doctor's exit and it actually being seen on screen. In the interim, the new Doctor had been cast, as had his new companion, and they had got well into recording the next series, with pictures of the location work being splashed across the press. On 3 January 2009, almost a year before Matt Smith's on-screen debut, there had even been a special *Doctor Who Confidential* programme to announce his accession to the role, which had won an extraordinary rating of 6.3 million viewers in an unaccustomed BBC One slot, making it the channel's sixteenth most viewed programme of the week. The situation was somewhat akin to that where a new US President is elected in the November of one year but does not take up office until the January of the next, the outgoing incumbent often being referred to as a 'lame duck President' during the period in between. There was a real danger here that Tennant's Doctor could come to be seen as something of a 'lame duck Doctor', with all of the public interest and attention turning to his successor long before the on-screen handover actually happened.

Another consequence of having a run of specials was that Davies obviously felt

---

[62] Presumably viewers would also have been deprived of Tennant's appearances in 'The Wedding of Sarah Jane Smith' two-parter of *The Sarah Jane Adventures* and in the 'Dreamland' animated story.

under an obligation to make them all ... well, special. They all aspire to a grand-scale, epic quality, like a holiday blockbuster movie. That's fine, of course, for viewers who particularly enjoy that type of *Doctor Who*; but one of the things that has always made the show so hugely appealing is the varied nature of its stories. With this succession of one-off, feature-length epics, there was no room to fit in a lower-key, quirkier type of episode, like 'Love & Monsters' (2006) or 'Gridlock' (2007) or 'Midnight' (2008); the type of episode that helps to provide balance and ensure a pleasing mix of styles in a full, 13-part series. This is really rather a pity.

If one looks at the specials as a kind of 'mini series' in their own right, then 'The End of Time' Part Two takes the place of the series finale, and as with all previous series finales, Davies tries to ramp everything up to make it the most stunning, spectacular, dramatic climax ever. The trouble is, the specials are already so big and so epic that it is really impossible to do that without it over-extending the show's resources and going completely over the top. And that, in a nutshell, is exactly what happens.

The absence of a regular companion for the specials has both positive and negative aspects. On the plus side, all of the one-off companions or quasi-companions that are brought in instead – Jackson Lake, Christina de Souza, Adelaide Brooke and the returning semi-regular Wilf Mott – are interesting characters, and very well portrayed by the respective guest cast members. On the minus side, however, the viewer is deprived of the opportunity of really getting to know a companion over the course of several episodes, and of seeing an ongoing friendship develop between her (or him) and the Doctor, which is normally one of the great pleasures of a full series.

The main reason for the absence of a regular co-star was Davies's desire to explore how the Doctor would be affected by the lack of ongoing human companionship, following up on Donna's observation in 'The Runaway Bride', 'Sometimes I think you need someone to stop you.' This culminates in the scene toward the end of 'The Waters of Mars' where the Doctor allows his hubris to get the better of him and declares himself to be the 'Time Lord Victorious'; a shocking development that starts him down the road that will ultimately lead to his regeneration. From that point on, the tenth Doctor becomes a much darker, more self-absorbed, more self-pitying character than before. This affords Tennant some excellent dramatic material to play, which he really gets his teeth into and does a great job with, but robs the show of much of the joyous sense of fun that has so characterised it since its return to TV in 2005. Consequently, whereas that sense of fun is very much in evidence in 'The Next Doctor' and 'Planet of the Dead', which are both highly entertaining, it is largely absent from 'The Waters of Mars' and 'The End of Time', which are much grimmer and more downbeat in tone. Perhaps that is only fitting for the trilogy of episodes that mark the end of the era of this hugely popular Doctor, but it does mean that Tennant bows out in rather atypical style.

In the final assessment, it has to be said that while there is much to admire and enjoy in the five gap year specials, and they certainly add a good deal to the show's status and mythology, they nevertheless make for a rather disjointed and dissatisfying conclusion to the tenth Doctor's highly successful tenure.

PART FIVE
THE END OF AN ERA

THE RUSSELL T DAVIES LEGACY

Doctor Who fans should count themselves very fortunate: the show's return to TV in 2005 could so easily never have happened, leaving the Doctor's ongoing adventures to continue to be told only through the tie-in media of novels, audio CD dramas and comic strips. The fact that it did happen can be put down to a set of happy coincidences, which saw just the right people being in just the right place at just the right time.

The right people were: Jane Tranter, then the BBC's Controller of Drama Commissioning, who recognised the potential appeal of *Doctor Who* to a 21st Century audience and was the driving force behind its revival; Lorraine Heggessey, then the Controller of BBC One, who gave her seal of approval and made the not inconsiderable commitment to an initial series of 13 episodes; Alan Yentob, then the BBC's Director of Drama, and a long-time supporter of the show, who secured the return of the rights from BBC Films, where they had languished since shortly after the production of the Paul McGann-starring TV movie of 1996; and Russell T Davies, an acclaimed scriptwriter with a life-long love of *Doctor Who*, who made it a condition of his going to work for the BBC that he would be allowed to bring the show back to TV.

The right place was BBC Wales, which was then in the process of being transformed into a major production centre as part of the BBC's commitment to increased regionalisation of its programme-making capacity, and which had just seen the highly talented Julie Gardner appointed as its Head of Drama.

The right time was 2003, when the BBC's finances were in a relatively healthy state, some four years before they were hit by the twin blows of a parsimonious new TV licence fee settlement from the Government and the advent of a global credit crunch that would blight the broadcasting industry as much as any other. Had the idea of reviving *Doctor Who* come up in 2007 rather than 2003, there would have been very little chance of it getting off the ground – and even less chance of it subsequently spawning two spin-off shows in *Torchwood* and *The Sarah Jane Adventures*.

Bringing *Doctor Who* back to TV was one thing; making a success of it was quite another. Many industry pundits believed that family-appeal dramas were a thing of the past in Britain, and that any attempt to resurrect this outmoded genre was doomed to failure. In their eyes, there was now a sharp divide between the audience for adult programmes and the audience for children's programmes (of which fewer and fewer were actually being made), with no viable middle ground between them. Even long-time fans of *Doctor Who*, who were confident that it still had the potential to appeal to a broad spectrum of viewers, were concerned that the producers of any new version might feel the need to revamp the format to such an extent that it would lose its essential ethos and cease to be the same show they knew and loved.

As it turned out, all of these fears and portents of doom proved unjustified. Not only did the new *Doctor Who* delight the great majority of existing fans with its adept and respectful updating of the original concept, but it also – and more importantly from the BBC's perspective – won far higher ratings and far greater critical acclaim than even its most optimistic supporters could have hoped for. More impressive still, its popularity grew ever greater with each passing year, and led to a resurgence in family drama programming more generally, with shows such as the BBC's *Robin Hood* and *Merlin* and ITV's *Primeval*. Further evidence of just how big a hit this new *Doctor Who* was could soon be found in shops up and down the country, which became packed with all manner of tie-in products, surpassing even the level of merchandising seen in the Dalekmania era of the mid-1960s. By 2009, *Doctor Who* had cemented its position as one of Britain's top favourite TV programmes and reaffirmed its status as a cherished national institution.

This incredible success can be credited largely to one man: Russell T Davies. During his five years as showrunner – a position of overall creative control previously almost unknown on British TV productions but commonplace on American ones – Davies wrote more episodes than anyone else, rewrote (sometimes heavily) most of the others and, crucially, set the artistic direction for every aspect of the show. His reputation and influence in the industry, already high before he took on this project, soared to new levels, and saw him given an OBE in the Queen's 2008 Birthday Honours, while *Doctor Who* itself was positively showered with awards.

Of course, Davies did not achieve all of this single-handed. Working alongside him he had his fellow executive producers Julie Gardner and, for Series One only, Mal Young, then the BBC's Controller of Continuing Drama Series. Another important collaborator was Phil Collinson, who served as line producer for Series One to Three and much of Series Four. The numerous skilled directors who were brought in to handle particular episodes also contributed much to the show. Then there was a multitude of other gifted behind-the-scenes team members, both from BBC Wales's own internal production departments and from firms of freelance contractors such as the Mill, responsible for CGI effects work, and Millennium FX, tasked with supplying monster prosthetics. The show's stars, too, were a big factor in its appeal, with two superb Doctors in Christopher Eccleston and David Tennant and a succession of memorable companions, including the hugely popular Billie Piper as Rose Tyler. Casting director Andy Pryor deserves considerable praise, as well, for helping to find not only these fantastic leads but also a whole host of wonderful guest cast members. But as important as all of these other contributors undoubtedly were, in their own respective ways, it was Davies who oversaw everything and provided the strong and focused creative vision that was needed for *Doctor Who* to maintain a level of quality and consistency befitting its newfound status as one of the BBC's flagship drama productions.

Davies realised right from the start that if the new *Doctor Who* was to win a big audience, it would need to counter the then popular perception of the show as a cheap, gaudy fantasy with wobbly sets and makeshift special effects. Although this perception was a largely unfair one, it was deeply ingrained through years of disdainful jibes by newspaper journalists and TV comedians. In order to address this, Davies chose a serious and distinguished lead actor in Eccleston – far removed from the kind of celebrity names previously bandied about in the press, such as magician Paul Daniels and *Baywatch* star David Hasselhoff – and paid careful attention to every aspect of the show's production to make sure that it always looked high-budget and classy. The new Doctor was given a dark-toned, down-to-earth costume with no hint of eccentricity, and his companion was made an ordinary working-class shop girl from the present day. Another good example of Davies's approach is the way he rehabilitated the image of the Daleks, ensuring it was made immediately clear that they could not be defeated simply by climbing a flight of stairs – a misconception that had previously seen them become the butt of countless jokes – and that other aspects of their design that might at first have seemed comical, such as their sink-plunger arm attachments, actually had a deadly purpose. Davies also determined to avoid featuring unconvincing alien planet settings that the viewing public of 2005 might have found hard to take seriously. Instead, he focused the stories on Earth, and mainly contemporary Earth, and gave them a strong domestic context by including semi-regular appearances by Rose's mother Jackie and on-and-off boyfriend Mickey. In this way, he made the show readily accessible to a modern audience by ensuring that, in aesthetic terms, it resembled the popular mainstream dramas with which they were already acquainted.

By the time of Series Two, the public had become sufficiently familiar with and fond of the show that some of these earlier strictures could start to be relaxed. The tenth Doctor was made a rather quirkier character than the ninth, and this was also reflected in his regular costume and hairstyle, which harked back more to the eccentricity of those of his classic-era predecessors. The show also started to feature alien planet settings and more offbeat storylines, 'Love & Monsters' (2006) being the prime example of the latter. These trends continued in Series Three and Four as, with the advent of *Merlin*, *Primeval* and the like, the viewing public became increasingly comfortable with and receptive to fantasy-orientated dramas – a type of programming that, prior to the return of *Doctor Who*, had been largely absent from mainstream British TV for many years.

Throughout all of these developments, Davies had his finger firmly on the pulse of the public's tastes, being careful never to alienate the audience by pushing the fantasy aspects of the show further than they would accept. In addition, Davies made the show more emotionally engaging than it had ever been before, in large part through the introduction of an element of romantic tension between the Doctor and his companions; and again this was made more overt as time went by. By the end of Series Four, there was really no mistaking that Davies was writing the relationship between the Doctor and Rose as an out-and-out love story. This broadened the show's narrative canvas and again helped to secure its phenomenal popularity with the general viewing audience.

Another crucial factor was that, being a long-time fan of *Doctor Who* himself, Davies had a very sound understanding of its established strengths and weaknesses, and knew what his fellow long-time fans wanted to see. He had sufficient faith and confidence in the enduring appeal of the show's great icons to resist any temptation to have them radically overhauled for a modern audience. So there was never any question of commissioning a brand new theme tune, or changing the TARDIS exterior from its anachronistic police box shape, or drastically altering the classic design of the Daleks. Davies was adamant, too, that his version of the show would be no remake, re-imagining or reboot. Despite his first series being referred to as Series One for production and promotional purposes, in story terms it was very much a continuation of the classic-era *Doctor*

Who that had run from 1963 to 1989 and the TV movie of 1996; and Christopher Eccleston's Doctor was always described as the ninth incarnation rather than the first. All of these things were crucial in securing the support and appreciation of the show's dedicated fan-base, which although tiny by comparison with the size of the general audience was extremely passionate and vocal, and could be very influential in shaping public opinion in relation to any potentially contentious innovations.

Davies's mastery of dialogue and character are really second to none, and the fantastic new companions he created for the Doctor – Rose Tyler, Captain Jack Harkness, Martha Jones and Donna Noble – became literally household names, as did some of the new monster races he introduced – the Slitheen and the Ood being perhaps the most memorable. This was really the first time since the 1970s that new *Doctor Who* characters had captured the public imagination in quite this way. The fact that some of the people in Davies's stories were openly gay or bisexual (or even omni-sexual) was highly unusual for family programming on British TV, and arguably served a valuable social purpose by depicting these characters and their relationships in a completely matter-of-fact way that, remarkably, attracted no significant controversy at all – something that would have been unthinkable just a few years earlier.

It seemed, too, that Davies had the happy knack of being able to juxtapose a whole variety of different story elements in ways that fit together perfectly and struck a real chord with the viewing audience, often by reflecting real-world concerns or aspects of contemporary British life – weapons of mass destruction, reality TV shows, mobile phones, sat-navs, political corruption, diet pills, celebrity cameos and so on. Ongoing plot strands such as the Bad Wolf arc in Series One and the Torchwood arc in Series Two were another highly effective innovation that Davies brought to the show.

This is not to say, of course, that Davies's *Doctor Who* scripts were perfect. Sometimes they were marred by poor plotting, with holes big enough to drive a bus through, and he had an occasional tendency to over-egg some of his story ideas – for instance, having the cloned test subjects in 'New Earth' (2006) unbelievably infected with every disease under the sun, rather than just certain specific ones, or setting the main action of 'Utopia' (2007) in the ridiculously far-distant year 100 Trillion. His frequent disregard of basic scientific principles meant that the Doctor could sometimes seem more like a wizard than a Time Lord, using his sonic screwdriver as a magic wand to solve any problem he encountered – unless this was awkward in plot terms, in which case a 'deadlock seal' would be all-too-conveniently discovered. This would no doubt have horrified *Doctor Who*'s principal creator, Sydney Newman, had he been alive to see it, as he was always keen that the Doctor's adventures should have a sound scientific basis, helping to give the show a semi-educational dimension.

Particularly toward the end of his time as showrunner, Davies also made some questionable choices in his characterisation of the Doctor, and allowed the stories to become too self-referential and over-reliant on the show's own mythology, essentially repeating a mistake made by his predecessor John Nathan-Turner in the mid-1980s, albeit thankfully not to such a damaging extent. In addition, his determination to make each series, and each series finale in particular, bigger and more dramatic than the last ultimately resulted in the stories becoming overblown and excessive. Davies himself apparently expressed concern to Julie Gardner that 'The End of Time' might seem like a piece of continuity-heavy fan fiction, and that description is not too far wide of the mark. As at the end of Jon Pertwee's era as the Doctor, from which Davies had arguably drawn more inspiration than any other in the show's history, it seemed that a certain loss of freshness and impetus was setting in. However, an excess of ambition is certainly a far more forgivable sin than a lack of ambition, and all things considered, the weaknesses in Davies's scripts were still far outweighed by the strengths.

Not only was Davies a great writer for *Doctor Who*, but he was also a great production team leader – a rare combination of talents. His sheer delight with the show that he and his colleagues were making, as frequently expressed in *Doctor Who Confidential* interviews, episode podcasts and the like, struck some fans as being smug and self-congratulatory, but was evidently entirely genuine. His relentlessly upbeat tone and obvious pride in his team's achievements had an inspirational effect on all those who worked with him, motivating many to contribute in ways that went far beyond the call of duty – putting in additional hours, making extra effort and, in the case of freelance contractors such as the Mill, even occasionally doing pieces of unbudgeted work for free, simply as a favour. This not only made the production a very happy one to be a part of, as attested to in countless interviews with people from both behind and in front of the cameras, but was also very much to the show's benefit in terms of the quality of the transmitted episodes.

While it could sometimes seem from the unstintingly complimentary comments of his closest associates that Davies had essentially surrounded himself with a group of 'yes men' (and women) who were entirely uncritical of all his scripting and production decisions, this was to some extent a public façade that did not fully reflect the behind-the-scenes reality. Any high-pressure working environment is bound to produce the occasional row, and nerves were particularly frayed during parts of the making of Series One, when everyone was still learning the ropes and getting to grips with the production. It was certainly not all sweetness and light, whatever those involved might have sought to suggest. More generally, Julie Gardner, Phil Collinson and others did occasionally challenge Davies over aspects of his work about which they had reservations. Fundamentally, though, they saw it as their job to assist Davies in putting his vision of *Doctor Who* on screen. His was the guiding hand and the creative wellspring, and the rest of the team were there essentially to support him in achieving his aims.

In doing this, they were helped considerably by the fact that they had a sympathetic BBC hierarchy, and a canny and ever-growing inside knowledge of the workings of the organisation. This enabled them to get the best out of the BBC's resources and keep the show to the forefront of the management's attention. Amongst the many benefits this brought, there were the two spin-off shows, *Torchwood* and *The Sarah Jane Adventures*; two factual series, *Doctor Who Confidential* and *Totally Doctor Who*; two special scenes produced for the *Children in Need* telethon; two animated series, 'The Infinite Quest' and 'Dreamland'; the 'Attack of the Graske' interactive game; a wealth of online content, including a specially-shot 'Tardisode' trailer for each of the Series Two episodes; two major *Doctor Who* concerts, including the 2008 Proms event, complete with the 'Music of the Spheres' mini-episode; and a whole host of other publicity-generating activities. This all helped to make the experience of being a *Doctor Who* fan at the beginning of the 21st Century a very rich and rewarding one indeed.

This, then, is the Russell T Davies legacy: a five-year odyssey of largely wonderful *Doctor Who* episodes that left the show deservedly more popular and critically-lauded than at any other time in its long history, and that stand as testament to his brilliance both as a writer and as an executive producer. Truly a golden age for *Doctor Who*.

PART SIX
APPENDICES

APPENDIX A
DREAMLAND

'Dreamland' was the sixth animated *Doctor Who* story to be produced, following on from 'Death Comes to Time' (2001), 'Real Time' (2002), 'Shada' (2003), 'Scream of the Shalka' (2003) and 'The Infinite Quest' (2007).[63] However, of those earlier serials, only 'The Infinite Quest' had been made for TV broadcast – the others had all been conceived as webcasts for the official *Doctor Who* website, and in the first three instances had been more audio dramas set to pictures than true animations. It was thus 'The Infinite Quest' that served as the main precedent for 'Dreamland', which was also intended from the outset to be shown on TV – initially split into six short episodes[64] on the BBC's Red Button interactive service, formerly known as BBCi, then in omnibus form on BBC Two, BBC HD and CBBC. As with 'The Infinite Quest', the omnibus version was also to be released subsequently on DVD. One important difference between 'The Infinite Quest' and 'Dreamland', though, was that whereas the former had utilised 2D Flash animation, the latter was to be realised with more ambitious 3D computer animation produced by the Brighton-based Littleloud Studios.

Commissioned to script 'Dreamland' was Phil Ford who, quite apart from his prior credits on 'The Waters of Mars' and several episodes of *The Sarah Jane Adventures*, had extensive experience of writing for animation on *Gerry Anderson's New Captain Scarlet* (ITV, 2005). Ford was given a free hand in devising the story, and chose to base it around the aftermath of the supposed UFO crash at Roswell, New Mexico, in the summer of 1947.[65] He wanted 'Dreamland' to have something of the feel of a 1950s B-movie, with familiar elements of UFO lore such as Men in Black, cattle mutilations and stereotypical Grey aliens, and to be the kind of story that *Doctor Who* would not have the budget to achieve as a live-action production. As in the five main gap year specials, the Doctor would be travelling alone, but would team up with some new friends during the course of events.[66]

---

[63] The earliest serious attempt to make an animated series was in the early 1990s. This was to have been produced by Nelvana for the Canadian Broadcasting Corporation, but fell through after the completion by artist Ted Bastien of initial concept drawings, which he worked on for almost a year. Some of these drawings have since been made available to view online at: www.cbc.ca/planetofthedoctor/tb_gallery.html.

[64] The original plan was to have seven episodes, but it was then decided that the first two should be combined into one approximately double-length instalment, reducing the total to six.

[65] Ford had earlier written the Roswell flying saucer into his story 'Prisoner of the Judoon' (2009) in Series Three of *The Sarah Jane Adventures*, and the one in 'Dreamland' was drawn to match that design, preserving continuity between the two.

[66] Although transmitted after 'The Waters of Mars', 'Dreamland' may take place

In the director's chair was *Doctor Who* script editor Gary Russell, who had taken on the same responsibility on 'The Infinite Quest' and had extensive past experience of working on the *Doctor Who* audio CD dramas produced by Big Finish. Big Finish's regular London recording venue, Moat Studios, was also used for the voice work on 'Dreamland', which was carried out in two sessions, on Monday 4 May and Saturday 9 May 2009 respectively. Amongst the guest cast members performing alongside David Tennant as the Doctor were Georgia Moffett and Tim Howar as one-off companions Cassie and Jimmy; David Warner as Lord Azlok, leader of the monstrous Viperox; and Stuart Milligan as Colonel Stark of the US military. Moffett, the daughter of fifth Doctor actor Peter Davison, had previously appeared as Jenny in the Series Four episode 'The Doctor's Daughter' and was Tennant's real-life girlfriend. She adopted an American accent for 'Dreamland', drawing on that of her mother, US-born actress Sandra Dickinson.

The main part of the animation work was done after the voice recording was completed, over the summer of 2009, with the pictures being matched to the dialogue.

The six episodes of 'Dreamland' were first transmitted over six consecutive days from 21 November 2009, leaving a good month's interval before the tenth Doctor's regeneration in 'The End of Time'. Fan response was largely positive. Ford's scripts in particular drew many plaudits for their sharp and witty dialogue, exciting action sequences, strong ideas and sound plotting. The actors' performances were also widely admired. Reaction to the animation was more mixed. The detailed and well-realised backgrounds were generally praised, but the character likenesses were felt by some to be rather crude, certainly by comparison with those in 'The Infinite Quest', and their jerky and unrealistic style of movement drew heavy criticism, being commonly likened to that of the puppets in Gerry Anderson's famous 'Supermarionation' shows such as *Stingray* and *Thunderbirds*.

---

before that in terms of the Doctor's timeline. His demeanour betrays no feelings of angst about his forthcoming regeneration, as might be expected if this was set between 'The Waters of Mars' and 'The End of Time'.

DREAMLAND

Writer: Phil Ford
Director: Gary Russell

DEBUT TRANSMISSION DETAILS

BBC Red Button
Episode One. Date: 21 November 2009. Time: 7.25 pm. Duration: 12' 46".
Episode Two. Date: 22 November 2009. Time: 5.15 pm. Duration: 7' 33".
Episode Three. Date: 23 November 2009. Time: 4.00 pm. Duration: 7' 23".
Episode Four. Date: 24 November 2009. Time: 4.00 pm. Duration: 6' 49".
Episode Five. Date: 25 November 2009. Time: 4.00 pm. Duration: 7' 34".
Episode Six. Date: 26 November 2009. Time: 4.00 pm. Duration: 7' 37".

BBC Two
Omnibus. Date: 5 December 2009. Time: 10.00 am. Duration: 44' 20"

CAST

David Tennant (The Doctor), Georgia Moffett (Cassie Rice), Tim Howar (Jimmy Stalkingwolf), David Warner (Lord Azlok), Stuart Milligan (Colonel Stark), Peter Guinness (Mister Dread), Clarke Peters (Night Eagle), Nicholas Rowe (Rivesh Mantilax), Lisa Bowerman (Saruba Velak), Ryan McCluskey (Soldiers).

PRODUCTION TEAM

Animation Studio: Littleloud
Animation Director: Darren Garrett
Art Director and Character Design: Paul Simpson
Animation Co-Director: Nik Faulkner
Visual Effects: Jim Howells
3D Design: Rebecca Green, Robin Konieczny, Adam Sharp
Lead Animator: Tim Sanpher
Animator: Nora O'Sullivan, Kristian Antonelli, Stu Short
Concept Design: Tiernen Trevallion
Sound Design: Dan Ward
Offline Editor: Dominic Jones
Online Editor: Matt Mullins
Production Assistant: Sara Khangaroot, Alice Parsons
Animation Producer: David Jacklin, Georgina Muggeridge, Saffron Allwood

With thanks to the BBC National Orchestra of Wales
Original Theme Music: Ron Grainer

Casting Director: Andy Pryor CDG
Music: Murray Gold
Sound Effects: Paul Jefferies, Darran Clement, Howard Eaves
Dubbing Mixer: Peter Jeffreys
Music Editor: Doug Sinclair
Voice Recording: The Moat Studios
Production Executive: Julie Scott

Interactive Producer: Ed Cross
Senior Producer: Mat Fidell

Executive Producer, Interactive: Anwen Aspden
Executive Producer for CBBC: Sarah Muller
Executive Producer: Russell T Davies, Julie Gardner, Piers Wenger

CBBC

PLOT

Eleven years after the June 1947 crash of a UFO in Roswell, New Mexico, the Doctor visits Nevada in search of chilli. At a diner, he meets a young waitress, Cassie Rice, and her Native American friend, Jimmy Stalkingwolf. After being confronted by some mysterious men in black and attacked by a huge monster – a Viperox battle drone – the three of them are rescued by the US Air Force and taken to their nearby base, Area 51, otherwise known as Dreamland. There they meet the base commander, Colonel Stark, who turns out to be in an alliance with the Viperox leader, Lord Azlok. The Viperox are trying to obtain a genetic warfare weapon that a race of grey-skinned aliens, whose planet they have ravaged, intend to use to destroy them. One of these aliens, Saruba Velak, was found alive aboard the ship that crashed in 1947 and is now being held captive at Dreamland. Her husband, Rivesh Mantilax, has come to Earth to try to rescue her, but has so far been prevented from doing so by the military. Colonel Stark wants the weapon for his own purposes: to wipe out the US's Cold War adversary, the Soviet Union. The men in black are robots working for the Alliance of Shades, who also want the weapon, their mission being to hide alien activities on primitive planets like Earth. The Doctor eventually gains control of the weapon and adapts it to release a powerful ultra-sonic wave that drives the Viperox – who will one day become a peace-loving race – away from Earth. Reunited, Saruba Velak and Rivesh Matilax leave in the latter's spaceship. The Doctor gives the weapon to Colonel Stark, who has seen the error of his ways, to ensure that the Viperox do not return. He then departs in the TARDIS, leaving Cassie and Jimmy holding hands.

PRESS REACTION

- '[In] a year of *Doctor Who* specials, this little gem deserves to be embraced as every bit as special as its live-action counterparts. And that's saying something, considering the CG animation is, to put it politely, basic … But "Dreamland" is a perfect example of that old adage that a decent story is more important than flashy visuals. A hugely entertaining romp liberally sprinkled with some killer one-liners ...., it feels like a Pertwee adventure given a Russell T Davies spit and polish. Oh yes, as the Doctor would say, underground bases, lots of running and plenty of chances for our errant Time Lord to deflate pompous military authority.' Dave Golder, *SFX* website, 3 December 2009.

APPENDIX B
DOCTOR WHO AT THE PROMS

On Sunday 27 July 2008, the Royal Albert Hall in London hosted the first *Doctor Who* Proms concert. This was inspired in part by the success of the *Doctor Who – A Celebration* event staged at the Millennium Centre in Cardiff on 19 November 2006 for the BBC's *Children in Need* charity appeal. Like that earlier event, it featured selections of Murray Gold's incidental music from *Doctor Who*, on this occasion with some classical pieces interspersed, all played by a full orchestra and complemented by appropriate episode clips shown on a number of large video screens suspended around the auditorium, the main screen being right above the stage. The *Doctor Who* pieces were conducted by Ben Foster, and Gold himself also appeared on stage toward the end of the concert, playing piano.

The main presenter was Freema Agyeman, while certain pieces of music were introduced by guest presenters Camille Coduri and Noel Clarke and, making a surprise unpublicised appearance, Catherine Tate. Actors in various monster costumes meanwhile moved amongst the audience, and even Davros put in an appearance, portrayed as in 'The Stolen Earth'/'Journey's End' (2008) by Julian Bleach. David Tennant was unable to attend in person, owing to his work on the RSC production of *Hamlet*, but appeared in the specially-recorded mini-episode 'Music of the Spheres'.[67]

The concert was broadcast live on BBC Radio Three and BBC iPlayer, and could be accessed for seven days afterwards via the 'listen again' facility on the BBC website. It was also, however, video-recorded for later TV transmission. That transmission eventually took place on BBC One and BBC HD at 1.50 pm on 1 January 2009, and took the form of a 59' 10" selection of highlights, omitting all of the non-*Doctor Who* music, the Camille Coduri and Noel Clarke segment and the Tim Phillips-performed vocal number 'Song for Ten'. 1.7 million viewers tuned in, representing a 12.6% audience share. This version of the concert was subsequently included as an extra on the DVD release of 'The Next Doctor' from 2 Entertain. A longer, 94' 16" version of the concert was made available to view on continuous loop on the BBC's Red Button interactive service on Sunday 11 January. This reinstated the previously-omitted material, but had a slightly altered running order. It has not been commercially released at the time of writing.

The on-screen credits for the concert were as follows. Those marked with an asterisk were given only on the 94' 16" version.

---

[67] See *Monsters Within – The Unofficial and Unauthorised Guide to Doctor Who 2008* (Telos Publishing, 2008) for full details of this production.

APPENDIX B: DOCTOR WHO AT THE PROMS

CREDITS

Presented by: Freema Agyeman
Guest Presenter: Catherine Tate, Camille Coduri*, Noel Clarke*
Music Composed by: Murray Gold
Original Theme Music: Ron Grainer

'Music of the Spheres'
Writer: Russell T Davies
Director: Euros Lyn
Producer: Catrin Defis

Soloist: Melanie Pappenheim, Tim Phillips*
Conductor and Arranger: Ben Foster
Conductor: Stephen Bell*

BBC Philharmonic
Leader: Yuri Torchinsky

London Philharmonic Choir

For BBC Philharmonic
Senior Producer: Mike George
Programme Manager: Stephen Rinker
Projects Manager: Martin Maris

Monsters
Davros: Julian Bleach
Voice of the Daleks: Nicholas Briggs
Dalek Operator: Barnaby Edwards
The Graske: Jimmy Vee
Hero Monsters: Paul Kasey
Commander Skorr: Dan Starkey
Other Monsters: Scott Baker, Alain Glet, Ian Hilditch, Ken Hosking, Andy Jones,
Ruari Mears, Adam Sweet, Joe White

Animatronics: Colin Newman
Prosthetics and Creatures: Millennium FX
Costume Design: Louise Page

Engineering Manager: Jeremy Turner
Camera Supervisor: Vince Spooner
Lighting Gaffer: Mark Gardiner
Lighting Desk Operator: David Bishop
Event Sound: Phil Wright, Sound by Design
Floor Manager: Richard Wyn Jones, Donna Tait
Projections: Anna Valley Display
Screen Sequence Editor: Gary Skipton

END OF TEN

Screen Sequence Edit Producer: Paul Symonds
Production Team: Lindsey Sisk, Llywela Jones, Sue Perry-Grech, Anwen Rees
Screens Vision Mixer: Llinos Metcalf
Screens Director: Rhian Williams
Production Assistant: Sian Parry
Vision Mixer: Hilary Briegel
Sound Supervisor: Julian Gough
Dubbing Mixer: Peter Jeffreys
Colourist: Jon Everett
Film Editor: Dylan Goch
Lighting Director: Bernie Davis
Movement Director: Denni Sayers
Production Designer: Eryl Ellis
Brand Executive: Edward Russell
Production Executive: Julie Scott
Line Producer: Jo Marks
Executive Producer: Julie Gardner, Russell T Davies
Producer: Paul Bullock
Director: Rhodri Huw

BBC Wales

APPENDIX C
DOCTOR WHO CONFIDENTIAL

As had been the case for every other episode of *Doctor Who* since it returned to TV in 2005, each of the five gap year specials was accompanied by its own dedicated *Doctor Who Confidential* documentary on BBC Three. In addition, six other programmes from the same team were transmitted: 'Christmas Moments' on Christmas Day 2008; 'Confidential – At the Proms', viewable only on the Red Button interactive service, on 1 January 2009; 'The Eleventh Doctor' on 3 January 2009; and three themed specials with the umbrella title 'Doctor Who's Greatest Moments' on 20 August ('The Doctor'), 27 August ('The Companions') and 3 September 2009 ('The Enemies') respectively.[68] Full debut transmission details are given below.

'The Eleventh Doctor', uniquely, went out on BBC One rather than BBC Three, and was the vehicle used by the BBC to announce Matt Smith's casting as the eleventh Doctor. As such, it attracted a remarkable 6.30 million viewers; by far the largest audience that an episode of *Doctor Who Confidential* had ever had. Generally, the show attracted around half a million viewers on its BBC Three debut transmissions, although 'Allons-y!', the episode accompanying 'The End of Time' Part Two, was exceptional in reaching 1.21 million.

Unusually, full-length versions of the regular *Doctor Who Confidential* programmes were included on the DVD releases of their respective *Doctor Who* specials, rather than shorter cut-down versions as in previous years. There were just a few music substitutions made and, in the case of 'Confidential Christmas 2008', the episode accompanying 'The Next Doctor', a few minor edits. In fact, in a very surprising first, the DVD version of 'Desert Storm', the episode accompanying 'Planet of the Dead', was over eight minutes *longer* than the debut transmission version, running to 57' 03". This longer version did not receive a TV screening until 1 January 2010, when it was shown on the BBC HD channel.

The 'Doctor Who's Greatest Moments' programmes also received a full-length DVD release, on a bonus disc packaged with the 'Dreamland' animated adventure, although again with some music substitutions.

---

[68] A short non-broadcast *Doctor Who Confidential* production was also included on the *Cybermen Collection* DVD release from 2 Entertain. This was an introduction by David Tennant, with clips from new-era *Doctor Who* episodes featuring the Cybermen, and ran to 9' 54".

SERIES CREDITS[69]

Narrated by: Anthony Head (4.14, 4.16, 4.17, 4.18, CM, PR, ED), Noel Clarke (4.15), Jo Whiley (GM1, GM2, GM3)

PRODUCTION TEAM

Camera: Mark Chandler (4.14, CM), James Daniels (4.14, 4.17, 4.18, CM, GM2), Dewi Davies (4.14, CM), Justin Davies (4.14, CM, PR), Alex Hansen (4.14, CM), Eric Huyton (4.14, 4.16, 4.17, 4.18, CM), Aled Jenkins (4.14, 4.16, 4.17, 4.18, CM, GM1, GM2, GM3), Andy Smith (all except PR), Huw Walters (4.14, CM), Mark Bond (PR), Roy Estabrook (PR), Richard Stevenson (ED), Paul Mongey (4.15), Jon Rees (4.15, 4.16, 4.17, 4.18), Mark Thompson (GM1, GM2, GM3), Oli Russell (GM2)
Camera Assistant: John Shuker (ED)
Sound: Steve Hoy (4.14, 4.15, CM, ED, GM1, GM2, GM3), Kevin Meredith (4.14, 4.15, CM), Brian Murrell (4.14, CM), Will Planitzer (4.14, CM, PR, GM2), Jon Thomas (4.14, 4.16, 4.17, 4.18, CM, GM1, GM2, GM3), David Ferguson (PR), Mazyar Tajiki (4.15, PR), Dafydd Parry (4.16, 4.17, 4.18), Brian Ullah (4.17, 4.18), Rob Kreeger (GM1, GM2, GM3), Ryan Windley (GM1, GM2, GM3), Jonny Stothert (GM2)
Runner: Stuart Laws (4.14, PR), Claire Riley (all except 4.15), Robert Wootton (4.14), James Bowen (4.14, 4.16, 4.17, 4.18, GM1, GM2, GM3)
Edit Assistant: Claire Riley (4.15)
Researcher: Nathan Landeg (PR), Robert Wootton[70] (4.15, 4.16, 4.17, 4.18, ED, GM1, GM2, GM3), Matthew Andrews (4.15, 4.16, 4.17, 4.18, GM1, GM2, GM3), Stuart Laws (4.16, 4.17, 4.18, GM1, GM2, GM3)
Assistant Producer: Ian Hay (4.14, 4.15, 4.16, 4.17, 4.18, CM, ED, GM1, GM3), Hannah Williams (all except ED), Donovan Keogh (4.16, 4.17, 4.18), James Brailsford (GM1)
Production Accountant: Kevin Rickwood
Production Team Assistant[71]: Emma Chapman (4.16, 4.17, 4.18)
Production Co-ordinator: Tors Grantham (4.14, 4.15, 4.16, 4.17, 4.18, CM, PR), Megan Pinches (4.16, 4.17, 4.18, GM1, GM2)
Production Manager: Katy Cartwright, Kirsty Reid (4.14, PR), Nathalie McCarty

---

[69] Where an episode number (or more than one) appears in brackets after a person's name in the listing, this means that they were credited only on the episode (or episodes) indicated. Otherwise, the person concerned was credited on all episodes. The episode numbers given are the same as for the corresponding *Doctor Who* specials, i.e. 4.14 = 'The Next Doctor'; 4.15 = 'Planet of the Dead'; 4.16 = 'The Waters of Mars'; 4.17 = 'The End of Time' Part One; 4.18 = 'The End of Time' Part Two. The six additional episodes made by the *Doctor Who Confidential* team are identified with the following initials: CM = 'Christmas Moments'; PR = 'Confidential – At the Proms'; ED = 'The Eleventh Doctor'; GM1 = 'Doctor Who's Greatest Moments: The Doctor'; GM2 = 'Doctor Who's Greatest Moments: The Companions'; GM3 = 'Doctor Who's Greatest Moments: The Enemies'.
[70] Credited as 'Rob Wootton' on ED.
[71] Credit given on 4.16 as 'Team Assistant'.

(CM)
Production Executive: Stan Matthews
Titles & Graphics: Component Graphics (GM1, GM2, GM3)
Title Music: Slam & Saw Productions (GM1, GM2, GM3)
Editor: James Brailsford (4.14, PR, ED), Simon Horobin (CM), Rob Mansell (ED)
Colourist: Jon Everett (4.14, 4.15, 4.17, 4.18, GM3), Duncan Bragg (CM), Matt Mullins (4.16)
Online Editor: Matt Mullins (4.14, PR), Mark Hardyman (GM1, GM2)
Dubbing Mixer: Mark Ferda
Offline Editor: Rob Mansell (GM1), Marius Grose (GM2), Rahim Mastafa (GM3)
Editor: Gary Skipton (4.15), Lizzie Minnion (4.16), John Parker (4.17, 4.18)

Edit Producer: Paul Symonds (4.16), Philip Powell (GM1), James Brailsford (GM2, GM3), Ian Hay (GM2)
Executive Producer: Mark Cossey
Executive Producer for *Doctor Who at the Proms*: Paul Bullock (PR)
Executive Producer for *Doctor Who*: Russell T Davies, Julie Gardner, Steven Moffat (ED), Piers Wenger (ED)

Producer: Zoë Rushton, Adam Page (GM1, GM2, GM3)
Series Producer: Gillane Seaborne

BBC Wales

EPISODE GUIDE

The episode durations quoted below are for the versions as originally transmitted. They may be a few seconds shorter than the timings of the complete programmes on the BBC's master tapes, as each episode tended to be cut into very slightly by the preceding and/or following continuity caption and announcement.

REGULAR EPISODES

4.14 – CONFIDENTIAL CHRISTMAS 2008

DEBUT TRANSMISSION DETAILS

BBC Three
Date: 25 December 2008. Scheduled time: 7.00 pm. Actual time: n/k.
Duration: 57' 26"

PUBLICITY BLURB

Doctor Who Confidential goes behind the scenes for a double dosage of the Doctor this Christmas. Catch up with the two Doctors and find out what makes this year's *Doctor Who* Christmas special so special.

4.15 – DESERT STORM

DEBUT TRANSMISSION DETAILS

BBC Three
Date: 11 April 2009. Scheduled time: 8.30 pm. Actual time: n/k.
Duration: 48' 39"

PUBLICITY BLURB

Doctor Who goes abroad! The cast and crew travel to Dubai to film the Easter special and *Confidential* are there to capture every shot, scene and sandstorm. How do you get a double decker bus to the desert? How do you shoot a drama in horrendous weather conditions? And how do you match a vast Arabian landscape with the cold Cardiff winter? The answers are revealed in this hour-long *Confidential* special.

4.16 – IS THERE LIFE ON MARS?

DEBUT TRANSMISSION DETAILS

BBC Three
Date: 15 November 2009. Scheduled time: 8.00 pm. Actual time: 8.01 pm.
Duration: 57' 54"

PUBLICITY BLURB

It is the beginning of the end for David Tennant's Doctor, and *Confidential* is on a mission to Mars to capture the strange goings-on in Bowie Base One. The programme goes behind the mask of the monsters as the waters rise, causing the production team a variety of problems. There are explosions, robots and gallons of water as the Doctor meets one of his heroes and battles against his greatest foe – time itself.

4.17– LORDS AND MASTERS

DEBUT TRANSMISSION DETAILS

BBC Three
Date: 25 December 2009. Scheduled time: 7.00 pm. Actual time: n/k.
Duration: 57' 00"

PUBLICITY BLURB

Doctor Who Confidential goes behind the scenes for the tenth Doctor's penultimate episode. It's the beginning of the end for the Doctor, and the cast and crew go on an action-packed journey towards the final showdown. With stunts more ambitious than ever and interviews with all the key players, *Confidential* gives an up close and personal account of the most thrilling two-part finale a viewer could wish for. Featuring interviews with David Tennant, John Simm and Bernard Cribbins.

4.18 – ALLONS-Y!

DEBUT TRANSMISSION DETAILS

BBC Three/BBC HD
Date: 1 January 2010. Scheduled time: 7.55 pm. Actual time: 7.56 pm.
Duration: 57′ 41″

PUBLICITY BLURB

Doctor Who Confidential gets up close and personal with David Tennant as he contemplates his last days as the Doctor. On set for his final episode, his final scenes, his final words, the tenth Doctor's time has come to an end and *Confidential* is there to follow him every step of the way.

Witnessing everything from his final showdown, his poignant goodbyes and, of course, his regeneration, this intimate account of TV history pulls out all the stops for the ultimate *Doctor Who* finale.

NOTES

- This was the first episode of *Doctor Who* to be simultaneously broadcast on BBC Three and BBC HD. Other episodes had also been shown on BBC HD, but at a later time or date than their debut BBC Three transmission.

ADDITIONAL EPISODES

CHRISTMAS MOMENTS

DEBUT TRANSMISSION DETAILS

BBC Three
Date: 25 December 2008. Scheduled time: 8.00 pm. Actual time: n/k.
Duration: 10′ 03″

PUBLICITY BLURB

A look back at the best moments from the Doctor's festive adventures.

NOTES

- Publicity material and programme listings for this episode gave the title as 'Top 5 Christmas Moments'. However, the on-screen title was just 'Christmas Moments'.
- On debut transmission, this went out directly after 'Confidential Christmas 2008'.

CONFIDENTIAL – AT THE PROMS

DEBUT TRANSMISSION DETAILS

BBC Three
Date: 1 January 2009. Scheduled time: n/a. Actual time: n/a.
Duration: 28' 02"

PUBLICITY BLURB

None.

NOTE

- This episode was made available to view only on the BBC's Red Button interactive service, where it was shown in a continuous loop over a period of several hours from 2.50 pm onwards.

THE ELEVENTH DOCTOR

DEBUT TRANSMISSION DETAILS

BBC One
Date: 3 January 2009. Scheduled time: 5.35 pm. Actual time: 5.34 pm.
Duration: 34' 44"

PUBLICITY BLURB

It has been 45 years since the TARDIS first landed on BBC One. Join us as we look at the lives of the ten Doctors, their most heroic moments and terrifying adventures, as well as the monsters, costumes and companions which have defined them.

NOTE

- Initial publicity for this episode gave it the title 'The Ten Doctors' and made no mention of the fact that it was to announce Matt Smith as the eleventh Doctor. This was to help preserve the secrecy and surprise.

DOCTOR WHO'S GREATEST MOMENTS: THE DOCTOR

DEBUT TRANSMISSION DETAILS

BBC Three
Date: 20 August 2009. Scheduled time: 8.00 pm. Actual time: n/k.
Duration: 56' 25"

PUBLICITY BLURB

Series taking viewers on a journey through time and space to relive action from the legendary sci-fi show, featuring exclusive interviews with key actors offering unique insights on the classic moments. David Tennant, John Barrowman, David Morrissey and *The League of Gentlemen*'s Mark Gatiss look back at the Time Lord's greatest moments.

DOCTOR WHO'S GREATEST MOMENTS: THE COMPANIONS

DEBUT TRANSMISSION DETAILS

BBC Three
Date: 27 August 2009. Scheduled time: 8.00 pm. Actual time: n/k.
Duration: 56' 00"

PUBLICITY BLURB

Series taking viewers on a journey through time and space to relive action from the legendary sci-fi show, featuring exclusive interviews with key actors offering unique insights on the classic moments. David Tennant, Billie Piper, Catherine Tate, Freema Agyeman and John Barrowman go through the greatest moments of the Doctor's finest companions.

DOCTOR WHO'S GREATEST MOMENTS: THE ENEMIES

DEBUT TRANSMISSION DETAILS

BBC Three
Date: 3 September 2009. Scheduled time: 8.00 pm. Actual time: n/k.
Duration: 56' 30"

PUBLICITY BLURB

Series taking viewers on a journey through time and space to relive action from the legendary sci-fi show, featuring exclusive interviews with key actors offering unique insights on the classic moments. The Doctor has faced a whole galaxy full of formidable foes. David Tennant and a host of stars including John Barrowman, Derek Jacobi, Zoe Wannamaker, Freema Agyeman and Sarah Parish look through the greatest moments of his deadliest enemies.

APPENDIX D
RATINGS AND RANKINGS

Series Four had closed with *Doctor Who*'s ratings hitting a remarkable high, 'Journey's End' being watched by an amazing 10.57 million people on its BBC One debut – no less than 49% of the total TV audience at that time – and capturing the coveted number one spot in the weekly viewing chart for the very first time in the show's long history. This capped a season that had achieved an average debut-transmission rating of 8.05 million viewers – the highest since the show returned to TV in 2005. The big question was, would this phenomenal level of popularity be maintained for the gap year specials, or would the lack of a full new series in 2009 see public interest in *Doctor Who* start to wane?

The table below shows what happened. It gives, for each special, the estimated total number of viewers aged four and over (corrected and adjusted to include those who recorded the episode to watch within the same week), in millions, for all of the BBC One, BBC HD and BBC Three transmissions that occurred within a fortnight of the BBC One debut. It also gives, in the fourth column, the number of hits recorded on the BBC's iPlayer service. The final column then gives a total audience reach figure.

EPISODE	BBC ONE DEBUT	BBC HD DEBUT	BBC THREE DEBUT	BBC ONE REPEAT	BBC HD REPEAT	BBC THREE REPEAT	BBC iPLAYER	ALL
'The Next Doctor'	13.10	n/a	0.39	2.27	n/a	n/a	0.58	16.34
'Planet of the Dead'	9.54	0.21	0.91	1.98	0.06	0.56	0.67	13.93
'The Waters of Mars'	9.94	0.38	0.70	n/a	n/a	n/a	0.61	11.63
'The End of Time' Pt 1	11.57	0.47	1.18	2.24	0.10*	0.50*	0.81	16.87*
'The End of Time' Pt 2	11.79	0.48	0.70*	1.91	0.10*	0.50*	0.77	16.25*
Average	11.19	n/a	n/a	n/a	n/a	n/a	0.67	14.99*

n/a = Not applicable, as there was no such transmission with a fortnight of the BBC One debut transmission. Column averages are given only in columns where there is an entry for each of the five specials.
* = Estimated, as the exact figure is not known.

Source for viewing figures: Broadcasters' Audience Research Board (BARB)
Source for iPlayer figures: BBC

While it is difficult to discern any meaningful trend from these figures in relation to those for Series Four, particularly in view of the impact of seasonal scheduling factors, there is one thing that comes across loud and clear: the gap year specials saw *Doctor Who* continuing to enjoy an incredible level of popularity. 'The Next Doctor', 'The End of Time' Part One and 'The End of Time' Part Two all had a total audience reach comparable to, if not slightly better than, that of around 16 million achieved by 'Voyage of the Damned' at Christmas 2007; and 'Planet of the Dead' and 'The Waters of Mars', the first specials not to be transmitted over a Christmas period, also did exceptionally well by any standards. The BBC One debut figures invariably put *Doctor Who* in the upper reaches of the TV chart for the week of transmission. In fact, the 11.79 million for 'The End of Time' Part Two was sufficient to see it secure the number two spot in the chart, just behind the episode of *EastEnders* that immediately followed it on air – an order that would have been reversed, giving *Doctor Who* its second number one placing, were it not for the fact that (arguably rather strangely) the chart does not take into account viewers who tune in to simultaneous BBC HD broadcasts.

The specials were not only watched by large numbers of people but also greatly enjoyed by them. The BBC's official Appreciation Index (AI) figures for the five BBC One debut transmissions were a uniformly excellent 86, 88, 88, 87 and 89 respectively, giving an average of just below 88. The average figures for Series One to Four were 82, 84, 86 and 88 respectively, so there is no doubt that the five specials maintained *Doctor Who*'s level of success on that measure too.

An indication of the quality of the specials from the point of view of fans can be gleaned from the online polls conducted on the most popular *Doctor Who* fan forum on the internet – specifically, Outpost Gallifrey for 'The Next Doctor' and 'Planet of the Dead' and Gallifrey Base, the *de facto* successor to Outpost Gallifrey when the latter closed down in the summer of 2009, for 'The Waters of Mars' and the two parts of 'The End of Time'. An average of 3,847 voters participated in these polls, ranging from a low of 3,672 for 'The Next Doctor' to a high of 3,941 for 'The End of Time' Part Two. In the Outpost Gallifrey polls, each special was given a mark of between one and five by each voter, with five being the highest. In the Gallifrey Base polls, the marks were out of ten, with ten being the highest. The percentages in the table below have been calculated by adding together the total number of marks received by each special (as of 10 May 2010) and dividing by the maximum that could have been achieved if everyone who voted had given top marks.

EPISODE	FAN RATING
'The Next Doctor'	73.55%
'Planet of the Dead'	70.03%
'The Waters of Mars'	83.11%
'The End of Time' Part One	72.08%
'The End of Time' Part Two	81.30%

Based on these scores – which show rather more variation than the AI figures for the general viewing audience – the fans' order of preference for the specials was:

1. 'The Waters of Mars'
2. 'The End of Time' Part Two
3. 'The Next Doctor'
4. 'The End of Time' Part One
5. 'Planet of the Dead'

Comparing the percentages with those recorded in previous years, it would seem that the specials were not amongst the fans' favourite episodes. The average fan ratings for Series One to Four were a fairly consistent 82%, 82%, 81% and 81% respectively, with each series having several episodes over 90%, reaching a high of 95% for 'The Family of Blood' (2007). Judged in this context, it would seem that even the most well-received of the specials – 'The Waters of Mars' and 'The End of Time' Part Two – were no better than average, by the fans' reckoning. 'Planet of the Dead' in particular clearly failed to strike much of a chord, ranking sixth lowest of all the 60 episodes produced during Russell T Davies's time as showrunner, albeit still quite a bit above the all-time low of 65% gained by 'Fear Her' (2006).

To conclude, set out below, for what it's worth, is this author's own ranking of the specials, again working downwards from favourite to least favourite – although I should perhaps add that my views on this tend to change from time to time!

1. 'The End of Time' Part One
2. 'The Next Doctor'
3. 'Planet of the Dead'
4. 'The Waters of Mars'
5. 'The End of Time' Part Two

APPENDIX E
ORIGINAL NOVELS

During the period covered by this book – from the build up to transmission of the gap year specials through to the end of the tenth Doctor's era – BBC Books published a further nine titles in their ongoing range of hardback *Doctor Who* novels, plus another two paperback Quick Reads books. Summary details are as follows.

28: THE STORY OF MARTHA

Writer: Dan Abnett with David Roden, Steve Lockley & Paul Lewis, Robert Shearman, and Simon Jowett
Publication date: 26 December 2008
Series Consultant: Justin Richards; Project Editor: Steve Tribe; Cover Design: Lee Binding

PUBLICITY BLURB

For a year, while the Master ruled over Earth, Martha Jones travelled the world telling people stories about the Doctor. She told people of how the Doctor has saved them before, and how he will save them again. This is that story. It tells of Martha's travels from her arrival on Earth as the Toclafane attacked and decimated the population through to her return to Britain to face the Master. It tells how she spread the word and told people about the Doctor. The story of how she survived that terrible year. But it's more than that. This is also a collection of the stories she tells – the stories of adventures she had with the Doctor that we haven't heard about before. The stories that inspired and saved the world. Featuring the Doctor and Martha as played by David Tennant and Freema Agyeman in the hit series from BBC Television.

NOTES

- The main narrative of this book takes place alongside the events of the Season Three story 'Last of the Time Lords' (2007). Dan Abnett wrote the umbrella story for the book, while the individual tales that Martha tells people of her adventures with the Doctor were contributed by the other credited authors.

29: THE EYELESS

Writer: Lance Parkin
Publication date: 26 December 2008
Series Consultant: Justin Richards; Project Editor: Steve Tribe; Cover Design: Lee Binding

PUBLICITY BLURB

At the heart of the ruined city of Arcopolis is the Fortress. It's a brutal structure placed here by one of the sides in a devastating intergalactic war that's long ended. Fifteen years ago, the entire population of the planet was killed in an instant by the weapon housed deep in the heart of the Fortress. Now only the ghosts remain. The Doctor arrives, and determines to fight his way past the Fortress's automatic defences and put the weapon beyond use. But he soon discovers he's not the only person in Arcopolis. What is the true nature of the weapon? Is the planet really haunted? Who are the Eyeless? And what will happen if they get to the weapon before the Doctor? The Doctor has a fight on his hands. And this time he's all on his own. Featuring the Doctor as played by David Tennant in the hit series from BBC Television.

30: BEAUTIFUL CHAOS

Writer: Gary Russell
Publication date: 26 December 2008
Series Consultant: Justin Richards; Project Editor: Steve Tribe; Cover Design: Lee Binding

PUBLICITY BLURB

Donna Noble is back home in London, catching up with her family and generally giving them all the gossip about her journeys. Her grandfather is especially overjoyed – he's discovered a new star and had it named after him. He takes the Doctor, as his special guest, to the naming ceremony. But the Doctor is suspicious about some of the other changes he can see in Earth's heavens – particularly that bright star, right there. No not that one, *that* one, there, on the left … The world's population is slowly being converted to a new path, a new way of thinking. Something is coming to Earth, an ancient force from the Dark Times. Something powerful, angry, and all-consuming … Featuring the Doctor and Donna as played by David Tennant and Catherine Tate in the hit series from BBC Television.

NOTE

Features the Mandragora Helix, as introduced in 'The Masque of Mandragora' (1976).

THE SONTARAN GAMES

Writer: Jacqueline Rayner
Publication date: 26 February 2009
Series Consultant: Justin Richards; Project Editor: Steve Tribe; Cover Design: Lee Binding

PUBLICITY BLURB

Every time the lights go out, someone dies ... The TARDIS lands at an academy for top athletes, all hoping to be chosen for the forthcoming Globe Games. But is one of them driven enough to resort to murder? The Doctor discovers that the students have been hushing up unexplained deaths. Teaming up with a young swimmer called Emma, the Doctor begins to investigate – but he doesn't expect to find a squad of Sontarans invading the academy! As the Sontarans begin their own lethal version of the Globe Games, the Doctor and Emma must find out what's really going on. But the Doctor is captured and forced to take part in the Sontaran Games. Can even a Time Lord survive this deadly contest? Featuring the Doctor as played by David Tennant in the acclaimed hit series from BBC Television.

NOTE

- A paperback in the Quick Reads range launched by the National Literacy Trust charity on World Book Day 2006 with the stated aim to 'provide fast-paced, bite-sized books by bestselling writers for emergent readers, anyone who had lost the reading habit or simply wanted a short, fast read'.

31: JUDGEMENT OF THE JUDOON

Writer: Colin Brake
Publication date: 16 April 2009
Series Consultant: Justin Richards; Project Editor: Steve Tribe; Cover Design: Lee Binding

PUBLICITY BLURB

Elvis the King Spaceport has grown into the sprawling city-state of New Memphis – an urban jungle, where organised crime is rife. But the launch of the new Terminal 13 hasn't been as smooth as expected. And things are about to get worse ... When the Doctor arrives, he finds the whole terminal locked down. The notorious Invisible Assassin is at work again, and the Judoon troopers sent to catch him will stop at nothing to complete their mission. With the assassin loose on the mean streets of New Memphis, the Doctor is forced into a strange alliance. Together with teenage private eye Nikki and a ruthless Judoon Commander, the Doctor soon discovers that things are even more complicated – and dangerous – than he first thought ... Featuring the Doctor as played by David Tennant in the hit series from BBC Television.

32: THE SLITHEEN EXCURSION

Writer: Simon Guerrier
Publication date: 16 April 2009
Series Consultant: Justin Richards; Project Editor: Steve Tribe; Cover Design: Lee Binding

PUBLICITY BLURB

1500 BC – King Actaeus and his subjects live in mortal fear of the awesome gods who have come to visit their kingdom in ancient Greece. Except the Doctor, visiting with university student June, knows they're not gods at all. They're aliens. For the aliens, it's the perfect holiday – they get to tour the sights of a primitive planet and even take part in local customs. Like gladiatorial games, or hunting down and killing humans who won't be missed. With June's enthusiastic help, the Doctor soon meets the travel agents behind this deadly package holiday company – his old enemies the Slitheen. But can he bring the Slitheen excursion to an end without endangering more lives? And how are events in ancient Greece linked to a modern-day alien plot to destroy what's left of the Parthenon? Featuring the Doctor as played by David Tennant in the hit series from BBC Television.

33: PRISONER OF THE DALEKS

Writer: Trevor Baxendale
Publication date: 16 April 2009
Series Consultant: Justin Richards; Project Editor: Steve Tribe; Cover Design: Lee Binding

PUBLICITY BLURB

The Daleks are advancing, their empire constantly expanding in to Earth's space. The Earth forces are resisting the Daleks in every way they can. But the battles rage on across countless solar systems. And now the future of our galaxy hangs in the balance … The Doctor finds himself stranded on board a starship near the frontline with a group of ruthless bounty hunters. Earth Command will pay them for every Dalek they kill, every eye stalk they bring back as proof. With the Doctor's help, the bounty hunters achieve the ultimate prize: a Dalek prisoner intact, powerless, and ready for interrogation. But where the Daleks are involved, nothing is what it seems, and no-one is safe. Before long the tables will be turned, and how will the Doctor survive when he becomes a prisoner of the Daleks? Featuring the Doctor as played by David Tennant in the hit series from BBC Television.

34: THE TAKING OF CHELSEA 426

Writer: David Llewellyn
Publication date: 3 September 2009
Series Consultant: Justin Richards; Project Editor: Steve Tribe; Cover Design: Lee Binding

PUBLICITY BLURB

The Chelsea Flower Show – hardly the most exciting or dangerous event in the calendar, or so Doctor thinks. But this is Chelsea 426, a city-sized future colony floating on the clouds of Saturn, and the flowers are much more than they seem. As the Doctor investigates, he becomes more and more worried. Why is shopkeeper Mr Pemberton acting so strangely? And what is Professor Wilberforce's terrible secret? They are close to finding the answers when a familiar foe arrives, and the stakes suddenly get much higher. The Sontarans have plans of their own, and they're not here to arrange flowers... Featuring the Doctor as played by David Tennant in the hit series from BBC Television.

35: AUTONOMY

Writer: Daniel Blythe
Publication date: 3 September 2009
Series Consultant: Justin Richards; Project Editor: Steve Tribe; Cover Design: Lee Binding

PUBLICITY BLURB

Hyperville is 2013's top hi-tech, 24-hour entertainment complex – a sprawling palace of fun under one massive roof. You can go shopping, or experience the excitement of Doomcastle, WinterZone, or Wild West World. But things are about to get a lot more exciting – and dangerous ... What unspeakable horror is lurking on Level Zero of Hyperville? And what will happen when the entire complex goes over to Central Computer Control? For years, the Nestene Consciousness has been waiting and planning, recovering from its wounds. But now it is ready, and its deadly plastic Autons are already in place around the complex. Now more than ever, visiting Hyperville will be an unforgettable experience ... Featuring the Doctor as played by David Tennant in the hit series from BBC Television.

36: THE KRILLITANE STORM

Writer: Christopher Cooper
Publication date: 3 September 2009
Series Consultant: Justin Richards; Project Editor: Steve Tribe; Cover Design: Lee Binding

PUBLICITY BLURB

When the TARDIS materialises in medieval Worcester, the Doctor finds the city seemingly deserted. He soon discovers its population are living in a state of terror, afraid to leave their homes after dark, for fear of meeting their doom at the hands of the legendary Devil's Huntsman. For months, people have been disappearing, and the Sheriff has imposed a strict curfew across the city, his militia maintaining control over the superstitious populace with a firm hand, closing the city to outsiders. Is it fear of attack from beyond the city walls that drives him or the threat closer to home? Or does the Sheriff have something to hide? After a terrifying encounter with a deadly Krillitane, the Doctor realises the city has good reason to be scared. Featuring the Doctor as played by David Tennant in the hit series from BBC Television.

CODE OF THE KRILLITANES

Writer: Justin Richards
Publication date: 4 March 2010
Series Consultant: Justin Richards; Project Editor: Steve Tribe; Cover Design: Lee Binding

PUBLICITY BLURB

'I blame those new Brainy Crisps. Since he started eating them, he's been too clever by half.'
Can eating a bag of crisps really make you more clever? The company that makes the crisps says so, and they seem to be right. But the Doctor is worried. Who would want to make people more brainy? And why? With just his sonic screwdriver and a supermarket trolley full of crisps, the Doctor sets out to find the truth. The answer is scary – the Krillitanes are back on Earth, and everyone is at risk! Last time they took over a school. This time they have hijacked the internet. Whatever they are up to, it's big and it's nasty. Only the Doctor can stop them – if he isn't already too late … A short, sharp shot of adventure, featuring the Doctor as played by David Tennant in the acclaimed hit series from BBC Television.

NOTES

• A paperback in the Quick Reads range launched by the National Literacy Trust charity on World Book Day 2006 with the stated aim to 'provide fast-paced, bite-sized books by bestselling writers for emergent readers, anyone who had lost the reading habit or simply wanted a short, fast read'.

APPENDIX F
ORIGINAL COMIC STRIPS

During the period covered by this book, *Doctor Who* fans could enjoy four different comic strip series presenting new adventures for the tenth Doctor and his companions. These appeared in: Panini's *Doctor Who Magazine*, which (under various different titles) had been home to a *Doctor Who* comic strip since 1979; *Doctor Who Adventures*, a now weekly (previously fortnightly) comic aimed at a pre-teen audience, published by BBC Magazines; *Battles in Time*, a fortnightly trading-card magazine pitched toward slightly older children, published by G E Fabbri; and *Doctor Who*, a US-only comic book, published by IDW.[72] Listed below are details of the stories from each of these four series in turn. The publication dates given are the cover dates or official publication dates and do not necessarily accord with when the issues actually went on sale.

DOCTOR WHO MAGAZINE

THINKTWICE

Story: Dan McDaid
Art: Martin Geraghty; Colours: James Offredi; Lettering: Roger Langridge; Editors: Tom Spilsbury and Scott Gray
Publication: Issue 400-402; 15 October 2008, 12 November 2008, 10 December 2008.

PLOT

Green-skinned interplanetary con artist Majenta Pryce is an inmate of ThinkTwice, a space station prison facility. Like all the other convicts there, she is unaware of her true identity, apparently due to repeated memory wipes supposed to have a reforming effect. The Doctor infiltrates the station and is surprised to find Majenta there: when he thwarted her last scheme, he assumed she would be sent to a less harsh facility for financial criminals. He discovers that the true purpose of ThinkTwice is to feed a race of mind parasites called the Memeovax. He defeats the Memeovax, and Majenta leaves with him in the TARDIS, insisting that he look after her as he is indirectly responsible for her condition.

NOTE

- Majenta Pryce first appeared in the story 'Hotel Historia' in Issue 394 of *Doctor Who Magazine*.

---

[72] IDW also brought out a series of classic *Doctor Who* comic books featuring stories of earlier Doctors reprinted, with newly-added colour, from earlier incarnations of *Doctor Who Magazine*.

THE STOCKBRIDGE CHILD

Story: Dan McDaid
Pencils: Mike Collins; Inks: David A Roach; Colours: James Offredi; Lettering:
Roger Langridge; Editors: Tom Spilsbury and Scott Gray
Publication: Issue 403-405; 7 January 2009, 4 February 2009, 4 March 2009.

PLOT

The Doctor's plan to take Majenta to a place called Panacea to try to cure her
amnesia is thwarted when the TARDIS materialises instead in the English village of
Stockbridge. In progress there is the Aurelia Winter Festival 2008, the re-enactment
of a medieval fayre, which the locals now celebrate instead of Christmas. The
Doctor's old friend Max Edison is conducting a protest against Khrysalis
Konstruction, a company carrying out a sinister digging project just outside the
village. The Doctor, Majenta and Max investigate and encounter the monstrous
Wyrrmen, who have been influencing the villagers and killing Max's fellow
protesters. The Wyrrmen target Max with energy beams from their eyes, causing
him to be taken over by a psychic manifestation of the Lokhus, an immature but
powerful entity from another universe. By threatening to blow up the site by using
a flaming torch to ignite the methane trapped in the tunnels beneath, the Doctor
causes the Lokhus to withdraw from Max's body and flee. However, one of the
Wyrrmen attacks the Doctor, inadvertently knocking the torch from his hand and
causing the site to explode. The Doctor manages to swing to safety on a rope.
Several days later, the villagers have forgotten all about Khrysalis and the Lokhus
and are celebrating Christmas. The Doctor and Majenta bid farewell to Max and
leave in the TARDIS. After they have gone, Max is accosted by four strange
creatures that read his mind to try to discover Majenta's whereabouts.

NOTE

• Max Edison and the village of Stockbridge featured in a number of previous
  Doctor Who Magazine comic strip stories, starting with 'The Tides of Time' in
  Issues 61 to 67.

MORTAL BELOVED

Story: Dan McDaid
Art: Sean Longcroft; Colours: James Offredi; Lettering: Roger Langridge; Editors:
Tom Spilsbury and Scott Gray
Publication: Issue 406-407; 1 April 2009, 29 April 2009.

PLOT

Again failing to reach Panacea, the Doctor and Majenta arrive on a rock floating in
space, which is shielded from a huge cosmic storm raging around it. There is a
grand house built upon the rock, guarded by a damaged robot called Owl. The
Doctor repairs Owl with his sonic screwdriver, and in the process activates a device

that transports him into a monochrome simulacrum of a smart cocktail party inside the house. Majenta meanwhile explores the house and gets into a fight with a girl called Violet, who closely resembles her and knows her name. At the party, the Doctor learns that the guests and their host, Wesley Sparks, are all solid light copies of real people, complete with memories and personalities. The Doctor is astounded when Wesley reveals that Majenta is his fiancée. The guests turn on the Doctor, Wesley and Owl, as their program files have been corrupted. Elsewhere in the house, Majenta encounters the emaciated directors of Sparktech, the company responsible for this place. She is then captured by a room full of Violets – solid light copies of herself – and faces being forced to marry a robot operated by the head of the real, much older Wesley. The Sparktech directors intervene, realising that the company is doomed to fail, and terminate themselves. The solid light copy of Wesley attacks and kills his real self, then decays and fades away in Majenta's arms. The Doctor tells Majenta that the remaining solid light occupants of the house will be fine, and that Violet will build the company up again. Majenta suspects that the Doctor brought her here on purpose to try to cure her amnesia, but he denies it. As she checks the TARDIS co-ordinates to confirm this, one of the strange creatures that earlier accosted Max Edison in Stockbridge tells her to 'Remember the Hand'.

THE AGE OF ICE

Story: Dan McDaid
Art: Martin Geraghty; Colours: James Offredi; Lettering: Roger Langridge; Editors: Tom Spilsbury and Scott Gray
Publication: Issue 408-41; 27 May 2009, 24 June 2009, 22 July 2009, 19 August 2009.

PLOT

The Doctor and Majenta arrive in Sydney, Australia, and are taken to a UNIT base under the harbour. Colonel Tom McCay tells them that temporal disturbances have recently affected the area, causing people to age prematurely and dinosaurs and other extinct creatures to appear. While the Doctor investigates an invisible spaceship hovering above the city, Majenta follows one of the UNIT team, Corporal Manning, to the Bestiary – a repository of artefacts from past alien invasion attempts. Instructed by a voice in his head, Manning reveals his true, green-skinned form to Majenta: he is her old partner in crime Fanson, although due to her amnesia, she does not recognise him. He and a number of the UNIT troops have fallen under the influence of the Doctor's old adversary, the Skith leader. The Doctor is captured by the controlled troops and taken to the leader. The leader explains that he is unable to access the spaceship above as it is phased out of time. He hopes to rectify this by killing the Doctor, knowing that causality bends around him. Suddenly, however, Skith from the spaceship appear and intervene. The Skith leader confronts the Skith general aboard the spaceship, and the latter throws the former to his death in its fusion core, believing that the time has come for the Skith to adopt a new way of thinking. The Doctor learns that the Skith home world has been destroyed by mysterious means – their central consciousness, the Mindcore, can show him only an image of a huge crimson hand. The Skith have developed a time ship called the SKARDIS using information gleaned from the Doctor when they last met, and now plan to travel back in time to prevent the loss of their world. Majenta appears to go over to the Skith side, but the Doctor tells her that the time travel information the Skith took from him was incomplete, so the SKARDIS will not work – hence the temporal disturbances that have hit Sydney. Majenta materialises the Skith spaceship above the UNIT base, allowing Colonel McCay to fire a captured Sontaran weapon at it. The Skith general tries to destroy Majenta for her betrayal, but Fanson interposes himself and is killed instead. With his dying breath, Fanson admits that it was he who wiped Majenta's memory, to protect her from knowing about something terrible she got involved with. Colonel McCay rescues the Doctor and Majenta from the spaceship just before it explodes, ending the Skith threat.

NOTE

• The Skith first featured in the comic strip story 'The First' in Issues 386-389 of *Doctor Who Magazine*.

THE DEEP HEREAFTER

Story: Dan McDaid
Art: Rob Davis; Colours: James Offredi and Rob Davis; Lettering: Roger Langridge; Editors: Tom Spilsbury and Scott Gray
Publication: Issue 412; 16 September 2009.

PLOT

The TARDIS brings the Doctor and Majenta to New Old Detroit, a colony world in the Proxima system, where they meet a half man, half fish private eye, Johnny Seaview, who has been shot in the back. As he dies, Johnny passes his hat to the Doctor. The Doctor and Majenta take refuge in Johnny's office, where they meet a *femme fatale* named Winter Palace, who turns out to be a robot operated from within by the diminutive gangster Tiny Danza. Danza demands to know the whereabouts of the World Bomb, a powerful weapon sought be every hoodlum in the city. Seaview found it, but Danza believes that one of his rivals, Red Morgan, got to the private eye first. Morgan has managed to convince the police that he is innocent of Seaview's murder, but then he too is shot down. The Doctor and Majenta are first on the scene, but are held at gunpoint by Half-Nelson, a man who has lost the whole left-hand side of his body in a transmat accident. Half-Nelson believes that the Doctor killed Seaview, but the Doctor denies this and tells him that he knows the key to the mystery. He takes off Seaview's hat and shows that written inside it are directions to look five fathoms down off a nearby dock. Half-Nelson and his gang take the Doctor and Majenta down in a submarine and find the Bomb in an underwater dome. They also encounter the real murderer: Hector Shellac, a lawyer from Alpha Centauri, who has grown tired of defending all the local gangsters and wants to use the Bomb against them. The Doctor and Shallac have a brief struggle, but then the Doctor deliberately detonates the Bomb. Instead of exploding, it transforms the city into an idyllic landscape of rolling green hills. The Doctor explains that the Worldsmiths, who made the Bomb, designed it to respond to the owner's will: he simply thought of England when he detonated it. The Doctor tosses Seaview's hat onto his nearby gravestone.

ONOMATOPOEIA

Story: Dan McDaid
Art: Mike Collins; Colours: James Offredi; Lettering: Roger Langridge; Editors: Tom Spilsbury and Scott Gray
Publication: Issue 413; 14 October 2009.

PLOT

The Doctor and Majenta arrive on a world where they find they are unable to speak. A floating stone head drops to the ground nearby, and they see malfunctioning circuitry within. Fleeing from a deafening shrieking noise, they meet a race of man-sized rodents. Investigating with their help, they discover that this is Graveworld 909, where many of the dead of the Seventh Galactic War are buried. Majenta manages to reboot the systems of the Groundskeeper – a giant stone creature – and, in return, it lifts the pall of silence it has imposed here for a hundred thousand years. Its task is to care for this world, but its droids – the floating stone heads – are now malfunctioning. It considers the rodents to be unwelcome vermin, and has been trying to eliminate them with the shrieking noise – a form of sonic attack. Majenta, however, persuades the Groundskeeper to let the rodents act as its helpers in place of the droids.

GHOSTS OF THE NORTHERN LINE

Story: Dan McDaid
Art: Paul Grist; Colours: James Offredi; Lettering: Roger Langridge; Editors: Tom Spilsbury and Scott Gray
Publication: Issue 414-415; 11 November 2009, 9 December 2009.

PLOT

The Doctor and Majenta investigate the appearance of ghosts in the tunnels of the London tube system. Hanging from the roof of one of the tunnels they encounter Mnemosyne, a robot-like alien with a glowing brain. She was created by the Corialiths of Masma to act as a mourning device, storing the engrams of their dead, but was abandoned on Earth 107 years ago when her master, who stole her and brought her here, was hounded and killed by the residents. Ever since, she has been storing memories of people who died on the tube; now she is becoming more proactive, and actually seeking out people to kill. Majenta persuades the ghosts to turn on Mnemosyne, promising that she will remember them when they are gone, as her mind is a blank slate. They pull the creature to the ground and Majenta stamps on the brain, killing it. The ghosts then fade away. The Doctor tells Majenta that they must get her to Panacea immediately, but suddenly a booming voice calls out to her, telling her that it is the voice of Justice and that Intersol has the planet surrounded. In space, a fleet of ships approaches.

THE CRIMSON HAND

Story: Dan McDaid
Pencils: Martin Geraghty; Inks: David A Roach; Colours: James Offredi; Lettering: Roger Langridge; Editors: Tom Spilsbury and Scott Gray
Publication: Issue 416-420; 6 January 2010, 3 February 2010, 3 March 2010, 31 March 2010, 28 April 2010.

PLOT

The Doctor and Majenta try to escape in the TARDIS, but it is pulled aboard an Intersol spaceship, where they encounter a woman nicknamed Zed – formerly Majenta's cellmate at ThinkTwice and now an Intersol agent. The Doctor realises that the only way Intersol could have taken control of the TARDIS is if it gave itself up to them; it has been trying to prevent him from getting Majenta to Panacea, and this is its last resort. He concludes that there is something deadly in Majenta's mind, and asks Zed for help in preventing Intersol from releasing it. By tapping into the Justice computer that has been interrogating Majenta, the Doctor witnesses a deeply-buried memory of her joining the Crimson Hand, a powerful criminal gang, who address her as Lady Scaph. The four mysterious creatures who lead the Crimson Hand arrive on the Intersol ship and destroy Justice. Fleeing to the TARDIS, Majenta tells the Doctor that she left the Crimson Hand after she refused their test of turning their most powerful weapon, the hand-shaped Manus Maleficus, on a planet of her choosing, and they then used it to destroy the Skith home world instead. However, they still need her, because the Manus will not work properly without her. This is why Fanson wiped her memory. The Crimson Hand set about destroying the Intersol ship, and Majenta uses the power bestowed on her by the Manus to blast both the Doctor and the TARDIS to nothingness. The Crimson Hand offer her a chance to rejoin them and shape the universe, and she accepts. Later, Majenta rules over the planet Vessica. The resistance she encounters from some of its people is only one of her problems, as a rift in time and space has appeared above the planet. The Doctor and the TARDIS are meanwhile suspended in a pocket universe. A projection of Majenta appears and tells the Doctor that she sent him there for his own safety, as the Crimson Hand would have destroyed him. A party that Majenta is holding on the blue moon of Vessica descends into chaos as the moon falls into the rift, but Majenta and Zed find themselves safe in the TARDIS. The Doctor tells them that the rift is the Morass, signifying the unravelling of time caused by the Manus. The only way to stop it is to cut the Crimson Hand off from the Manus and allow time to heal itself. Majenta gives the Doctor a red crystal with which to destroy the Manus, but when he tries to use it, it does not work. Majenta then joins with the Manus and uses it to destroy the four leaders of the Crimson Hand. She has saved the universe, but at the cost of her own life. The Manus starts to fade away into the Morass, but the Doctor leaps after it. He uses the Manus to bring Majenta back to life, and leaves her with Zed on the idyllic world of New Old Detroit, now renamed Redemption.

DOCTOR WHO ADVENTURES

THE MAN IN THE MOON

Script: Nev Fountain
Art: John Ross; Colours: Alan Craddock; Letters: Paul Vyse
Publication: Issues 88-89; 30 October 2008, 6 November 2008

PLOT

The TARDIS is hovering above the Moon when it receives a transmission from a traffic warden robot telling the Doctor that it is illegally parked in a no orbiting zone. Materialising on the Moon's surface, the Doctor and Donna start to explore. They find another of the robots, this one wrecked, and meet an elephant-like creature named Chevron. The creature has been stuck here for a billion and a half years, and has built up a huge parking fine, putting him in conflict with the robots. The robots attack in force, and while Chevron holds them off, the Doctor tries to take Donna back to the TARDIS, as her spacesuit has developed a leak. However, the TARDIS has been 'clamped' by the robots, rendering it inaccessible. The Doctor manages to remove the clamp, and he, Donna and Chevron take refuge inside the TARDIS. The Doctor manages to repel the humourless robots by beaming a joke at them, so Chevron is at last free to leave. However, it turns out that Chevron's spaceship is the Moon itself. If he takes it out of orbit, the Earth will be devastated. When he tries to move the Moon, however, it will not budge, and the Doctor realises that it has been clamped not only by the robots but by every other local galactic authority that has ever looked after this part of space. Chevron declines the Doctor's offer of a lift, determining to stay and argue his case with these authorities for another billion years.

TIME FLIES

Script: Trevor Baxendale
Art: John Ross; Colours: Alan Craddock; Letters: Paul Vyse
Publication: Issues 90-92; 13 November 2008, 20 November 2008, 27 November 2008

PLOT

The TARDIS hits turbulence in the time vortex, and the Doctor makes an emergency materialisation. He and Donna find themselves at a science convention. There they meet Professor Eustace Krosson, whose multi-wave time-vector detector, designed to function as a hairdryer, caused the turbulence. Suddenly everyone in the convention hall starts to fade away to nothing. The Professor's invention renders the culprits visible: vicious insect-like creatures, who are attacking the attendees. The Doctor identifies the creatures as the Imago, parasites from the fourth dimension, sometimes called Time Flies. The Imago Queen appears and feeds on Donna's time stream, causing her too to fade away. However, as Donna is a time traveller, she is regurgitated, along with all the other convention attendees. Depleted of energy, the Imago are forced to retreat into their own dimension. The Doctor then dismantles the Professor's invention in order to prevent any more problems.

THE GIANT'S RING

Script: Jason Loborik
Art: John Ross; Colours: Alan Craddock; Letters: Paul Vyse
Publication: Issues 93-94; 4 December 2008, 11 December 2008

PLOT

The Doctor takes Donna to visit the lost civilisation of Kolvax. There they meet Lorkel, the last Guardian of Kolvax, who asks the Doctor to take him to Earth. The Doctor agrees, but suddenly some flame-like creatures appear and insist that Lorkel must not leave. Lorkel repels them with an energy beam from a ring on his finger. The Doctor and Donna then take Lorkel to England in the TARDIS. Once there, it transpires that he has tricked them. Attaching polarising stasis generators to some standing stones, he awakens a huge creature that has been lying dormant beneath the ground. This creature, Takurthi, explains that he was Kolvax's greatest star warrior, but his people feared he would take over their planet, so they buried him on Earth with the aid of human slaves. Lorkel dies from his exertions, and the Doctor puts on his ring and uses it to try to overpower Takurthi. Donna helps by using the sonic screwdriver to liberate more of the flame-like creatures from the standing stones – they were left there as Takurthi's jailers. This is still not enough to defeat Takurthi, so instead the Doctor adapts Lorkel's stasis generators to turn them into a molecular destabiliser, shrinking Takurthi until he disappears.

FROSTY THE SNOWDEMON

Script: Christopher Cooper
Art: John Ross; Colours: Alan Craddock; Letters: Paul Vyse
Publication: Issue 95; 18 December 2008

PLOT

The Doctor takes Donna to a garden centre so she can buy a Christmas present for her grandfather. There, she encounters a living snowman who tells her that he is fleeing from alien pursuers. Meanwhile, inside a Santa's Grotto attraction, the Doctor encounters some green-skinned aliens who have arrived by teleport. It is these aliens, the Pixees, who are hunting the snowman – or, as they call him, the Snowdemon. The Snowdemon is a criminal, and they are trying to apprehend him. The Pixees and the Doctor teleport back to the garden centre, and the Doctor traps the Snowdemon in the hothouse, where it melts. The Doctor, Donna and the Pixees then enjoy the garden centre's Christmas buffet.

THE CHROMOSOME CONNECTION

Script: Christopher Cooper
Art: John Ross; Colours: Alan Craddock; Letters: Paul Vyse
Publication: Issue 96; 2 January 2009

PLOT

In Edinburgh, 2009, the Doctor meets a girl who has encountered a ghostly apparition of a woman in 19th Century clothes being chased by a monster. The Doctor identifies the monster as a Mozhtratta. He also realises that the girl is fuzzy with residual vortex radiation, and speculates that he knew one of her ancestors, gaining confirmation of this when she introduces herself as Heather McCrimmon. The Mozhtratta has been trapped by the vortex radiation ever since it attacked the woman Heather saw, who must have been one of her ancestors. The Doctor takes Heather in the TARDIS back to 1815 and helps the woman to resist the Mozhtratta's attack, saving Heather from the monster's influence. Heather joins the Doctor on his travels.

NOTES

• It is implied, though not explicitly stated, that Heather is a descendent of the Doctor's former companion Jamie McCrimmon.

THE AQUARIUS CONDITION

Script: Trevor Baxendale
Art: John Ross; Colours: Alan Craddock; Letters: Paul Vyse
Publication: Issue 97; 8 January 2009

PLOT

The TARDIS lands at the bottom of the English Channel, and the Doctor and Heather explore in diving suits. They are amazed to see the Big Ben clock tower under the water. Then they are taken prisoner by ferocious creatures identified by the Doctor as the Spaeron, from the planet Oceanus Pacifika. Taken to the Spaeron shoal's queen, Askelia, they learn that the creatures have aquaformed the planet and claimed it as their own. The Doctor and Heather swim for their lives and meet a group of human divers, led by Captain Harris of the Sub-Aqua Division. He tells them that Earth entered into an alliance with the Spaerons to allow them to live in the oceans after their own planet was destroyed by the Daleks, but the creatures flooded everything by melting the polar ice caps. The Doctor determines to return the ice caps to their proper state, and agrees to take the Spaeron to live on the ocean world Kerun Za with his friend Sea-Rah.

NOTE

• Sea-Rah featured in the earlier *Doctor Who Adventures* story 'Sea-Rah'.

GLUM CULTURE

Script: Christopher Cooper
Art: John Ross; Colours: Alan Craddock; Letters: Paul Vyse
Publication: Issue 98; 15 January 2009

PLOT

The TARDIS has brought the Doctor and Heather to a run-down habitation pod that is home to a glum couple named Mr and Mrs Olbec. The TARDIS falls through the floor, and the Doctor and Heather climb after it into the building's central hub. There they meet a lowly ServoBot, Trundle-y, who tells them that the beautiful city outside is being used by the other ServoBots, which are all on a recharge cycle. The Doctor and Heather visit City Hall to talk to the MayorBot, but instead find the city presided over by Maya De La Grotzka, a one-time model who disappeared 20 years earlier. Maya tells them that she dropped out of society because she no longer wanted all the public attention. She is horrified to learn that there are still residents living in squalid conditions in the Podworld – she had been assured they had been rehoused. Mr and Mrs Olbec and the other residents are released from their pods into the city, to be looked after by the ServoBots, while Trundle-y promises to protect Maya's privacy.

THE GREAT RAIN ROBBERY

Script: Craig Donaghy
Art: John Ross; Colours: Alan Craddock; Letters: Paul Vyse
Publication: Issue 99; 22 January 2009

PLOT

The Doctor has taken Heather home for her to fetch some clothes. The weather is stormy, but the Doctor realises that although the lightning is real, the rain is artificial. It has been created by the Cran Movement, whose own world dried up and who now steal the rain from others. The Doctor points out the insect-like Cran ship, the wings of which are designed to catch clouds. He decides to materialise the TARDIS on board the ship. Once there, he lowers the ship's shields and it is struck by lightning, severely damaging it. The Doctor tells the Cran he will give them a tow outside of the atmosphere, where the Shadow Proclamation can arrest them.

THE PARRIAN PROPOSAL

Script: Craig Donaghy
Art: John Ross; Colours: Alan Craddock; Letters: Paul Vyse
Publication: Issue 100; 29 January 2009
PLOT

The Doctor takes Heather to the supposedly beautiful planet Delquis, only to find it in chaos. They visit the Delquesian Shell Judge and she tells them that Parrian war birds have been attacking them for months. The Doctor is puzzled, as the Parrian are the Delquesian's formerly-peaceful neighbours. He and Heather journey to the Parrian Palace to speak to their Prince. He explains that he did not tell the birds to attack; they were performing a traditional proposal ceremony. He has fallen in love with the Shell Judge, and did not intend the Delquesian cities to be destroyed. At his command, the war birds set about repairing the damage they have done. The Shell Judge asks the Doctor to tell the Parrian Prince that she finds his intensions honourable. It seems that love is in the air.

HITCHING POINT

Script: Christopher Cooper
Art: John Ross; Colours: Alan Craddock; Letters: Paul Vyse
Publication: Issue 101; 5 February 2009

PLOT

Explorer Hiram Bingham discovers Machu Picchu, the lost city of the Incas ... only to find that the Doctor and Heather have got there first, and are in the process of rigging up equipment to get rid of a 'temporal hiccup'. The Doctor recognises Hiram, but knows that he is not due to discover the city until the following day. Hiram is accidentally sucked into the time hole, and suddenly the Doctor and Heather find themselves in a futuristic city. The Doctor realises that the whole course of history has been changed. They meet an unkempt old man who begs them to save the Earth from the tyranny of the lizard-like Incasaurs, who now inhabit the city. He takes them to a monument, the inscription on which identifies it as the 'Hitching Point of the Sun'. A time portal opens above it, and they see Hiram, who has fallen back in time to Machu Picchu in the era of the Incas. The Doctor tells him that he is at the centre of a temporal cataclysm. A group of Incasaurs arrive and explain that the used the portal to come to this Earth from their own parallel dimension as their sun was dying. The Doctor realises that the old man is an alternate version of Hiram, kept alive by the time portal. The two Hirams shake hands, and there is a huge discharge of temporal energy, which restores history to its proper state. The Doctor and Heather leave Hiram unconscious in Machu Picchu, ready to wake up and discover it the following day.

STORE WARS

Script: Nev Fountain
Art: John Ross; Colours: Alan Craddock; Letters: Paul Vyse
Publication: Issue 102; 12 February 2009

PLOT

The Doctor takes Heather to the Waltox Worldstore, the largest supermarket in the galaxy, to get some of his favourite zongaberry jam. They find the place run-down and devoid of shoppers. The store manager, Lenid Strimmer, tells them that the store's automated systems went mad after one customer took eight items to the 'seven items or less' checkout. The store is now planning to destroy what it believes to be a competitor – the Earth. Using the sonic screwdriver to change the store's orbit around the Earth, the Doctor restores it to normal. He realises that from the orbit the Worldstore was in, the continents of Earth appeared to spell out the word 'supermarket' in Waltoxian writing. Now, in its new orbit, they read simply 'Beware the pink warthog'. The Doctor and Heather return to the TARDIS with several boxes of zongaberry jam.

THE SUBMARINERS

Script: Trevor Baxendale
Art: John Ross; Colours: Alan Craddock; Letters: Paul Vyse
Publication: Issue 103; 19 February 2009

PLOT

During the Battle of the Atlantic in September 1944, a German U-Boat submarine is sunk by an Allied depth charge that knocks out its main motor. The TARDIS arrives on board, and the Doctor and Heather are taken prisoner. The Doctor offers to fix the motor, although Heather is troubled, as her great-grandfather was killed on a ship sunk during the War and, if repaired, this U-Boat could go on to take more Allied lives. The Doctor realises it is more likely that the U-Boat will eventually be destroyed by the Allies. He succeeds in fixing the motor, and he and Heather leave in the TARDIS. The U-Boat surfaces, and an Allied warship, the HMS Worthy, forces it to surrender. The War is over for the U-Boat crew, but their lives have been saved.

THE GREED OF THE GAVULAV

Script: Christopher Cooper
Art: John Ross; Colours: Alan Craddock; Letters: Paul Vyse
Publication: Issue 104; 26 February 2009

PLOT

The Doctor takes Heather to enjoy a show on Broadway, New York City, in the year 2018. There they witness some policemen succumbing to mind possession by some mysterious black-suited men. They follow them all to the New York Stock Exchange, where a blue-skinned alien in a huge, scorpion-like vehicle orders the 'Children of the Gavulav' – a crowd of other mind-controlled people – to begin trading and accumulating wealth. The Doctor tells Heather that the Gavulav are a race of hyper-intelligent computer hackers who have made a galactic fortune by fleecing the economies of a thousand worlds. While Heather distracts the Gavulav by pretending to be a health and safety officer, the Doctor counteracts the computer virus and blocks the psychic web. The freed people turn on the Gavulav and he flees, vowing not to return.

THE SECRET ARMY

Script: Simon Guerrier
Art: John Ross; Colours: Alan Craddock; Letters: Paul Vyse
Publication: Issue 105; 5 March 2009

PLOT

The Doctor pilots the TARDIS to the Empty Nebula so that it will be safe while he carries out some repairs. The ship hits something, and the Doctor is knocked unconscious. Opening the doors, Heather encounters a race of monsters, who have hidden their space fleet in the Nebula so that they can make a surprise attack on the Empire of Whap. Believing Heather to be a spy, they prepare to eat her. The recovered Doctor tries to materialise the TARDIS around Heather to rescue her but, as he has disconnected the dimensional control while effecting his repairs, it instead materialises, giant size, around the whole alien fleet. Heather gets back on board and the Doctor sorts out the dimensional muddle. He drops the alien fleet off where they can be arrested by the Whap Border Patrol.

NOTE

- Issue 105 is the last to feature a regular 'Letters' credit on the comic strip. This credit will appear only sporadically in future issues, as indicated in the listing below.

THE SILVER BULLET

Script: Michael Stevens
Art: John Ross; Colours: Alan Craddock
Publication: Issue 106; 12 March 2009

PLOT

The Doctor is taking Heather on a train trip on the Silver Bullet across the Fluxos Desert of the planet Flexella. Heather sees a large pink creature, a Flexellan Octopod, being chased through the train. Later, when she retires to the sleeper carriage, she sees one of the creature's tentacles tapping on the outside of her window. The Doctor is unconcerned but agrees to take Heather to the guards' van to investigate. There, they see that the Octopod has been apprehended by ticket inspectors. The Octopod manages to produce its ticket, and all is well – the creature simply had a nervous disposition.

THE INVISIBLES

Script: Trevor Baxendale
Art: John Ross; Colours: Alan Craddock
Publication: Issue 107; 19 March 2009

PLOT

The Doctor and Heather get back to the TARDIS just in time to escape the pursuing Mohagan Horde, a race of vicious purple creatures. Heather becomes invisible, and the Doctor takes her to a space station housing the Institute for Exo-Contamination Treatment, or InFECT for short. There, Professor Aldrin Strykt concludes that Heather has picked up a retro-photonic virus. In order to find a cure, the Doctor has to return to Mohaga. He finds the organic protein extract he needs, and returns to the Institute, where everyone has caught the virus and become invisible. Luckily the Doctor is immune, and is able to synthesise an antidote.

GOOD OLD DAYS

Script: Simon Guerrier
Art: John Ross; Colours: Alan Craddock
Publication: Issue 108; 26 March 2009

PLOT

The Doctor and Heather visit an outer-space old people's home where the artificial gravity has failed due to an attack by a band of meerkat-like space pirates. The pirates explain that they were dumped here after their spaceship was stolen by a rival group, who are crab-like in appearance. The Doctor, the pirates and the old people board the spaceship and fight off the crabs with lemon juice. The meerkats and crabs call a truce and decide to live in peace in the old people's home, while the old people take over the spaceship and set out looking for adventure.

THE ABOMINATION GAME

Script: Trevor Baxendale
Art: John Ross; Colours: Alan Craddock
Publication: Issue 109; 2 April 2009

PLOT

The Doctor sprains his ankle while he and Heather are exploring an alien world and is given hospitality by Krolo, one of the indigenous population. Krolo explains that every week, volunteers from his community have to brave the Mountain of Death. Those who survive return with lots of treasure and are free to leave the planet to start a new life in the stars. The rest are never seen again. The Doctor and Heather investigate the mountain and narrowly avoid some robot guards. They enter a chamber full of treasure, but the Doctor is more interested in a computer a finds there. He realises this is the remains of an ancient Abomination Game, which involved passing a series of challenges in order to win the treasure. The people of this world are descendents of the original contestants; although the game ended long ago, no-one switched the computer off. The Doctor rectifies this, and tells Krolo that his people are all winners now.

T.R.O.L.

Script: Christopher Cooper
Art: John Ross; Colours: Alan Craddock
Publication: Issue 110; 9 April 2009

PLOT

The Doctor takes Heather to the supposedly serene planet Tranquillity, only to find it in chaos. One of the local people, the Bereft, explains that at the stroke of midnight, the whole planet started shaking itself to pieces. Everyone is now taking refuge in a single area of tectonic stability, beyond Eternity Canyon. The Doctor helps the Bereft to reach the safe area across a light bridge, but suddenly a huge flying robot appears from the Canyon, telling them they have entered a restricted zone. This robot is a Tactical Response and Offensive Leveller – TROL for short. The Doctor gets control of the robot and pilots it below the planet's crust, to a military complex that is the last remnant of the Bereft's warlike pre-history. A long-defunct weapon has activated and caused the disruption to the planet. The Doctor holds it in check long enough for the Bereft to escape on rescue ships.

CYCLOPS

Script: Steve Lyons
Art: John Ross; Colours: Alan Craddock
Publication: Issue 111; 16 April 2009

PLOT

The TARDIS has arrived in 1918 on the ship USS Cyclops, shortly to vanish without trace in the Bermuda Triangle. The Doctor is taken prisoner by Captain Worley, the commanding officer, who believes him to be a stowaway. He is rescued by Heather, who has discovered a piece of a telegram in German and concluded that there must be a spy on board. Suddenly the ship is menaced by a huge sea creature, which the Doctor identifies as an Octopod – a weapon created by the alien Rutans, whose spaceship must have crash-landed nearby. The Doctor gets Captain Worley and his crew to throw the USS Cyclops' cargo of manganese ore at the Octopod. This reacts with its magnetic field and causes it to lose its grip on the ship. The Doctor and Heather leave in the TARDIS, having saved the USS Cyclops for now – although its mysterious fate in the Bermuda Triangle still awaits it.

NOTE

- The Rutans, perennial adversaries of the Sontarans, featured in the TV story 'Horror of Fang Rock' (1977).

THE CRYSTAL PALACE

Script: Christopher Cooper
Art: John Ross; Colours: Alan Craddock
Publication: Issue 112; 23 April 2009

PLOT

The Doctor aims to take Heather to visit the Crystal Palace in South London in 1854 but instead arrives in the 1930s to find a group of military and scientific men gathered with a purple-robed alien around an alien device called an Atomic Event Extender. The men see the device as a weapon, but the robed alien is aiming to use it to awaken Victumas the Conqueror to reclaim her empire. The huge, foliage-entwined Victumas appears, and kills her robed servant, who has now fulfilled his purpose. The Doctor explains that Victumas is the Queen of the Dominion Sisterhood, and that he previously trapped her in the Antimatter Realm. He routes the Atomic Event Extender's output through the iron framework of the Crystal Palace, turning it into a giant magnet. As antimatter and magnets 'don't mix', Victumas is destroyed. The Crystal Palace overheats and bursts into flames, burning to the ground.

THE SPIRIT OF ASHGAR

Script: Trevor Baxendale
Art: John Ross; Colours: Alan Craddock
Publication: Issue 113; 30 April 2009

PLOT

The Doctor and Heather are visiting a famous tourist attraction: the tomb of the evil Ashgar, most feared of all the Star-Demons of Kroul. The Doctor is concerned that Ashgar might actually still be alive, because the psychic paper is picking up his name. Venturing into the vault, he and Heather manage to get past some ferocious robot gargoyles left to guard the place. They discover that Ashgar is dead after all, but his will lives on. Ashgar explains that he has turned over a new leaf since dying, and now wants only to help people. It is his benign influence that has led the people of nearby worlds to prosper.

MONSTER IDOL

Script: Steve Lyons
Art: John Ross; Colours: Alan Craddock
Publication: Issue 114; 7 May 2009

PLOT

Auditions are under way for the Monster Idol TV show on Space Station Apple Theta, the aim being to find new bodyguards for the two judges, the King and

Queen of Meritoria. Suspecting there is something more sinister afoot, the Doctor uses the psychic paper to establish his credentials as a third judge. Heather is left to investigate behind the scenes. She learns that the real King and Queen are unconscious in their dressing room and have been replaced by impostors. The Doctor discovers a bomb in the TV camera and disarms it, while Heather tackles the impostors. It transpires that the whole show was a sham designed to allow the impostors – in truth, a pair of purple-skinned monsters – to wipe out all their rivals with the bomb. The culprits are arrested.

THE SLAKKEN CAT

Script: Craig Donaghy
Art: John Ross; Colours: Alan Craddock
Publication: Issue 115; 14 May 2009

PLOT

The TARDIS picks up a strange signal, which the Doctor and Heather trace to a Slakken Cat collar in a wood on Earth, 1969. There they encounter a large, green-skinned alien who introduces himself as the Hunter. He is also seeking the Slakken Cat, which is supposedly a dangerous animal without its collar. The Cat has been found by a pair of hippies, and the Doctor notices that it actually seems quite docile. The Hunter admits that it is actually the collars that make the Slakken Cats dangerous, and so more fun for him and his kind to hunt. The Slakken Cat jumps on the Hunter and overpowers him. The Doctor then determines to take them both home and put a stop to the hunts.

CODE FREEZE

Script: Christopher Cooper
Art: John Ross; Colours: Alan Craddock
Publication: Issue 116; 21 May 2009

PLOT

The TARDIS arrives on a space station in response to a distress call. They meet a crew member who tells them that the distress call was supposed to be a quarantine warning about a computer virus, but was reprogrammed by the virus itself. The Doctor realises that the virus consists of ByteMites – two types of nano-bots locked in a centuries-long civil war across the cosmos. The Doctor decides to flush them out by using as bait the computer brain of the station's robot servant, Glomp. The ByteMites leave the station's systems and take over Glomp, who goes on the rampage. However, Glomp's emergency back-up processor reboots itself, attracting the ByteMites to it, and it is then ejected from the station airlock, allowing things to return to normality.

HEAR NO EVIL

Script: Steve Lyons
Art: John Ross; Colours: Alan Craddock
Publication: Issue 117; 28 May 2009

PLOT

The Doctor has lost the sonic screwdriver, and it has been found by an old lady named Agnes Hardcastle. Annoyed by the sound of partying from the flat next door, Agnes uses the device to set up a standing wave, broadcasting a 'bubble of silence'. The Doctor traces the wave to its source, and finds the sleeping Agnes being menaced by a purple creature. Unable to make himself heard, the Doctor uses the psychic paper to give Agnes a message, telling her to switch off the sonic screwdriver. She does so and, as sound returns, the creature fades away. The Doctor tells Heather that the creature was just trying to communicate, but its method of communication is deadly to people, just as their form of communication – sound – is deadly to it. Now that sound has returned, the creature has been banished to its own dimension. The Doctor and Heather depart, but Agnes is now afraid of silence, and plays loud music to dispel it – annoying the people in the flat next door …

NOTE

• This story was also included in a special edition of *Doctor Who Adventures* given away free with an edition of the *Daily Mirror* newspaper.

TERROR IN THE TARDIS

Script: Christopher Cooper
Art: John Ross; Colours: Alan Craddock
TARDIS Design: Matthew Lee
Publication: Issue 118; 4 June 2009

PLOT

The TARDIS has got time sickness after encountering an anomaly in the vortex. Recovering from a daze, Heather and the Doctor see that the ship's interior has acquired a new design, and that there are a number of chicks loose inside. The chicks transform into huge, scary bird creatures that chase them through the ship until they reach the redesigned console room. Heather realises that the chicks were created by the TARDIS itself to get them to come here. The Doctor uses the sonic screwdriver – the only part of the TARDIS that is still the same as before – to restore his ship to normality.

THE BALL AND CHAIN GANG

Script: Craig Donaghy
Art: John Ross; Colours: Alan Craddock
Publication: Issue 119; 11 June 2009

PLOT

The Doctor escorts Heather to the Edinburgh University summer ball. They are alarmed by a strange screeching noise made by the band's singer, and suddenly the hall is overrun by shaggy green monsters, identified by the Doctor as prison ship escapees called Kulgaris. The Doctor realises that the singer is a Gumpii – a race too lazy to conquer a planet on their own but happy to control any mindless creatures they come across. Using the sound of his sonic screwdriver, amplified through the singer's microphone, the Doctor causes the Kulgaris to explode. He then restrains the Gumpii in the Kulgaris' prison chains.

NOTE

•   This story was also included in a special edition of *Doctor Who Adventures* given away free with an edition of the *Daily Mirror* newspaper.

THE MEMORY COLLECTIVE

Script: Craig Donaghy
Art: John Ross; Colours: Alan Craddock
Publication: Issue 120; 18 June 2009

PLOT

The Doctor and Heather arrive on the beautiful planet Uriel – to the Doctor's surprise, as it was supposed to have been destroyed the previous year by a vicious race called the Supress. They meet a number of other creatures who have also been drawn here. The Doctor deduces that the planet is bringing back prior visitors in the order they visited – which means that the Supress will be next to come. Heather is giving off a mysterious glow, and by seeing in which direction this is strongest, the Doctor traces the source of the problem to a large metal box. This as a memory collective: a galactic force sub-atomic standard terraforming computer that rebuilds destroyed worlds. It has gone into overdrive, pulling back all the planet's visitors as well. The reason Heather is glowing is that she is the only one who has never been here before. This enables her to get through the force shields surrounding the memory collective and put it in reverse, blasting the Supress away from the planet. The machine is then switched off, allowing everyone to leave.

THE BLUE STAR BOMB

Script: Trevor Baxendale
Art: John Ross; Colours: Alan Craddock
Publication: Issue 121; 25 June 2009

PLOT

The Doctor and Heather visit a private detective, Jake Krumb, in Los Angeles in 1938. They are trying to find his mother, as a clever and cunning Blue Star bomb has concealed itself within her. Arriving at her home, they find her being menaced by an alien. The alien is trying to retrieve the bomb for his paymasters. The Doctor is able to extract the bomb from Mrs Krumb and deactivate it. He then gives it to the grateful alien, who leaves in his spaceship.

FLIGHT OF THE GIURGEAX

Script: Christopher Cooper
Art: John Ross; Colours: Alan Craddock
Publication: Issue 122; 2 July 2009

PLOT

An Austrian boy named Wolfgang with an interest in alien sightings encounters the Doctor and Heather just as he is about to board an plane home after finishing a stint as an exchange student in Australia. Intrigued by what he hears of their conversation, he follows them onto a plane where the passengers are sitting in a dazed state with their oxygen masks over their faces and the cockpit is occupied by the brain of a purple alien called a Giurgeax. The Doctor and Heather are seized by the alien, but the Doctor is able to warn Wolfgang that the plane itself is actually the alien's disguised body, and he is in its stomach. Reasoning that the Giurgeax must be drawing sustenance from the passengers, Wolfgang pulls out its feeding tubes. The alien then dissolves. As Wolfgang has missed his flight, the Doctor and Heather offer to give him a lift in the TARDIS.

STARSTRUCK

Script: Craig Donaghy
Art: John Ross; Colours: Alan Craddock
Publication: Issue 123; 9 July 2009

PLOT

The Doctor takes Heather and Wolfgang – known as Wolfie for short – to an autograph signing by a famous alien actor named Stario Glovit. Stario starts behaving erratically and, using his sonic screwdriver, the Doctor reveals that he is actually a robot. Stario's agent admits that the real actor went missing 20 years earlier. However, the time travellers have noticed a crowd member with a strange device strapped to his body. The Doctor identifies this device as a Banjoor disguise belt. With the belt switched off, the crowd member is revealed to be the real Stario. Stario explains that he decided to hide for a while as his agent was pushing him too hard, only to find himself replaced with the robot. The agent starts planning Stario's comeback.

THE GENIUS TRAP

Script: Steve Lyons
Art: John Ross; Colours: Alan Craddock
Publication: Issue 124; 16 July 2009

PLOT

The Doctor takes Heather back to Edinburgh University so she can visit her friends. Wolfie notices that a lot of people are playing on purple hand-held games consoles. Making enquiries at a computer shop, the Doctor learns that these games are the latest brain-training craze, called the Tesseract, the aim of the puzzle being to build a virtual, four-dimensional cube – which is almost impossible. The Doctor solves the puzzle, and this attracts the attention of an alien monster. Heather meanwhile finds that all her friends are ignoring her, as they are completely immersed the game, and that there are posters of missing students all over the campus. Wolfie is seized by some thugs who mistakenly believe that he is the one who solved the puzzle. He is taken before the monster, the Bacothormean, which explains that it evolves by stealing the brains of geniuses to add their intellects to its own. Wolfie realises that the games consoles were a trap for geniuses. The Doctor and Heather track Wolfie down, and the Doctor defeats the Bacothormean by overloading its mind with ten lifetimes' worth of memories in one big burst. The monster reverts to its usual self – dumb and peaceful – and the Doctor, Heather and Wolfie take it away from Earth in the TARDIS, leaving UNIT to arrest its henchmen.

NOTE

• Wolfie's surname is revealed in this story as Ryter.

THE RISING TIDE

Script: Eddie Robson
Art: John Ross; Colours: Alan Craddock
Publication: Issue 125; 23 July 2009

PLOT

The Doctor and his companions are enjoying a day at the seaside when suddenly a huge monster, Octron, emerges from the waves and announces that it has come to Earth to take control of the oceans. While the Doctor shouts a warning to the holidaymakers on the beach, Octron and several others of its kind whip up a sandstorm. This makes it difficult for people to breath, causing them to collapse, and the monsters start taking them into the sea – including Wolfie! The Doctor commandeers an ice cream van and, having adapted its equipment with the sonic screwdriver, shoots a blast of quick-frozen air at the sea. This causes the sea to freeze over, trapping the monsters and freeing their hostages. The monsters accept the Doctor's offer to take them away from Earth to an uninhabited planet.

SWEET DREAMS

Script: Craig Donaghy
Art: John Ross; Colours: Alan Craddock
Publication: Issue 126; 30 July 2009

PLOT

The Doctor brings Heather and Wolfie to the planet Lurbos 3 to search for all the explorers who have gone missing there. They find the explorers lying on the ground in rows, asleep. The Doctor realises that they have been bitten by a Dream Sucker, a small creature that sends its victims to sleep and then feeds off their dreams. Heather is bitten by the creature, and falls fast asleep. The Doctor deliberately allows himself to be bitten too, challenging the Dream Sucker to feed on his darkest memories. The Dream Sucker starts to grow in size and is eventually overwhelmed, releasing all the dreams it previously consumed. Heather and the explorers then return to normal. The Dream Sucker will need a few months' sleep, but will eventually recover.

COPYCAT

Script: Eddie Robson
Art: John Ross; Colours: Alan Craddock
Publication: Issue 127; 6 August 2009

PLOT

The Doctor becomes separated from Heather and Wolfie while they are exploring the Great Forests of the planet Yellan. They were supposed to meet back at the TARDIS, but multiple copies of the police box have appeared amongst the trees. The Doctor finds Wolfie and they see a huge tentacle disgorging a further copy of the TARDIS. Exploring inside the tentacle, they find it is part of an alien creature that keeps objects within itself and creates duplicates of them – including the trees of the forests outside. The Doctor locates both Heather and the TARDIS, and he and his friends depart.

SHADOW OF THE VAIPID

Script: Christopher Cooper
Art: John Ross; Colours: Alan Craddock
Publication: Issue 128; 13 August 2009

PLOT

The Doctor has taken Heather and Wolfie to Carnaby Street in London in 1967, the height of the 'swinging sixties'. They are alarmed to see a strange shadow fall, draining the colour from everything within it and making everyone miserable. Returning to the TARDIS, they learn that the haze is wrapped around the Earth's upper atmosphere like a shroud. They trace its source to a grey spaceship inhabited by grey aliens, the Vaipid, who take them before their Committee for processing. The Committee are surprised that the Doctor has resisted the effects of the haze, which they describe as the Cloud, and contemplate dissecting him to find the reason. They explain that the Cloud recreates the atmospheric conditions of their own planet, which have robbed them of the warmer emotions for a thousand generations. The want to study human reaction to it in the hope of discovering the secret of happiness. The Doctor takes Vaipid representatives to Earth and shows them that there is no great secret to happiness – in the words of the Beatles, all you need is love.

SNAKES ALIVE!

Script: Steve Lyons
Art: John Ross; Colours: Alan Craddock
Publication: Issue 129; 20 August 2009

PLOT

In the 1920s, the Doctor, Heather and Wolfie are visiting Fat Eddie's club when the room is raked with gunfire by a group of snake-skinned intruders calling themselves the Sidewinder Syndicate. While Heather and Wolfie take cover, Fat Eddie tells the Doctor that these aliens have been muscling in on his turf for weeks with their ray guns. Later, Heather and Wolfie confront the aliens at a snake oil store that they are using as a cover. The Doctor meanwhile breaks in at the back door and carries out his own investigation. He learns that the Syndicate are criminal exiles from the planet Serpentine. They fell to Earth by chance and thought they could blend right in. The Doctor fixes their spaceship's navi-pod, enabling them to leave, but they tell him they would rather stay and amass a fortune through their gangster activities. The Doctor warns them that they will soon have to deal with the planet's 'real heavies', and shows them pictures of a shark, a leopard and a rhino in an animal book. Scared off, the Syndicate leave Earth in their spaceship.

THE SPARKLING PLANET

Script: Steve Lyons
Art: John Ross; Colours: Alan Craddock
Publication: Issue 130; 27 August 2009

PLOT

The TARDIS arrives in the cargo hold of a space freighter, which is pulling itself apart. The owner, McKendrick, tells the Doctor that it is struggling to escape the gravitational pull of a planet. The Doctor identifies the planet as Adamas, which is supposed to be off-limits to space travellers. Heather and Wolfie meanwhile encounter a sparkling diamond creature trapped in the hold. As the creature breaks out, the Doctor observes that McKendrick chose the wrong type of diamond to smuggle – a living one. He explains that this is an Adamasian, which is actually part of the planet below, and the planet doesn't want to let it go. The Doctor blasts the creature out of the freighter's airlock. McKendrick, however, prevents Heather from operating the control to close the door, so the Doctor is also ejected. By threatening to destroy all the cargo in the hold, Heather and Wolfie force McKendrick to retrieve the Time Lord with the freighter's traction beam. McKendrick is free to go, but will have to spend all the credits he owns in order to repair the damage caused to the freighter. The Adamasian, meanwhile, falls back home to its planet.

THE CURSE OF VLADULA

Script: Christopher Cooper
Art: John Ross; Colours: Alan Craddock
Publication: Issue 131; 3 September 2009

PLOT

In a forest, the Doctor, Heather and Wolfie meet a young girl being chased by a monster. Realising that the monster is a type of banned cyborg slave, the Doctor manages to switch off its mind with his sonic screwdriver. The girl tells Heather of the curse of Castle Wrath, said to be responsible for the disappearance of a number of villagers. Having got the cyborg under control, the Doctor and his friends pretend that Heather is its prisoner in order to gain access to the Castle. They make their way to a laboratory in the dungeon, where a huge creature attended by a green-skinned servant named Philo is waiting to feed. This is Vladula, Queen of the Leviathan Leeches. The girl from the forest has meanwhile gathered the local villagers to attack the Castle, and Vladula flees the planet in her spaceship.

PHOTO FINISH

Script: Eddie Robson
Art: John Ross; Colours: Alan Craddock
Publication: Issue 132, 10 September 2009

PLOT

The Doctor takes Heather and Wolfie to London, 1880, to visit his old friends the Brunswick family. Curiously, the father, George, initially fails to recognise the Time Lord, who once saved his life. The Doctor then finds a photograph of the family, with horrified expressions on their faces. Heather and Wolfie are taken by the daughter, Anne, to look around the house, but when they return, they are strangely different, and the Doctor sees that Anne is holding a similar photograph of them. Dashing upstairs, the Doctor finds a camera-like device, which he throws into reverse with the sonic screwdriver. The family, along with Heather and Wolfie, are drawn into the device, but they are merely duplicates, and their real selves are then released from the photographs where they have been trapped. The Doctor explains that the 'camera' contains several creatures from the Scree Dimension, who came here to relieve their dull existences.

BRAIN TRAIN

Script: Christopher Cooper
Art: John Ross; Colours: Alan Craddock
Publication: Issue 133; 17 September 2009

PLOT

The Doctor, Heather and Wolfie are taking a train to visit Heather's Aunty Jen. Wolfie is playing on his GamePod console when it automatically downloads a new puzzle. All the other train passengers are focusing trance-like on exactly the same puzzle, which has appeared on their newspapers, magazines and games consoles. The Doctor finds hidden aboard the train a Neuronic Receptor, which is harvesting the passengers' brain waves. The Doctor and Heather are chased by two men in military clothing and find themselves in the front section of the train, which is full of futuristic equipment. The woman in charge explains that the passengers' brain energy is to be used to power a scientific breakthrough, accelerating the train past the speed of light. This will occur when the train passes through the Sydenham Hill tunnel, protecting London from the resultant shockwave. The Doctor points out one thing the woman has overlooked: the train will jump half way across the galaxy into deep space, and everyone on board will be killed! The Doctor reverses the neuron flow and destroys the equipment, leaving Wolfie and the other passengers none the wiser when they emerge from their trances.

FOOT SOLDIERS

Script: Eddie Robson
Art: John Ross; Colours: Alan Craddock; Letters: Paul Vyse
Publication: Issue 134; 24 September 2009

PLOT

The Doctor has taken Heather and Wolfie to a shoe shop so that he can buy a new pair of trainers. He is alarmed when the trainers start marching him around of their own accord. The sonic screwdriver stops them in their tracks, and the Doctor discovers electronic components in the soles – they are robotic! Emerging on to the street, the three time travellers see that everyone else is experiencing the same problem with their shoes. A flying saucer appears in the sky, and the creatures within announce that they have planted the robot shoes in Earth's shops so that they can round everyone up and take them to their own planet, Rhastis, to create energy by operating treadmill generators. As the aliens prepare to teleport the first batch of people up to their ship, the Doctor commandeers the shopping centre's PA system and broadcasts a signal that makes all the left shoes think they are right shoes, and vice versa. Consequently everyone starts walking in circles. The Doctor receives a transmission from Prylin of the Rhastin, and they make a bargain: the Rhastin will give up their scheme, and the Doctor will help them fix their energy problems.

BAD WOLFIE

Script: Christopher Cooper
Art: John Ross; Colours: Alan Craddock
Publication: Issue 135; 1 October 2009

PLOT

The Doctor takes his companions to visit the temple of Angkor Wat in 12th Century Cambodia. There, Wolfie falls prey to a telepathic influence and becomes host to the reborn Lychaos the Unforgiving, a Aztlan warrior. He transforms into a ferocious wolf-like creature and starts to create havoc. The Doctor is knocked unconscious but, by appealing to Wolfie's mind within the beast, and reminding him of all their travels together, Heather is able to help him throw off the alien influence. Lychaos is banished, and the Doctor and Heather take Wolfie back to his home in Salzburg to recuperate. He decides to stay there with his parents and give up travelling in the TARDIS.

CITY OF LIGHT

Script: Eddie Robson
Art: John Ross; Colours: Alan Craddock
Publication: Issue 136; 8 October 2009

PLOT

The Doctor takes Heather to see Luminous, a bright city orbiting a dead planet in the Higlag system. Suddenly an alarm shatters the peace, and a group of winged purple creatures swoop down from the sky. The city's inhabitants, believing themselves to be under attack, fire at the creatures with ray guns. The Doctor, however, realises that the creatures are simply attracted to the globe of light at the city's centre, like moths to a flame. He turns up the interior lights in the TARDIS, luring the creatures inside, and tells Heather that they can now drop them off at a nice, bright, quiet star somewhere.

THE GUARDIAN OF MURCHER

Script: Craig Donaghy
Art: John Ross; Colours: Alan Craddock; Letters: Paul Vyse
Publication: Issue 137; 15 October 2009

PLOT

The Doctor takes Heather back to Edinburgh to see her friends, but suddenly the area transforms into a purple alien landscape! Retreating to the TARDIS, they establish that they are still on Earth, but someone is projecting a 3D hologram onto the planet. The Doctor materialises the TARDIS at the source of the projection, the Murcher Moon. Some men working to repair a transmitter tower explain that when it broke, it knocked off course their planet's disguiser – the cause of the problem on Earth. They need the disguiser because their otherwise defenceless planet is covered in Skongolian glitter vines, and if the Seebees find out, they will harvest them. The Seebees' spaceships arrive in the sky, but the Doctor scares them off by using his sonic screwdriver and the Murcher transmitter to display a giant image of an ant that he found back in Edinburgh, making it appear monstrous.

NIGHT OF THE BURNT TOAST

Script: Christopher Cooper
Art: John Ross; Colours: Alan Craddock
Publication: Issue 138; 22 October 2009

PLOT

The Doctor takes Heather to an exclusive alien party celebrating the grand opening of the Hirnathaan Tower, the tallest building in the galaxy. The Doctor knows that the Tower never actually opened, and now he is about to find out why. Suddenly the guests are attacked by Acrylamide Assassins – energy beings that have smuggled themselves in inside the ChefBots' power cells. To the horror of the architect, Mr Vawn, it transpires that the creatures have been paid by the building contractor, Blubb, to prevent the Tower opening and thereby cover up his shoddy work. Having already been paid, the Assassins depart, leaving Blubb to be arrested by a Judoon patrol.

THE GHOST FACTORY

Script: Craig Donaghy
Art: John Ross; Colours: Alan Craddock
Publication: Issue 139; 29 October 2009

PLOT

The Doctor and Heather have arrived in a factory on the Nurburr Asteroid in response to a distress signal. They meet a purple-skinned alien called Watnul, who tells them that he has been here alone for years and has started hearing distressing noises. The factory has been in his family for years, and there has been talk of ghosts. Venturing to the lowest level of the factory, where faulty parts are sent to be incinerated, they encounter a robot that has constructed itself out of pieces of scrap. It is this that has been making the noises, as it has been trapped and lonely. The robot can now be Watnul's friend and help him in the factory.

SKYDIVE!

Script: Trevor Baxendale
Art: John Ross; Colours: Alan Craddock
Publication: Issue 140; 5 November 2009

PLOT

The Doctor and Heather visit Sky City, a floating city that is the showpiece of Earth's civilisation in the 453rd Century. A stranger barges past and gives Heather an egg-shaped metallic device. She passes this to the Doctor, but is arrested by two guards, who believe her to be an AAA – Anti-Antigravity Activist. Later, the Doctor confronts the stranger, Laydon, in the City's Club District. The metallic device is a gravity converter that would improve the City's antigravity engines by a power of ten, saving huge amounts of energy. However, Laydon believes that the Sky City's rulers wouldn't like this, so the AAA have to keep pestering them. The Doctor uses the converter to fly above the city and escape the guards. It transpires that the rulers had mistakenly thought that the AAA wanted to sabotage the City. The Doctor tells them that Laydon's invention will make a big difference to everyone who lives there, and they owe him an apology.

HIGHWAY ROBBERY

Script: Steve Lyons
Art: John Ross; Colours: Alan Craddock
Publication: Issue 141; 12 November 2009

PLOT

Stranded in a forest, the Doctor and Heather see a horse-drawn coach being held up by a highwayman. The highwayman demands of the passenger, Lady Harrington-Fletcher, that she give up her ammonium carbonate, and makes off with her smelling salts – leaving all her jewellery behind. The Doctor, Heather and Lady Harrington-Fletcher give chase and discover that the highwayman is actually a robot. The Doctor reprograms it to take them to its creator, and it leads them to a crashed Cyrronak space pod. The pilot was knocked insensible in the crash, and the robot needed carbon to repair the pod and get him back to Cyrronak for treatment. A mob of local constables appears outside the pod – they too have tracked the highwayman. While Lady Harrington-Fletcher distracts the constables, the space pod lifts off. The exhaust fumes cause the constables to fall asleep, and they will remember nothing of this when they awake. The Doctor and his friends, however, are protected by nose filters found in the pod.

DOOMSILK

Script: Trevor Baxendale
Art: John Ross; Colours: Alan Craddock
Publication: Issue 142; 19 November 2009

PLOT

In the far future, the TARDIS lands on an unknown planet, the surface of which seems to be made of silk. Two menacing creatures rise up from the silk, and suddenly the ground gives way beneath the Doctor and Heather, causing them to fall into a cavern below. There they find a giant spider, now dead. There is some green slime on the ground, and the remains of other visitors are hanging cocooned in silk above. The Doctor deduces that the slime killed the spider but gave life to its web silk. Now silk creatures have spread across the whole planet. The two that rose up earlier based their forms on the Doctor and Heather themselves, as they have no natural forms of their own – they just copy whatever creatures land on their world. Having solved the mystery, the Doctor and Heather depart in the TARDIS.

ONE CAREFUL OWNER

Script: Eddie Robson
Art: John Ross; Colours: Alan Craddock
Publication: Issue 143; 26 November 2009

PLOT

The Doctor and Heather are exploring a city on an alien planet when a petty thief named Ronnu Thanjess makes off with the TARDIS. They track it to a nearby used car lot, where the owner, Ronnu's brother Briak, is just recovering from being attacked. He explains that he sold the TARDIS to a customer, a local crook named Ludo Farltrati, who could not get it to work and came back to exact revenge, taking Ronnu away with him to try to get him to operate the ship. Posing as mechanics, the Doctor and Heather enter Ludo's warehouse and gain access to the TARDIS. They take Ronnu and Ludo on a short trip to 'test' the ship – and materialise in the local police station, where the two criminals are arrested.

THE GARDEN REBELLION

Script: Christopher Cooper
Art: John Ross; Colours: Alan Craddock
Publication: Issue 144; 3 December 2009

PLOT

The Doctor takes Heather to visit London's Hyde Park, only to find that it has been paved over and turned into a car park. The hear an explosion from the direction of the Royal Albert Hall and, investigating, find that the place looks like a war zone. Strange plant creatures in transparent globes atop spider-like legs fire ray weapons at them, and the Doctor falls into a hole in the ground, while Heather is taken captive. The Doctor meets a group of people sheltering below ground, afraid that the creatures – out-of-control eco-drones called Gardenizens – will 'monoxise' them. Heather is just one of many people captured and taken to prison camps, the nearest and main one being at Kew Gardens. The Doctor goes there, and is taken into the Gardenizens' command centre, which is presided over by their super-brain, a ferocious purple plant. The Doctor persuades it to shut-down the Gardenizens and trust the humans to work with it to save the planet's ecology.

THE GOATS OF CHRISTMAS PAST

Script: Eddie Robson
Art: John Ross; Colours: Alan Craddock
Publication: Issue 145; 10 December 2009

PLOT

The Doctor and Heather visit Norway to buy a Christmas tree to take to Heather's granny. They learn from the locals that the trees are mysteriously disappearing, and soon discover the cause – goat-like alien creatures, recognised by the Doctor as Capranom, that consume a huge amount of food by shrinking it down with rays from their horns and then storing the energy like a living battery. The Doctor formulates a plan and, later, the Capranom group together to concentrate their rays on a tree that refuses to shrink, not understanding that it is made of plastic rather than wood. The Doctor and Heather start to round the creatures up while they are distracted. Their owner then arrives, and they persuade him to keep the Capranom in check until after Christmas, when they can eat all the dead trees they like. The Doctor and Heather leave in the TARDIS with the Christmas tree they came to get.

A MERRY LITTLE CHRISTMAS

Script: Eddie Robson
Art: John Ross; Colours: Alan Craddock
Publication: Issue 146; 17 November 2009

PLOT

The Doctor and Heather are spending Christmas in the village of Stillmuir with Heather's granny. The Doctor sees the whole village suddenly disappear, but the villagers initially fail to realise that anything is amiss. Heather and her friends notice a group of blue-skinned elf-like aliens working on a machine – a weather agitator – that causes the ground to shake and snow to fly about. The aliens try to escape through a portal that opens up in the sky, but while one of them, Selby, gets away, the other, Kernow, gets trapped under their own machine. The Doctor discovers that the whole village has been transported across space, shrunk in size and placed in a transparent globe, like a snow-globe toy. The aliens explain that they wanted to study the odd, primitive festival of Christmas. The Doctor tells them that they won't understand it by sealing it in a laboratory. He persuades them to put the village back where it belongs on Earth, and join Granny McCrimmon as guests for Christmas. Fortunately, Granny McCrimmon is short sighted, and assumes that the aliens are simply blue with the cold.

WE WILL ROCK YOU

Script: Christopher Cooper
Art: John Ross; Colours: Alan Craddock
Publication: Issue 147; 30 December 2009

PLOT

The Doctor takes Heather to Cardiff's Millennium Stadium in the year 2000 so that she can see a performance by the rock band Unattended Article. The support band, the Mondegreens, turn out to be lobster-like aliens, whose music puts the audience into a trance. The Doctor manages to rescue Heather with the sonic screwdriver, but all the others start to turn to stone as a result of their DNA being altered by a phonic boom. The Doctor invades the stage to try to stop the band playing, but they open fire with weapons concealed in their instruments. The Doctor and Heather stage dive, then crowd surf their way to the mixing desk. By reversing the phonic boom, the Doctor manages to save the crowd, while the aliens are turned to stone – at least until the Shadow Proclamation arrive to arrest them. All is returned to normality in time for Unattended Article to make their appearance.

NOTE

- From this issue onwards until the end of the run of tenth Doctor comic strips in *Doctor Who Adventures*, the stories bore the caption 'The Tenth Doctor's Untold Stories'. This reflected the fact that readers had by this point already seen David Tennant's Doctor regenerate into Matt Smith's on TV.

THE HIGHEST STAKE

Script: Eddie Robson
Art: John Ross; Colours: Alan Craddock
Publication: Issue 148; 7 January 2010

PLOT

On the planet Jelsen, the Doctor and Heather have been captured and forced to take part in a flying car race. Their opponents in the other car, Jossi and Karter, are likewise unwilling participants. The Lords of Jelsen, in charge of the race, decide to make things more interesting by letting loose on the cars a multitude of flying N-Fish. In amongst these creatures, the Doctor and Heather see the ghost-like forms of other cars. These are the losers of earlier races, trapped into making the same circuit over and over again. The Doctor and Heather spot the finish line, but slow down so that the car with Jossi and Karter in crosses it at the same time. The race is a dead heat. While the Lords are confused, the Doctor and Heather bail out of their car and set it on a collision course with the race's control tower. With the tower destroyed, all the trapped cars are released.

HOOK, LINE AND SINKER

Script: Christopher Cooper
Art: John Ross; Colours: Alan Craddock
Publication: Issue 149; 14 January 2010

PLOT

An alien pod falls to Earth in the ocean and cracks open, releasing the creature within, which gets caught in the nets of the research ship Deep Ocean 7. Months later, the Doctor and Heather are visiting an underground aquarium in Las Vegas when the same creature bursts out of one of the tanks, sending water cascading everywhere. The Doctor identifies it as a Thalatth, one of the universe's most fearsome underwater predators. He realises that the way to combat it is to lure it outside into the heat of the Nevada Desert. They succeed in doing this by tempting it with amplified whale song – the sound of fresh food. The sun's rays accelerate the creature's life cycle and it generates a chrysalis, from which emerges its final form: a beautiful Solarix Prizmatterfly; a creature literally made of stardust.

THE UNWELCOME VISITORS

Script: Eddie Robson
Art: John Ross; Colours: Alan Craddock
Publication: Issue 150; 21 January 2010

PLOT

On another world, the Doctor and Heather explore a farmstead and encounter a three-armed, one-eyed alien creature who runs away in alarm. Soon, more of the creatures appear and take the Doctor and Heather prisoner, considering them hideous monsters. The Defence Force are summoned to deal with them, despite the Doctor's protestations that they were only sightseeing. The Defence Force decide to study the two time travellers by dissecting them, but their appeals to reason have influenced one of the creatures, Private Grodax, who helps them to escape. They leave in the TARDIS, pleased that Grodax is prepared not to take things at face value.

JUNK FOOD

Script: Christopher Cooper
Art: John Ross; Colours: Alan Craddock
Publication: Issue 151; 28 January 2010

PLOT

The Doctor and Heather are in the near future, attending the opening of a new factory that promises to end world hunger using a process that recycles rubbish into food. The Doctor is suspicious, and they hide away inside the factory until it closes for the night. Exploring, they are attacked by a one-eyed, many-tentacled creature, and Heather is transported to a distant planet, which is where all the rubbish is really going. Back on Earth, the Doctor gets inside the factory's machinery and finds a Supermassive Matter Transporter, big enough to teleport an invasion force. Heather captures and questions one of the aliens, and it admits that its race, the Benjix, plan to attack as soon as the supposed food canisters, each of which contains one of their number, are exported to every continent of Earth. Heather teleports back to Earth, and the Doctor then uses his sonic screwdriver to adapts the Transporter, ensuring that the Benjix end up back on their own planet, along with all the rubbish.

DEAD-LINE

Script: Christopher Cooper
Art: John Ross; Colours: Alan Craddock
Publication: Issue 152; 4 February 2010

PLOT

The Doctor takes Heather back to Edinburgh University to avoid her missing another tutorial. She finds her Professor tied up in a classroom, and is taken prisoner by some fellow pupils who are under the influence of the Mozhtratta – the monster that was apparently killed on the day Heather first met the Doctor.[73] The Mozhtratta explains that it was not killed, only weakened, and is now seeking revenge. It activates a device called the ReCohesion Cannon, allowing it to feed on the vortex radiation in Heather, and creating a number of ghostly duplicates of her. The Doctor realises that these duplicates are memories of times past. He tracks down the Mozhtratta and turns the Cannon on it, destroying it and knocking the controlled students unconscious. Heather is freed, but the Cannon has jiggled her molecules so severely that she no longer has any natural defences against vortex radiation. If she were to make even one further journey in the TARDIS, it would tear her apart, so she has to bid farewell to the Doctor. The TARDIS dematerialises as the students recover and prepare to untie the Professor, and Heather reflects that she has had the time of her life every day with the Doctor.

ARCTIC ECLIPSE

Script: Oli Smith
Art: John Ross; Colours: Alan Craddock
Publication: Issue 153; 11 February 2010

---

[73] As recounted in Issue 96.

PLOT

The Doctor, now travelling alone, visits the Arctic in 2019 to see a solar eclipse. When the eclipse occurs, a group of fierce-looking creatures break their way up through the ice. They tell the Doctor that they are the Antipho, and they want his help to free their spaceship, which is trapped beneath the ice. They are unable to emerge during daylight, as it is lethal to them. The Doctor uses his sonic screwdriver to cut through the ice, allowing the Antipho to blast off in their ship.

RETURN OF THE KLYTODE

Script: Trevor Baxendale
Art: John Ross; Colours: Alan Craddock
Publication: Issue 154; 18 February 2010

PLOT

The TARDIS materialises in the Oval Office of the White House, Washington DC, in the year 4041. The US President announces that this is an historic day: the ambassador from the Aktren Galaxy has promised a new, perfect ecology for the Earth. The Doctor realises that the ambassador is really the Klytode, who has tried to destroy the planet twice before.[74] The Klytode claims to be a reformed character who comes in peace, but the Doctor is highly sceptical. The President explains that the Klytode's androids are already approaching all of the Earth's weather control stations, ready to change the environment. The Doctor realises that the Klytode plans to cause the androids to explode, destroying the stations and wreaking havoc on Earth. The androids turn on the Klytode, and it is put safely under lock and key … for the time being.

NOTE

• The US President in this story bears an uncanny likeness to *Doctor Who* showrunner Russell T Davies.

CREATURE FEATURE

Script: Cavan Scott
Art: John Ross; Colours: Alan Craddock
Publication: Issue 155; 25 February 2010

PLOT

The Doctor arrives in what seems to be the middle of an attack by a green, tentacled alien, and rescues a woman from the monster's clutches. It turns out that he has made a mistake: he has interrupted filming of a special effects sequence for a movie called *The Blob from Beyond*. The director has him thrown off the set, but the

---

[74] As recounted in Issues 26-27 and 44-45.

leading lady – the woman he 'rescued' – tells him that there is a reason why the monster looked so convincing: it is a real alien, one of a race called the Thrunn, whose ship crashed in the desert six months earlier. The Doctor frees the Thrunn and repairs their ship. The director come on board and insists that no-one can leave until his movie is finished, but the Doctor scares him off with a holo-projector image of an even fiercer monster – a real special effect this time!

MUDSHOCK

Script: Christopher Cooper
Art: John Ross; Colours: Alan Craddock
Publication: Issue 156; 4 March 2010

PLOT

The Doctor arrives in Dustville, a frontier town on the planet Arkansas XVI. The place seems deserted, but the Doctor quickly learns that the settlers are hiding below ground from a raid by 'bandits' – huge, crystalline monsters. A man named Ben McGill explains that the bandits attack each day at noon to steal their supplies. The following morning, the Doctor and Ben explore the Wastes, and see the monsters rise up from the ground. Hurrying back to Dustville, the Doctor confronts the monsters when they arrive for their daily raid. He appeals to them to share the planet in peace with the humans, but they refuse. The Doctor then signals Ben to use the sonic screwdriver, causing the TARDIS to shoot a beam of energy into the sky that makes icy rain fall – the first rain this planet has seen in a thousand centuries. The rain breaks the monsters down into puddles, which the Doctor has the settlers collect in buckets so that he can take them to a world they can make all their own.

PROJECT UFO

Script: Christopher Cooper
Art: John Ross; Colours: Alan Craddock
Publication: Issue 157; 11 March 2010

PLOT

In London in March 1970, civil servant George Baldwin is being pensioned off and his project closed down, despite all the evidence it has gathered of UFO sightings. Suddenly the Doctor arrives, presenting an old UNIT identity card and asking George for his help in stopping certain information from falling into the clutches of an approaching squad of Chukwa Fel Interrogators. The armoured attackers arrive, and George and the Doctor take refuge in the building's vault. The Doctor explains that if the Chukwa Fel get hold of one particular file – the one for the Bromley Common landing of 1969 – they'll start a galactic war, and Earth will be caught in the crossfire. As the Chukwa Fel break into the vault, George finds the file and hands it to the Doctor. While George stalls the attackers, the Doctor surreptitiously makes amendments to a circuit diagram within the file. George then hands the file to the Chukwa Fel's leader, and they teleport away. The Doctor takes George in the TARDIS to see what happens next. In space, the Chukwa Fel try to activate a Solar Obliterator but, thanks to the Doctor's amendments, they have actually built an Inverted Space Warp Catapult, and it shoots them to the other side of the galaxy. The Doctor takes George home, where he can now retire feeling he has earned it.

BORROWED TIME

Script: Oli Smith
Art: John Ross; Colours: Alan Craddock
Publication: Issue 158; 18 March 2010

PLOT

Each day for the past 20 years, Irene has woken in her home on the mini-moon of Delphi and gone to the greenhouse to water the last surviving example of a Pink Cichorium, while man-eating alien weeds mass beyond the glass. Each day, too, she has sent a distress signal. This is finally answered by the Doctor, who makes his way through the weeds and enters the greenhouse. Irene asks him to take the Pink Cichorium away to somewhere safe, and he agrees. Irene herself does not want to be rescued, however. She intends to fight off the weeds with shears and a tank of weed-killer. The Doctor takes the Pink Cichorium and plants it in the fields of Centauri-Beta.

LUCKY HEATHER

Script: Christopher Cooper
Art: John Ross; Colours: Alan Craddock
Publication: Issue 159; 26 March 2010

PLOT

Heather McCrimmon is in London's Science Museum at midnight, trying to fend off a meteorite superbrain that is using a psychic signal to create a mechanical body out of the Museum's exhibits. She is delighted to run into Wolfie Ryter, who tells her he is also there chasing aliens and getting into trouble. They wrap the superbrain in a stealth blanket, blocking the psychic signal and causing the bric-a-brac creature to collapse. However, their success is short-lived as the superbrain breaks free and reassembles the creature. Heather and Wolfie take refuge in the space exploration gallery, but their situation looks grim. Suddenly the Doctor arrives and, using a Mezon Energy Marble, reactivates the engine of a rocket exhibit, blasting the meteorite monster to pieces. Silently, the Doctor returns to the TARDIS and departs. Heather remarks, 'I think he was saying goodbye'.

NOTE

- This story was devised as a 'missing scene' from the Doctor's succession of farewell appearances to his companions at the close of 'The End of Time' Part Two.

BATTLES IN TIME

THE TIME STEALER / SCHOOL OF THE DEAD / GHOSTS FROM THE PAST / THE BATTLE FOR TIME

Written by: Jason Loborik
Inks: Lee Sullivan; Colours: Alan Craddock
Publication: Issues 53-56; 10 September 2008, 17 September 2008, 24 September 2008, 1 October 2008.

PLOT

The Doctor and Donna arrive in an old house in 1908 where they encounter the Koltroxa, an old hag who drifts endlessly back and forth in time but will be trapped at the point of her death. The Koltroxa drains some of Donna's life force into herself, causing Donna to age by 50 years. The Doctor, who knows that the Koltroxa's presence here is causing a time fracture that could spread and destroy the vortex, makes a bargain with her. He gives her some of his own life force, and in return she restores Donna and leaves the house. The Doctor and Donna follow in the TARDIS, knowing that if she isn't stopped, she will kill again. They arrive 100 years later at the same house, which has now become a school. The Koltroxa has drained the pupils' life force, reducing them to zombies. She tries to blast the Doctor with time energy, but he has managed to seize her pendant, which is really a device for protecting her from the effects of time travel. The pendant absorbs the time energy, which the Doctor then transfers to the school pupils, returning them to their normal selves. However, the Koltroxa snatches the pendant and escapes again. The TARDIS next brings the Doctor and Donna to the same house once more, but in the year 2109. A scientist named Professor Rubenstein has constructed a time-flux analyser machine, which the Koltroxa tries to use to absorb the energy of the time vortex, causing people from many different historical periods to appear. A Roman soldier strikes at the machine with his sword, destroying both it and the house. The Doctor and Donna are protected by the Koltroxa's pendant, but the Koltroxa takes refuge in the TARDIS's time rotor. She takes the TARDIS back to the same house in 1908, before she originally left. The resulting time paradox destroys the house and the Koltroxa with it, but the Doctor and Donna, still protected by the pendant, escape.

CARNAGE ZOO / FLIGHT AND FURY / THE LIVING GHOSTS / EXTERMINATION OF THE DALEKS

Written by: Steve Cole
Inks: Lee Sullivan; Colours: Alan Craddock
Publication: Issues 57-60; 8 October 2008, 15 October 2008, 22 October 2008, 29 October 2008.

PLOT

The Doctor, now travelling alone, is on Earth in the future, visiting a zoo containing alien animals. The zoo has been infiltrated by the Daleks, who steal a cage containing a rare creature called a Krikoosh. Assuming that the Daleks want to learn the secret of the Krikoosh's ability to pass through solid matter at will, the Doctor daringly infiltrates their base and rescues the creature. What the Daleks really wanted, though, was not the Krikoosh but its cage. They already possessed an intangibility weapon; now, with the cage, they have a means to protect themselves from its effects. The use the weapon to turn everyone on Earth into living ghosts who, unable to eat, will soon die. However, the Doctor has befriended the Krikoosh and draws on its powers to regain solid form. He then reverses the settings on the Daleks' weapon, returning the Earth's population to normal and rendering the Daleks intangible instead. Rather than suffer this fate, the Daleks self-destruct.

DA VINCI'S ROBOTS / METAL MANIA

Written by: Simon Furman
Inks: Lee Sullivan; Colours: Alan Craddock
Publication: Issues 61-62; 5 November 2008, 12 November 2008.

PLOT

The Doctor visits his old friend Leonardo da Vinci, who is apparently working on constructing some deadly robots. Leonardo's assistant Ludovico distracts one of the robots when it attempts to kill the Doctor, and the Doctor is able to deactivate it. The Doctor realises that Leonardo is being controlled by a spider-like alien creature. The creature explains that its old host body was ruined when it crashed here and it needs a new one. The Doctor tricks the creature into leaving Leonardo and entering one of the robots, where he traps it, intending to return it to its home planet. He leaves Leonardo to sleep off the effects of his ordeal, which he is unlikely to remember.

ABOUT LAST NIGHT / DARK SIDE OF THE MOON

Written by: Alan Campbell
Inks: Lee Sullivan; Colours: Alan Craddock
Publication: Issues 63-64; 19 November 2008, 26 November 2008.

PLOT

The TARDIS is fired on in space by a warship. The Doctor materialises inside, where he meets a seemingly peaceful creature named Florian. Florian explains that 300 of his people – the Palomians – woke from their previous night's sleep to find themselves mysteriously on board this ship, which is patrolled by killing drones. As the warship moves to the dark side of Palomia, Florian and his people begin to change into vicious, snarling creatures. The Doctor realises that the previous 'night' actually lasted 42 years, as Palomia's orbit had taken it deep inside the Tyranean Nebula. During this time, the Palomians adapted into a hostile life-form. As the warship moves back into sunlight, the Doctor having changed its course, Florian and his people revert to their previous peaceful selves, remembering nothing of what has happened.

NOTE

- The robotic killing drones in this story closely resemble the Trods, as featured in a number of the 1960s *Doctor Who* comic strips in *TV Comic*, although they are not actually named as such.

THE DAY THE EARTH WAS SOLD / THE KING OF EARTH

Written by: Keiran Grant and Neil Corry
Inks: Lee Sullivan; Colours: Alan Craddock
Publication: Issues 65-66; 3 December 2008, 10 December 2008.

PLOT

Three alien races, the Nin, the Ssraarl and the Hoolox, all claim that they have made a deal to buy the Earth from the King of Earth himself. The Doctor discovers that the so-called King is a young boy named Robbie. Robbie found an alien communications device and, thinking it was a game, pretended to offer the Earth for sale in return for bars of gold. As the Nin, Ssraarl and Hoolox confront each other on the Nin spaceship, the Doctor uses the communications device to summon its former owner: Fliant Wormbleeder, estate agent to and of the stars. Leaving Wormbleeder to find new planets for the three races, the Doctor takes Robbie back to Earth.

THE GUARDIANS OF TERROR / THE REBIRTH OF CORAH

Written by: Jason Loborik
Inks: Lee Sullivan; Colours: Alan Craddock
Publication: Issues 67-68; 17 December 2008, 24 December 2008.

PLOT

On the planet Corah, the Doctor encounters a military survey team, some of whose members have gone missing. The Doctor realises that the missing men have been transformed into stone statues by a large, pool-dwelling creature that has absorbed all the water from their bodies. To the annoyance of the team's scientific adviser, Professor Slade, one of the soldiers opens fire on the creature, enraging it. Fleeing from the creature on skimmer vehicles, the Doctor and the survey team members find a disused weather control station built by the planet's lost civilisation. The station was intended to stop a drought overtaking the planet, but it didn't work, and it has not rained here for thousands of years. The Doctor repairs the station's equipment, causing rain to fall, and the creature returns to its pool. It should now be willing to restore the missing team members to their normal state, as they have just been in a form of suspended animation.

THE HOUSE AT THE END OF THE WORLD / THE END

Written by: Steve Cole
Inks: Lee Sullivan; Colours: Alan Craddock
Publication: Issues 69-70; 31 December 2008, 7 January 2009.

PLOT

The TARDIS has materialised in a white void where the Earth should be. All that is left of the planet is a single house, beset by dragons. The house's owner, an old man named Bob Manning, tells the Doctor that he has refused to be evicted by builders. The dragons are being controlled by an alien intelligence called the Absence, which wishes to wipe the Earth clean. It is being prevented from taking Bob's house by a similar intelligence that is inhabiting the cellar. This is the Presence, tutor and guardian to the Absence, which has been dormant since a freak collision in space damaged its systems. The Doctor realises that the Absence can be brought back under control if he allows the Presence access to power from the TARDIS. He is knocked unconscious by one of the dragons, but Bob takes the TARDIS key and opens the door. Power floods out, restoring the Presence, but killing Bob in the process. The Earth is now back to normal, and Bob's house is demolished by builders. The Doctor ensures that, from that day onwards, the wall of every house built on that spot has a plaque reading, 'Bob Manning Lived Here. The Man Who Saved the World'.

NOTES

• Issue 70 was the final issue of *Battles in Time*.

DOCTOR WHO

After the six-issue mini-series published between February and August 2008 (later reprinted in graphic novel form under the title *Agent Provocateur*)[75], IDW published a further six-issue mini-series, *The Forgotten*, between August 2008 and January 2009. This was followed between February and August 2009 by a number of one-shot, standalone stories (subsequently collected together in a graphic novel entitled *Through Time and Space*). Meanwhile, in July 2009, a new regular monthly series commenced, marketed to the trade under the title *Doctor Who Ongoing* but still called simply *Doctor Who* on the comic books themselves. This *Ongoing* series was subdivided into a number of multi-issue stories under separate titles.

---

[75] For details of the *Agent Provocateur* story see *Monsters Within: The Unofficial and Unauthorised Guide to Doctor Who 2008* (Telos Publishing, 2008).

MINI-SERIES

THE FORGOTTEN

Written by: Tony Lee
Cover: Nick Roche, colours by Charlie Kirchoff (1, 2, 3, 4, 5), Ben Templesmith (6)[76]
Art: Pia Guerra (1, 2, 4, 5), Stefano Martino (3), Kelly Yates (4, 6)
Inks: Kent Archer (1, 2, 4, 5), Shaynne Corbett (2), Rick Ketcham with Brian Shearer, John Wycough and Kelly Yates (6)
Colours: Charlie Kirchoff (1, 2, 4, 5), Kris Carter (2, 3, 4, 6), Liam Shalloo (3)
Letters: Neil Utetake (1), Richard Starkings (2, 3, 4, 5, 6)
Production: Neil Utetake (Parts 3, 4, 5, 6)
Edits: Chris Ryall and Tom Waltz (1), Denton J Tipton (2, 3, 4, 5, 6)
Publication: Part 1: 'Amputation', August 2008; Part 2: 'Renewal', September 2008; Part 3: 'Misdirection', October 2008; Part 4: 'Survival', November 2008; Part 5: 'Revelation', December 2008; Part 6: 'Reunion', January 2009

PLOT

The Doctor awakes from unconsciousness to find that he has no recollection of anything prior to his most recent regeneration. He is greeted by Martha Jones, and discovers that they are in a kind of museum apparently dedicated to him. The exhibits trigger memories of adventures he had in each of his previous nine incarnations, and eventually he encounters the creature responsible for his state of amnesia: Ex'cartrss, last of a race of cranial parasites called the Tractire, who was a prisoner on the Dalek Crucible when the Doctor visited it and stowed away aboard the TARDIS when he left. This museum has actually been forged in the virtual reality of the Matrix by virtue of the Doctor's telepathic link with the TARDIS, which sent a simulacrum of Martha to assist him. The current appearance adopted by Ex'cartrss is a cross between the duplicate Doctor left with Rose Tyler in her parallel universe, and the Doctor's old adversary the Master. Within the Matrix, the Doctor is able to join forces mentally with all his previous incarnations and defeat Ex'cartrss, who melts away to nothing; he based his appearance on a Time Lord body, but the Time Lords no longer exist.

NOTE

- This mini-series is notable for featuring appearances by all of the first nine Doctors, plus many of their companions and adversaries.

---

[76] Each issue was also published in a rarer alternative version with a photographic cover, as a 'retailer incentive'.

ONE-SHOT STORIES

THE WHISPERING GALLERY

Written by: Leah Moore and John Reppion
Cover: Ben Templesmith[77]
Art and Colours: Ben Templesmith; Letters: Richard Starkings; Edits: Denton J Tipton
Publication: February 2009

PLOT

The TARDIS brings the Doctor and Martha Jones to the Whispering Gallery on the planet Grått, where displays of emotion are forbidden. Each of the portraits hanging in the Gallery contains an imprint of the deceased subject's final thoughts before death. The Doctor tells Martha that he was once accompanied on his travels by a Gråttite girl named Grayla. They find Grayla's portrait in the Gallery, and learn that her final thoughts were a warning to the Doctor that her people were right to suppress their feelings. Investigating, the Doctor discovers that after Grayla left him, her influence on the Gråttites caused them to begin showing emotion, and this led to the awakening of the Mörkön, a monster that wreaked destruction on the planet. The Mörkön feeds on emotion, and Grayla was like a beacon to it. The other Gråttites consequently decided to keep Grayla sedated until her death, so that the monster would become dormant once more. The Doctor's own emotions reawaken the Mörkön but are so strong that they ultimately overwhelm and destroy it. The Doctor tells the Gråttites that Grayla would have achieved the same thing, had they not sedated her. On learning this, they erect a statue in her memory.

THE TIME MACHINATION

Written by: Tony Lee
Cover: art: Paul Grist; colours: Phil Elliott[78]
Art: Paul Grist; Colours: Phil Elliott; Letters: Malaka Studio; Design: Neil Uyetake; Edits: Denton J Tipton
Publication: May 2009

PLOT

In 1889, the Doctor enlists the help of his old friend H G Wells and scientist Jonathan Smith in refuelling the TARDIS with rift energy, while trying to dodge the attentions of two Torchwood agents. Smith is not who he appears to be: he is actually a time traveller from the 51st Century who has come to this era to prevent the death of his master Magnus Greel. The Doctor, however, has found out about

---

[77] Released with two different standard covers and one 'retailer incentive' cover, all with art by Ben Templesmith.
[78] Also published with a photographic 'retailer incentive' variant cover.

this, and has set a trap for Smith. Wells tells the Torchwood agents that Smith is the Doctor, and they take him prisoner. The Doctor assures Wells that Smith will eventually be released by a man named Harkness, but by that point, Greel will be dead.

NOTES

- This story ties in to events seen in 'The Talons of Weng-Chiang' (1977) and 'Timelash' (1985).

AUTOPIA

Written by: John Ostrander
Cover: art: Kelly Yates; colours: Kris Carter[79]
Art: Kelly Yates; Colours: Kris Carter; Letters: Kubikiri; Design: Neil Uyetake; Edits: Denton J Tipton
Publication: June 2009

PLOT

The Doctor and Donna Noble visit Autopia, a supposedly idyllic world whose people cut themselves off from the rest of the universe after inventing robots to do all their work. They meet a woman called Ixtalia who orders that they be put to death as intruders. However, the robot charged with this task, nicknamed Sam by Donna, decides that killing the two travellers would be morally wrong. At Donna's suggestion, the Doctor then alters Sam's programming to give him free will. The effect of this spreads to all the planet's other robots, who realise that they have been nothing but slaves. They determine to kill their former masters, but the Doctor objects, and says that if they do this, he could destroy them with a computer virus. Sam and the other robots relent, but point out that they no longer have a purpose. Donna supplies the answer: they should transform Autopia into a luxury spa.

ROOM WITH A DEJA VIEW

Written by: Rich Johnston
Cover: art: Tom Mandrake; colours: Charlie Kirchoff[80]
Art: Eric J; Colours: Kris Carter; Letters: Neil Uyetake; Edits: Denton J Tipton
Publication: July 2009

PLOT

Responding to a distress signal, the Doctor takes the TARDIS to a space station in the middle of nothingness. There, he is arrested by a group of alien armed guards and questioned by two green, tentacled detectives, Inspector Mozz and Inspector Looz. A creature named Tx is suspected of killing a Krotonic guard who tried to

---

[79] Also published with a photographic 'retailer incentive' variant cover.
[80] Also published with a photographic 'retailer incentive' variant cover.

prevent him sending the distress signal and thereby threatening the status of the space station as an isolated refuge from a plague that ravaged the galaxy centuries ago. Tx, however, is one of the Counter family, who live their lives backwards through time. The Doctor questions him with the aid of the TARDIS, and discovers that from Tx's perspective, he was not sending the distress signal but receiving it, and far from killing the Krotonic guard, wanted to revive him. He was trying to prevent the space station being destroyed in an explosion at some point in the future – which from his perspective is the time of his ancestors, the explosion being the cause of the family's creation. The Doctor tries to explain what he has learned to Mozz and Looz, but they take it as a confession by Tx. The following day, they prepare to execute him, but are surprised to find that the family are happy about this. The Doctor explains that for them, this is not Tx's death, but his birth. Finally understanding, Mozz and Looz carry out the execution/birth. The Doctor leaves in the TARDIS.

NOTE

- The names of the two detectives are loosely based on those of Inspector Morse and Inspector Lewis from the renowned series of crime novels by Colin Dexter, adapted for TV in the ITV1 series *Inspector Morse* (1987-2000) and *Lewis* (2006-).

COLD-BLOODED WAR

Written by: Richard Starkings
Story: Gary Russell
Cover: Adrian Salmon[81]
Art: Adrian Salmon; Colours: Kris Carter; Colour Assist: Ceri Carter; Letters: Richard Starkings; Design: Amauri Osorio; Edits: Denton J Tipton
Publication: August 2009

PLOT

The royal houses of Draconia are feuding. Some believe this has been caused by Earth joining the Galactic Federation; others consider it due mainly to the controversial appointment of a female, Lady Adjit Kwan, as Empress. The Doctor and Donna Noble arrive on Draconia by mistake, and pass themselves off as Earth Adjudicators. The Doctor is taken prisoner by followers of Fusek Kljuco, a Draconian renegade. Donna demands that he be rescued, and is supported in this by the Ice Lord commander of a force of Ice Warriors present on the planet to act as monitors. The Doctor manages to escape, rescuing also a young Draconian girl named Adjita – Kljuco's daughter. He returns to the Empress's throne room, where Donna's scathing criticism of the squabbling of the Draconian factions has brought a degree of order. Kljuco scales the walls of the palace, sneaks inside and tries to assassinate the Empress, who previously dismissed him as supreme commander of the Draconian forces, but Adjita is hit by his shot instead. As Kljuco is seized by the

---

[81] Also published with a photographic 'retailer incentive' variant cover.

Ice Warriors, Adjita dies in the Doctor's arms. The Ice Lord admonishes the Draconians, telling them they should all support Kwan's appointment as Empress and put Kljuco on trial for his crimes.

NOTES

- This story features the Ice Warriors, the Draconians, Alpha Centauri, the Adjudicators (as introduced in 'Colony in Space' (1971)) and an Adipose.
- The name Fusek Kljuco was drawn from those of actress Vera Fusek, who played the Earth President in 'Frontier in Space' (1973), and Cynthia Kljuco, the production designer of that story.

BLACK DEATH WHITE LIFE

Written by: Charlie Kirchoff
Cover: art: Guy Davies; colours: Charlie Kirchoff[82]
Art: Tom Mandrake; Colours: Charlie Kirchoff; Letters: Chris Mowry; Edits: Denton J Tipton
Publication: September 2009

PLOT

The Doctor and Martha Jones arrive in an English village in 1669, where they find apparent plague victims – surprisingly so, as this is three years after the last recorded outbreak of bubonic plague. The villagers tell them that the cloaked and masked plague doctors are angry that the victims are being cured by a mysterious Healer at the church. It transpires that the plague doctors are actually an alien macro-virus, trying to transform the village's inhabitants into others of their kind and intent on killing the Healer. The Doctor takes Martha to the Healer, who explains that he fled here after the macro-virus attacked his home world, Mimosa 3. The Doctor realises that the Healer and his kind are immunoglobulins. With the Doctor's encouragement, the Healer is able to subdivide into a new force of immunoglobulins, which destroy the macro-virus in the village. The Doctor then takes the immunoglobulins to Mimosa 3 in the TARDIS so that they can continue the fight there.

ONGOING SERIES

SILVER SCREAM

Written by: Tony Lee
Issue 1 Cover A: art: Paul Grist; colours: Phil Elliott
Issue 1 Cover B: Al Davison
Issue 1 Cover RI (retailer incentive): Tommy Lee Edwards
Issue 2 Cover A: art: Paul Grist; colours: Phil Elliott
Issue 2 Cover B: Al Davison

---

[82] Also published with a photographic 'retailer incentive' variant cover.

Issue 2 Cover RI (retailer incentive): Al Davison
Art: Al Davison; Colours: Lovern Kindzierski; Letters: Robbie Robbins (1), Chris Mowry (2); Edits: Denton J Tipton
Publication: Issues 1-2; July 2009, August 2009

PLOT

Visiting Hollywood in 1926, the Doctor attends a party thrown by silent movie star Archie Maplin. He meets movie executive Leo Miller and his actor friend Maximilian Love; a young United Actors studio runner, Matthew Finnegan; and an aspiring actress, Emily Winter, who is bemused when he tells her that she is connected with a fixed point in time that he is investigating. The following day, at the studio, the Doctor learns that Miller is using an alien device to extract emotions from young actors and actresses such as Emily and transfer them to Love. Miller and Love admit that they stole the device from a museum on their home planet, Terron V, where they were both actors until theatre was banned. They are now using it try to make Love a better actor. They tie the Doctor to the tracks of an approaching train, but he is rescued by Matthew and Emily. Returning to the studio, they find Love and Miller about to use the transference device on Maplin. The Doctor offers himself in Maplin's place, and Love is overwhelmed by the emotions he absorbs from the Time Lord. In order to survive, he agrees to forget, and the stolen emotions flow out of his head. The Doctor and Maplin then chase Miller through the studio, until eventually he is arrested by the police. Emily and Matthew ask if they can join the Doctor on his travels, but he refuses. At that moment, however, the Shadow Architect appears from a temporal vortex, accompanied by a force of Judoon, and arrests the Doctor for interfering with a fixed point in time. If found guilty, he will be executed.

NOTE

• Archie Maplin was originally intended to be Charlie Chaplin, but reportedly the name had to be changed for legal reasons. However, the character is still drawn with Chaplin's likeness.

FUGITIVE

Written by: Tony Lee
Issue 3 Cover A: art: Paul Grist; colours: Phil Elliott
Issue 3 Cover B and RI: art: Matthew Dow Smith; colours: Charlie Kirchoff
Issue 4 Cover A: art: Paul Grist; colours: Phil Elliott
Issue 4 Cover B and RI: art: Matthew Dow Smith; colours: Charlie Kirchoff
Issue 5 Cover A and RI: art: Paul Grist; colours: Phil Elliott
Issue 5 Cover B: art: Matthew Dow Smith; colours: Charlie Kirchoff
Issue 6 Cover A: art: Paul Grist; colours: Phil Elliott
Issue 6 Cover B and RI: art: Matthew Dow Smith; colours: Charlie Kirchoff
Art: Matthew Dow Smith; Colours: Charlie Kirchoff; Letters: Chris Mowry (3), Robbie Robbins (4), Neil Uyetake (5, 6); Edits: Denton J Tipton
Publication: Issues 3-6; September 2009, October 2009, November 2009, December 2009

PLOT

The Doctor is put on trial by the Shadow Proclamation for saving Emily Winter's life and thereby interfering with a fixed point in time. The prosecuting counsel is recognised by the Doctor as Mr Finch, a Krillitane in human guise. The defending counsel is a blue-skinned woman known as the Advocate. The Doctor survives an attempt on his life by a shape-shifting Gizou assassin, who is killed by a Judoon. However, he is found guilty in his trial and sentenced to be imprisoned in Volag-Noc. Mr Finch determines that the prison barge should meet with a fatal accident before reaching its destination. The barge is also carrying three alien delegates – a Sontaran, an Ogron and a Draconian – who were *en route* to a peace conference before they were arrested on false charges. The Doctor manages to enlist the help of the three delegates in seizing control of the barge and crash-landing it on a planet. They are pursued by traitorous Judoon loyal to Finch, but manage to hijack their ship and escape. Finch takes the Shadow Architect prisoner and orders his Judoon and Krillitane followers to destroy the Doctor. In the meantime, however, the three delegates have contacted their respective fleets, and they battle and defeat Finch's forces. The Doctor, having realised that 'Finch' is really another Gizou impostor, incapacitates him and frees the Shadow Architect. The peace conference is saved, and the Shadow Architect admits that the Doctor's trial was really just a sham set up to expose the conspirators. The Doctor is returned to the point in space and time from which he was taken, where he reluctantly agrees to allow Emily and Matthew to accompany him in the TARDIS. He is unaware that the plot against him was actually hatched not by 'Finch', who has now been imprisoned, but by the Advocate, who has placed something in the TARDIS that she believes will soon bring about his demise …

NOTES

- This story not only features the Shadow Proclamation, the Judoon, the Draconians, the Ogrons, the Sontarans and the Krillitanes, but is also packed with numerous other continuity references.
- In terms of the Doctor's timeline, this and the other stories in the Ongoing series appear to be set somewhere between 'Planet of the Dead' and 'The Waters of Mars'.

TESSERACT: TIME SMASH/IMPLOSION

Written by: Tony Lee
Issue 7 Cover A: art: Paul Grist; colours: Phil Elliott
Issue 7 Cover B and RI: Al Davison
Issue 8 Cover A: art: Paul Grist; colours: Phil Elliott
Issue 8 Cover B and RI: Al Davison
Art: Al Davison; Colours: Lovern Kindzierski; Letters: Neil Uyetake; Edits: Denton J Tipton
Publication: Issues 7-8; January 2010, February 2010

PLOT

The TARDIS's shields are breached by an Acari spaceship under the instructions of the Advocate. The control room disappears from its usual place, and the Doctor, Emily and Matthew search for it through the ship's interior, pursued by the Acari. Matthew meets the Advocate, who tries to turn his mind against the Doctor, while Emily encounters a group of fifth-dimensional creatures, the Tef'aree, who have infiltrated the stricken ship. With the Tef'aree's help, Emily is able to get to the control room, which the Doctor has also managed to reach. There they are able to expel the Acari spaceship, restoring the TARDIS – although the Doctor, unaware of the Advocate's involvement, is left to wonder how the Acari could have acquired the Shadow Proclamation technology used to breach his ship's shields in the first place. The TARDIS's telephone then rings; it is a call from Martha Jones, requesting the Doctor's help with a UNIT operation back on Earth.

DON'T STEP ON THE GRASS: OLD FRIENDS / OLD FRIENDS / WEED KILLER / [?][83, 84]

Written by: Tony Lee
Issue 9 Cover A and RI: art: Paul Grist; colours: Phil Elliott
Issue 9 Cover B: Blair Shedd
Issue 10 Cover Regular and RI: art: Paul Grist; colours: Phil Elliott
Issue 11 Cover Regular and RI: art: Paul Grist; colours: Phil Elliott
Art: Blair Shedd; Colours: Lovern Kindzierski (9), Charlie Kirchoff (10, 11); Letters: Robbie Robbins (9), Neil Uyetake (10, 11); Edits: Denton J Tipton
Publication: Issues 9-12; March 2010, April 2010, May 2010, June 2010

[UNKNOWN STORIES][85]

Publication: July 2010 in IDW's *Doctor Who Annual*

FINAL SACRIFICE[86]

Publication: Issues 13-16; August 2010, September 2010, October 2010, November 2010

---

[83] Part One and Part Two both had the same subtitle, 'Old Friends', printed on the inside front cover of their respective issue. It seems likely that this was an error, and that Part Two should have had a different subtitle.
[84] At the time of this book being written, Issue 11 of IDW's *Doctor Who* is the most recent to be published. The details given here are for Issues 9-11 only; the publication date given for Issue 12 is the planned date. No plot synopsis is provided, as the story has yet to be concluded.
[85] Not published at the time of this book being written. The publication date given is the planned date.
[86] Not published at the time of this book being written. The publication dates given are the planned dates.

NOTE

- This is IDW's final tenth Doctor comic strip story.

APPENDIX G
OTHER ORIGINAL FICTION

In addition to the novels and comic strip stories covered in the preceding Appendices, there were a number of other places where original, officially-sanctioned new series *Doctor Who* fiction could be found during the period covered by this book. Details are given below.

DOCTOR WHO AUDIOBOOKS

Following on from the success of 'Pest Control' and 'The Forever Trap' in 2008, BBC Audio released a further five double-CD talking books of tenth Doctor stories exclusive to the audio medium. These were as follows.

THE NEMONITE INVASION

Release date: 12 February 2009
Written by: David Roden
Read by: Catherine Tate
Produced by: Kate Thomas; Project editor: Steve Tribe; Executive producer: Michael Stevens; Music and sound effects composed and performed by Simon Hunt; Doctor Who theme music by Murray Gold

PUBLICITY BLURB

Catherine Tate reads this exclusive thrilling story, in which the Doctor and Donna take on a race of dangerous bloodsucking aliens. When the sky rips open somewhere over Dover, two objects hurtle out of the vortex and crash-land in the sea. One is the TARDIS, out of control and freefalling – but the other, a mysterious crystalline sphere, is far more sinister. The Doctor and Donna are rescued and taken to a secret command centre in the Dover cliffs. It's May 1940, and Vice-Admiral Ramsey is about to finalise one of the most daring plans of the Second World War: Operation Dynamo. But something else has got inside the war tunnels, a parasitic Nemonite from the crashed sphere. Its aim is to possess all humans and spawn millions of young. The Doctor and Donna must fight for their lives in order to save both Operation Dynamo and the world at large. 'The Nemonite Invasion' features the Doctor and Donna, as played by David Tennant and Catherine Tate in the hit BBC Television series *Doctor Who*. Written specially for audio by David Roden, it is read by Catherine Tate.

THE RISING NIGHT

Release date: 2 July 2009
Written by: Scott Handcock
Read by: Michelle Ryan
Produced by: Kate Thomas; Project editor: Steve Tribe; Executive producer: Michael Stevens; Music and sound effects composed and performed by Simon Hunt; Doctor Who theme music by Murray Gold

PUBLICITY BLURB

When Harry Winter goes out collecting rocks to repair the wall around his father's farm, he makes a fatal mistake. He disturbs Lucifer's Tombstone, and awakens something demonic and dreadful ... The TARDIS arrives in the 18th Century village of Thornton Rising in the Yorkshire Moors – a village cut off from the world by an all-consuming darkness, where the sun has not risen for three weeks. Farm animals have been attacked, people have gone missing, and strange lights have been seen in the sky. The Doctor soon becomes involved in a nightmarish adventure, helped by a young local woman named Charity. But who is feeding on the blood of the locals, and where will the carnage stop ...? Written specially for audio by Scott Handcock, 'The Rising Night' is read by Michelle Ryan, who played Christina in the TV episode 'Planet of the Dead'.

THE DAY OF THE TROLL

Release date: 8 October 2009
Written by: Simon Messingham
Read by: David Tennant
Produced by: Kate Thomas; Project editor: Steve Tribe; Executive producer: Michael Stevens; Music and sound effects composed and performed by Simon Hunt; Doctor Who theme music by Murray Gold

PUBLICITY BLURB

When the Doctor arrives on Earth in the far future, he is horrified to find the planet beset by famine and starvation. England is a barren wasteland, and scientists are desperately seeding the ground to make the crops grow again. But now it seems that something even worse is happening. Karl Baring, the owner of research facility the Grange, has been snatched away in the middle of the night. His sister Katy was with him when he vanished, but is now in catatonic shock – so it is up to the Doctor, with the help of the scientists at the Grange, to investigate. What is lurking under the old bridge, and why is it preying on people? The Doctor must find out, before it strikes again ... Written specially for audio by Simon Messingham and read by David Tennant, this brand new exclusive adventure features the Doctor as played by David Tennant in the acclaimed hit series from BBC Television.

DEAD AIR

Release date: 4 March 2010
Written by: James Goss
Read by: David Tennant
Produced by: Kate Thomas; Project editor: Steve Tribe; Executive producer: Michael Stevens; Music and sound effects composed and performed by Simon Hunt; Doctor Who theme music by Murray Gold

PUBLICITY BLURB

'Hello, I'm the Doctor. And, if you can hear this, then one of us is going to die.' At the bottom of the sea, in the wreck of a floating radio station, a lost recording has been discovered. After careful restoration, it is played for the first time – to reveal something incredible. It is the voice of the Doctor, broadcasting from Radio Bravo in 1966. He has travelled to Earth in search of the Hush – a terrible weapon that kills, silences and devours anything that makes noise – and has tracked it to a boat crewed by a team of pirate DJs. With the help of feisty Liverpudlian Layla and some groovy pop music, he must trap the Hush and destroy it – before it can escape and destroy the world … Written specially for audio by James Goss and read by David Tennant, 'Dead Air' features the Doctor as played by David Tennant in the acclaimed hit series from BBC Television.

THE LAST VOYAGE

Release date: 7 January 2010
Written by: Dan Abnett
Read by: David Tennant
Produced by: Heavy Entertainment; Project editor: Steve Tribe; Executive producer: Michael Stevens; Music and sound effects composed and performed by Simon Hunt; Doctor Who theme music by Murray Gold

PUBLICITY BLURB

The TARDIS materialises on board the maiden voyage of a pioneering space cruiser, travelling from Earth to the planet Eternity. The Doctor has just started exploring the huge, hi-tech Interstitial Transposition Vehicle when there is a loud bang, a massive jolt and a flash of light. Shortly afterwards, he discovers that nearly all the passengers and crew have disappeared. Unless the Doctor and flight attendant Sugar MacAuley can take control and steer the ship, they could crash-land – or keep slipping through space forever. And as if that wasn't enough, something awful awaits them on Eternity … Written exclusively for audio by Dan Abnett and read by David Tennant, 'The Last Voyage' features the Doctor as played by David Tennant in the acclaimed hit series from BBC Television.

THE DOCTOR WHO STORYBOOK 2010

This fourth entry in the *Storybook* series followed the now-familiar format of the previous three, with seven illustrated pieces of prose fiction and one comic strip story, *Space Vikings!*. Russell T Davies provided an Afterword in the form of *A Letter from the Doctor*. Like the gap year specials, the stories all had the Doctor travelling alone, without a regular companion. Mark Gatiss's *Scared Stiff* was notable for featuring a return appearance by the Gelth from 'The Unquiet Dead'. The frontispiece illustration by Andy Walker showed the tenth Doctor being advanced upon by three Voord from 'The Keys of Marinus' (1964), but these creatures did not feature in any of the stories. Story credits were as follows:

TOTAL ECLIPSE OF THE HEART
Written by Oli Smith. Illustrations by Martin Geraghty.

THE END OF THE RAINBOW
Written by Jacqueline Rayner. Illustrations by Brian Williamson.

SCARED STIFF
Written by Mark Gatiss. Illustrations by Ben Willsher.

BENNELONG POINT
Written by Keith Temple. Illustrations by Neill Cameron.

THE SHAPE ON THE CHAIR
Written by Matt Jones. Illustrations by David A Roach.

KNOCK KNOCK!
Written by Paul Magrs. Illustrations by Adrian Salmon.

THE HALDENMOR FUGUE
Written by Jonathan Moran. Illustrations by Andy Walker.

SPACE VIKINGS!
Written by Jonathan Morris. Art by Rob Davis & Ian Culbard.

DOCTOR WHO – THE OFFICIAL ANNUAL 2010

Whereas *The Official Annual 2009* had featured some quite substantial content, with three comic strip stories and two pieces of prose fiction, the 2010 equivalent had only two comic strip stories and no pieces of prose fiction at all. The rest of the pages were filled with factual features, quizzes and the like. Credits for the two comic strip stories were as follows:

THE VORTEX CODE
Written by Trevor Baxendale. Illustrations by John Ross. Colours by James Offredi.

HEALTH AND SAFETY
Written by Christopher Cooper. Illustrations by John Ross. Colours by James Offredi.

THE DARKSMITH LEGACY

In 2009, Penguin's BBC Children's Books imprint published ten books in a series with the umbrella title *The Darksmith Legacy*, featuring the tenth Doctor. The books were supplemented by online content available at www.thedarksmithlegacy.com. However, that website is no longer active.

1: THE DUST OF AGES

Publication date: 29 January 2009
Writer: Justin Richards
Cover Illustration: Peter McKinstry

PUBLICITY BLURB

It is a few years into our future, and there are bases on the Moon. A recent survey has shown something unusual, an unknown power source. When a tall, skinny, spiky-haired stranger turns up and announces he's from the Bureau of Alien Technology doing a spot check, the survey team know they've found something special. But is this special power source a blessing or a curse? This amazing ten-book series follows the Doctor on his exciting journey to discover the origins of the so-called Eternity Crystal and the powerful artisans who have created it – the Darksmiths.

2: THE GRAVES OF MORDANE

Publication date: 29 January 2009
Writer: Colin Brake
Cover Illustration: Peter McKinstry

APPENDIX G: OTHER ORIGINAL FICTION

PUBLICITY BLURB

The Doctor has discovered the Darksmiths' Eternity Crystal and is determined to destroy it before it falls into the wrong hands. But to find out more about the Crystal, the Doctor must travel to Mordane, the peaceful cemetery planet. But once the sun goes down, Mordane turns into a planet of nightmares. Will the Doctor manage to hold on to the Crystal and fight off the living dead? This amazing ten-book series follows the Doctor on his exciting journey to discover the origins of the so-called Eternity Crystal and the powerful artisans who have created it – the Darksmiths.

3: THE COLOUR OF DARKNESS

Publication date: 26 February 2009
Writer: Richard Dungworth
Cover Illustration: Peter McKinstry

PUBLICITY BLURB

The Doctor is in pursuit of the robot Agent and the Eternity Crystal. His travels have taken him to the forbidding planet of the Darksmith Collective, Karagula. Before the Doctor can reach the hidden Dark Cathedral, he arrives at a village without any children. It is a mystery that the Doctor must unlock before he can find the Crystal. Will the Doctor solve the mystery and will he find the Crystal before the Darksmiths retrieve it? This amazing ten-book series follows the Doctor on his exciting journey to discover the origins of the so-called Eternity Crystal and the powerful artisans who have created it – the Darksmiths.

4: THE DEPTHS OF DESPAIR

Publication date: 26 March 2009
Writer: Justin Richards
Cover Illustration: Peter McKinstry

PUBLICITY BLURB

The Doctor has arrived on planet Flydon Maxima – also known as 'Despair' since the whole planet is flooding. A scientific base has been monitoring the slow melting of the glaciers and their advanced equipment looks to have been created by Varlos, the Darksmith who created the Crystal. But why would Varlos risk visiting this planet? And who is the mysterious Gisella? This amazing ten-book series follows the Doctor on his exciting journey to discover the origins of the so-called Eternity Crystal and the powerful artisans who have created it – the Darksmiths.

5: THE VAMPIRE OF PARIS

Publication date: 30 April 2009
Writer: Stephen Cole
Cover Illustration: Peter McKinstry

PUBLICITY BLURB

The Doctor and his new companion, Gisella, have escaped the robot Agent and the rampaging Dreadbringers. The Doctor, more than ever, wants the Crystal destroyed and must find the Crystal's creator, Varlos. But Varlos has been dead for years. The Doctor and Gisella must travel back in time to Paris to find clues to Varlos' whereabouts. Will they find him in time or will the Darksmiths finally capture the Doctor? This amazing ten-book series follows the Doctor on his exciting journey to discover the origins of the so-called Eternity Crystal and the powerful artisans who have created it – the Darksmiths.

6: THE GAME OF DEATH

Publication date: 28 May 2009
Writer: Trevor Baxendale
Cover Illustration: Peter McKinstry

PUBLICITY BLURB

The hunter becomes the hunted as the Doctor tracks the Agent from Paris towards the Silver Devastation. The Doctor hopes the Agent will lead him to where the Crystal can be destroyed. Following the trail, Gisella and the Doctor arrive at an elegant country house where they are welcomed to join the game. The rules are simple: survive the night and you are the winner. But where is the robot Agent, and why did it come here? This amazing ten-book series follows the Doctor on his exciting journey to discover the origins of the so-called Eternity Crystal and the powerful artisans who have created it – the Darksmiths.

7: THE PLANET OF OBLIVION

Publication date: 25 June 2009
Writer: Justin Richards
Cover Illustration: Peter McKinstry

PUBLICITY BLURB

The Planet of Oblivion is where the Darksmiths met their clients. A once pleasant planet with lush jungles, it has now been reduced to a charred and scorched mess. A few surviving inhabitants desperately try to bring the planet back to life, with the help of the Dravidians. But are these technically accomplished insects helping for their own gain? Will the Doctor get closer to the identity of the Darksmiths' mysterious clients? This amazing ten-book series follows the Doctor on his exciting journey to discover the origins of the so-called Eternity Crystal and the powerful artisans who have created it – the Darksmiths.

8: THE PICTURES OF EMPTINESS

Publication date: 30 July 2009
Writer: Jacqueline Rayner
Cover Illustration: Peter McKinstry

PUBLICITY BLURB

The Doctor finds himself on trial before the Shadow Proclamation where the Crystal is legally returned to Gisella. The Doctor is ready to continue his mission until Gisella betrays him, staying with the Darksmiths. But she accidentally reveals where the Darksmiths are meeting their client. The Doctor arrives on the chosen planet, and becomes involved in an adventure involving missing eyes and souls. Will the Doctor solve this mystery and stop the hand-over of the Crystal? This amazing ten-book series follows the Doctor on his exciting journey to discover the origins of the so-called Eternity Crystal and the powerful artisans who have created it – the Darksmiths.

9: THE ART OF WAR

Publication date: 27 August 2009
Writer: Mike Tucker
Cover Illustration: Peter McKinstry

PUBLICITY BLURB

The Darksmiths have the Eternity Crystal and are eager to finally fulfil their contract with their mysterious client. The Darksmiths have also reprogrammed Gisella, the robotic 'daughter' of Varlos, who now seems to be working for them. The Doctor learns that the Darksmiths are due to hand over the Crystal to their client as a secret rendezvous on present day Earth. Will the Doctor be able to intercept the transaction in time? Or will the Crystal begin a war that will continue for all eternity? This amazing ten-book series follows the Doctor on his exciting journey to discover the origins of the so-called Eternity Crystal and the powerful artisans who have created it – the Darksmiths.

10: THE END OF TIME

Publication date: 24 September 2009
Writer: Justin Richards
Cover Illustration: Peter McKinstry

PUBLICITY BLURB

The Krashoks commissioned the Darksmith Collective to fashion a device that creates life. The Krashoks, after waiting for centuries, have finally had their contract fulfilled. They intend to detonate the Eternity Crystal unless the Doctor can stop them. To make matters worse, Gisella is trapped on board the Krashoks' ship. Can the Doctor save Gisella and destroy the Eternity Crystal once and for all? This amazing ten-book series follows the Doctor on his exciting journey to discover the origins of the so-called Eternity Crystal and the powerful artisans who have created it – the Darksmiths.

NOTE

- By a curious coincidence, this book had the same title as the two-part TV story that marked the end of the tenth Doctor's era, transmitted only three months later.

ABOUT THE AUTHOR

Stephen James Walker became hooked on *Doctor Who* as a young boy, right from its debut season in 1963/64, and has been a fan ever since. He first got involved in the series' fandom in the early 1970s, when he became a member of the original Doctor Who Fan Club (DWFC). He joined the Doctor Who Appreciation Society (DWAS) immediately on its formation in May 1976, and was an attendee and steward at the first ever *Doctor Who* convention in August 1977. He soon began to contribute articles to fanzines, and in the 1980s was editor of the seminal reference work *Doctor Who – An Adventure in Space and Time* and its sister publication *The Data-File Project*. He also became a frequent writer for the official *Doctor Who Magazine*. Between 1987 and 1993 he was co-editor and publisher, with David J Howe and Mark Stammers, of the leading *Doctor Who* fanzine *The Frame*. Since that time, he has gone on to write and co-write numerous *Doctor Who* books and articles, and is now widely acknowledged as one of the foremost chroniclers of the series' history. He was the initiator and, for the first two volumes, co-editor of Virgin Publishing's *Decalog* books – the first ever *Doctor Who* short story anthology range. More recently, he has written *Inside the Hub*, the definitive factual guide book on the *Doctor Who* spin-off *Torchwood*. He has a degree in Applied Physics from University College London, and his many other interests include cult TV, film noir, vintage crime fiction, Laurel and Hardy and an eclectic mix of soul, jazz, R&B and other popular music. Between July 1983 and March 2005 he acted as an adviser to successive Governments, latterly at senior assistant director level, responsible for policy on a range of issues relating mainly to individual employment rights. Most of his working time is now taken up with his role as co-owner and director of Telos Publishing Ltd. He lives in Kent with his wife and family.

Other Cult TV Titles
From Telos Publishing

Back to the Vortex: *Doctor Who* 2005
Second Flight: *Doctor Who* 2006
J Shaun Lyon

Third Dimension: *Doctor Who* 2007
Monsters Within: *Doctor Who* 2008
End of Ten: *Doctor Who* 2009
Cracks in Time: *Doctor Who* 2010
River's Run: *Doctor Who* 2011
Time of the Doctor: *Doctor Who* 2012 and 2013
Stephen James Walker

The Television Companion (*Doctor Who*) Vols 1 and 2
David J Howe, Stephen James Walker

The Handbook (*Doctor Who*) Vols 1 and 2
David J Howe, Stephen James Walker, Mark Stammers

Talkback (*Doctor Who* Interview Books) Vols 1, 2 and 3
Ed. Stephen James Walker

The Target Book (*Doctor Who* Novelisations)
David J Howe

Doctor Who Exhibitions
Bedwyr Gullidge

Inside the Hub (Guide to *Torchwood* Season 1)
Something in the Darkness (Guide to *Torchwood* Season 2)
Stephen James Walker

A Day in the Life (Guide to Season 1 of *24*)
Triquetra (Guide to *Charmed*)
A Vault of Horror (Guide to 80 Great British Horror Films)
The Complete Slayer (Guide to *Buffy the Vampire Slayer*)
Keith Topping

Liberation (Guide to *Blake's 7*)
Fall Out (Guide to *The Prisoner*)
By Your Command (Guide to *Battlestar Galactica*, 2 Vols)
Alan Stevens and Fiona Moore

A Family at War (Guide to *Till Death Us Do Part*)
Mark Ward

Destination Moonbase Alpha (Guide to *Space 1999*)
Robert E Wood

Assigned (Guide to *Sapphire and Steel*)
Richard Callaghan

Hear the Roar (Guide to *Thundercats*)
David Crichton

Hunted (Guide to *Supernatural* Seasons 1-3)
Sam Ford and Antony Fogg

Bowler Hats and Kinky Boots (Guide to *The Avengers*)
Michael Richardson

Transform and Roll Out (Guide to The Transformers Franchise)
Ryan Frost

**Songs for Europe (Guide to the UK in the
Eurovision Song Contest: 4 Volumes)**
Gordon Roxburgh

Prophets of Doom (Guide to *Doomwatch*)
Michael Seely and Phil Ware

**All available online from
www.telos.co.uk**